And There Was War in Heaven

A Guide to Understanding God's Purpose and His Plan

MARIE HUNTER ATWOOD

WESTBOW
PRESS

A DIVISION OF THOMAS NELSON

WestBow Press books may be ordered through booksellers or by contacting:

WestBow Press
A Division of Thomas Nelson
1663 Liberty Drive
Bloomington, IN 47403
www.westbowpress.com
1-(866) 928-1240

ISBN: 978-1-4497-9759-1 (sc)
ISBN: 978-1-4497-9760-7 (hc)
ISBN: 978-1-4497-9758-4 (e)

Library of Congress Control Number: 2013910261

Printed in the United States of America.

WestBow Press rev. date: 6/18/2013

Acknowledgements

I've been so fortunate to sit at the feet of not just one or two great teachers but many who have inspired me, strengthened me and nurtured my mind toward things spiritual. But it wasn't until a Wednesday evening class on the subject of the Book of Revelation at the Eastside church of Christ in Colorado Springs, CO that suddenly my heart was on fire to know more on this particular subject. It became almost an obsession and I have been a faithful student of the book in excess of the forty years that have since passed. For this reason, I want to express my gratitude to the one who was the inspiration, who presented the book in such a way that I could not choose *not* to continue the study.

To Roy Smalling, my gratitude and everlasting thanks.

In grateful memory of
my parents
who set me on the path
and to my children
grandchildren and great – grandchildren
who will carry the torch
and especially to my husband
Melvin Atwood
who left this world in 2012.
Thank you for your
confidence, belief and encouragement.

"And there was no longer a place for them in heaven. And the great dragon was thrown down, the serpent of old who is called the devil and Satan ... he was thrown down to the earth, and his angels ... with him."

—Revelation 12:7–9

Table of Contents

Introduction

I am a great-grandmother who loves reading and studying God's Word. I grew up in a Christian environment within a family that lived its spirituality. Don't misunderstand me. My family was not perfect, but I was able to recognize its imperfections and appreciate them anyway because I was also imperfect. Spiritually, my mother was the stronger of my parents. My father officially gave his life to God when I was nine after fourteen years of marriage and five children. (I am the youngest.) In retrospect I realize the atmosphere of the marriage set the stage for his active belief. Had it been an environment of dissension and condemnation, he would not have committed his life to God in all likelihood. I see the connection of the marriage and the commitment to the Lord in perfect symmetry because as I looked at my parents it was like a sunrise I didn't want to miss.

In an interesting quirk of human nature my husband and I shouted at each other quite frequently and had less overt harmony than my parents had. We were totally different in personality but without a smidgeon of difference in our goals. I was the one who studied and wrote about it. He, the gregarious one, studied less as he was earning a living for his family of seven, but he delved into it with patience and anticipation after his retirement. He marveled at things I felt I'd known most of my life that were just becoming his. Our best times together were in such discussions, and I could see his mind opening to the things he was learning like a flower responding to the sun. He was a special person who wanted to learn, a personification of the text "seek and you will find, knock and it will be opened to you" (Matthew 7:7–8). He has gone on to be in God's presence now. And when I join him, he will be the teacher, and I will be the student.

I began to write this book several years ago, and although the children had married and had left home, it was primarily for them. I felt something vital had been lost or never found in their biblical training, and I felt the responsibility was mine to rectify. I decided that the problem was one of continuity, or perhaps it was a problem I had, so I began to study from that point of view and decided in addition I would start at the beginning.

Of course we understand that God has always been without beginning or end—he is the Alpha and the Omega—but the rest of the inhabitants of the heavenly realm are created beings, as is Satan (Ezekiel 28:13). I feel it is vitally important to understand that Satan, as the antagonist of this story, is recognized as an unhappy, miserable, jealous character that didn't just happen to slip into this situation. It is not in error to say that he forced himself into it probably by issuing a challenge to God, who created him. For example, look at the challenge recorded in Job: "Does Job fear God for nothing?" Paraphrasing for Satan, he replied, "You have protected him and his possessions and blessed all that he has. Take away all that he has and he will curse you to your face" (Job 1:9). Satan is implying that God had bribed Job by blessing him. "Take away what you've given him," he replied, "And Job will worship me," so God allowed him to try his premise, but Job remained faithful. This Satan is a miserably unhappy character, full of hate and jealousy, a character that wants to be God and doesn't mind how much pain he inflicts in trying.

Why did God allow this turn of events? I can think of two reasons—His sameness and His impartiality. He would not treat man any differently than He had treated His angelic host. Man would have the same opportunity to deny Him and the same rewards for believing and obeying. Whether Satan realized it or not, there would eventually be a reckoning because freedom to choose always brings consequences. The interesting thing about it is one can only blame oneself for what follows because the self is the one who will make the choices.

The conclusion is that God's creation didn't just happen. He had a plan. In the same way mankind didn't just happen to come about on a day when God had nothing else to do. It, too, was a plan. He moved forward, setting goals and methods and assuring Himself that everything was in order. He understood that Satan would continue to undermine His work and that there would be problems where mankind was involved as a result of man's right to choose the direction for his life; however, it was a necessary part of the overall plan in order to achieve the proper results. Every man and woman would be assured of salvation if he or she wanted it, with no reworking of the plan. It had been an inspired moment, and He was pleased with the way it had turned out. He recognized it would require centuries of work, a long-term project by man's time but necessary to achieve the results He wanted. The timing of each project was not at all bad when He took everything into consideration, and because it was by His own design, He was confident of success.

This is a study that examines God's continuity, His sameness throughout the ages. It will look at beginnings and the foundation, which literally goes from Adam and Eve to the resurrection and ascension. It is a preview of all that will occur in between the foundation and the ascension, and in the process we will check out many of the happenings as they occur. In later sections, you will find both questions (and answers) regarding the purpose of the law, its necessity, and who benefited from its teaching. We will also explore those who were the beneficiaries of the teaching that occurred and the current status of the law.

The books of law, history, and prophecy will each be considered with a brief synopsis, one that will characterize each book. Prophecy will be grouped by time periods in which the prophecies were given, with consideration for periods of exile and post-exile. Books of history will be grouped (as closely as possible) in their own periods as nearly as text and/or history allows, while poetry will be designated by the time of the complete period of writing rather than individually. In addition to tracking continuity, *And There Was War in Heaven* will be helpful in understanding the stories and other incidents that we chiefly learned in our childhood. Together with other happenings throughout the ages they will also be useful in connecting the Scriptures as they demonstrate God's purpose and His plan.

There will be a few comments on the 430-year silence of God and an effort to glean from that time any information that affects God's continuity. This will be followed by the New Testament and the ministry of Jesus, His death, His burial, and His resurrection, and finally His ascension into heaven. This is the point at which Satan takes the war to heaven and is defeated. What follows is a graphic illustration of our war with Satan, in which we will first focus on the woman whose children are those "who keep the commandments of God and hold to the testimony of Jesus" (Revelation 12:17). This refers specifically to Christians.

Finally we will learn that no man is without an avenue of belief, so there is no excuse for those who do not believe. We will learn of false teachers who defile Scripture and in doing so are instruments of Satan, who leads man away from God. We will be given the key to obedience, which in turn gives assurance of God's love and desire for reconciliation. In the process of learning these truths we will connect the great moments of time in which God altered the way He communicates with man, while we are maintaining the concepts and principles from which His sameness flows.

I hope that you will benefit from bringing these events and times together and that you will be able to see and understand the continuity to the whole that has perhaps been missing for you.

Your questions or comments are welcome. Please submit to the publisher at the address in this book. Thank you.

—Marie Atwood

Chapter 1: God

The path to God can be littered with obstacles and often is. When we examine what we know about Him and what we don't know, it is somewhat miraculous that we reach our destination at all. However, each of us has the assurance that we will have the opportunity to find Him "because that which is known about God is evident within them; for God made it evident to them" (Romans 2:19). Call it conscience, intuition, a feeling, whatever. He took the first step toward us. The next step is up to us. The suggestions below may be viewed as starting points or as hindrances to becoming acquainted with God.

Where Do We Place Our Emphasis

God is the reason for the season. Shall we wear pins or phylacteries? I include this not because wearing a pin is wrong but because it isn't. We have to recognize that many things can separate us or keep us from finding God that are not wrong but have simply been placed in front of God in importance. We see this phrase often, especially in the Christmas season. Actually I wish we could change it, not because it is incorrect but because it implies that Christmas is "God time" whereas He is not necessary in other times. This of course is an exaggerated example, but it's one to consider. If it were up to me, I would change all such banners to read, "God is the reason for being." That is a statement that may seem to some as a bit radical, overboard, or at the very least not needed. My point is not that pins are wrong but that we need God constantly in order to love and trust. It is a life lived for Him that counts.

There is some similarity between these Christmas messages and the phylacteries worn by Jewish males after they reached the land of Canaan. Theirs were designed to remind them of all God had done for them in delivering them from the bondage of slavery. I don't know if we regard the Christmas season in that light, but it is actually true for us because it was by Jesus that we were delivered from the bondage of sin. The message here is not in the wearing or not wearing of pins—except that it is good to be reminded occasionally that sometimes our emphasis can prevent the finding of our Lord.

As I ponder the significance of the phylacteries of the Old Testament and the pins by which we would remind ourselves of our Savior, I wonder if they are beneficial to us today. I would suspect it depends on attitude. God designed the new covenant with the intent that His Word live in our hearts not by reason of pins or phylacteries. This would also apply to anything we place by emphasis before God.

The Art of Studying

Are we *studiers*? Part of studying is habit, pure and simple, but how can we know God's will if we don't read the manual? By *manual* I refer to the Bible. We understand this need for preparation for almost any job on the face of the earth, except when it comes to pleasing God. Some say they can't understand what the Bible says. If this is your problem, let me remind you that you probably didn't understand your first math book or English grammar text ... or your first day in a foreign language class ... or what you were supposed to do the first day in the chemistry lab ... or how to find a word in the dictionary. All learning has a beginning. You simply need to start. That's all there is to it. The only way to understand the text that you read is to begin. Read it and think about it. You might even be brave and approach God to ask for help in understanding. God is more than willing to help you. He wants to help you. All you have to do is ask. If you are not in the habit of studying, start with a simple task like the meaning of words you don't understand. Then thank God that you have the ability and the means to do that. Make studying a daily habit, and you will be blessed for it.

The Art of Prayer

Prayer is our conversation with God, and the Bible is His conversation with us. Prayer is not meant to be a handy pathway to present requests but a ready pathway to offer praise to the Father with requests added in. We need to praise Him for who He is and for what He is, for His love, for His faithfulness, for His sacrifice in giving His Son. We generally talk to the ones we love. How do you think God feels when we fail to approach His throne in loving conversation with Him? Prayer is nourishment to our souls. It is as important in our lives as the food we eat. I would urge you to open this path to the Father and use it regularly. You may talk with God silently all day and gradually add more formal prayers if you like. This practice could be termed as a prayerful attitude.

The Art of Making Good Decisions

Think about this seriously. God is allowing you to make the choices that will either reward you or punish you in eternity. When you really think about this, you will realize that in a sense, you are going to be your own judge when the time comes. How does this work? It doesn't mean that you can do whatever you want without the resulting circumstances. Let's look at an example. When King David saw Bathsheba and wanted her, he took her, and a whole lot of consequences began to pile up. He had Uriah, her husband, put on the front lines of battle, so he would be killed. The child who came from his union with Bathsheba died. Now here is the point we fail to remember because David repented and God forgave him; however, on his deathbed David still had to cope with his sin with Bathsheba and the fact that he had chosen to have many wives. Consequences don't go away. By backing Solomon, Bathsheba's son, another son named Adonijah lost his life. What a horrible choice to make. But David had created this situation a generation earlier in his life. The words *if only* are two very wretched words, don't you agree? I've wondered if David realized he had brought about Adonijah's death by his own poor choices a generation earlier.

These suggestions can all be starting points as one chooses to follow the path that leads to Him. Emphasis, studying, praying, and making choices are all important; however, approached in a negative manner they can also be hindrances. Analyze your life to determine if you are placing things, people, or circumstances before our Lord, and you will learn a lot about who you are. If necessary, then you can make a *course adjustment* to make sure you are headed in the right direction. See on which side of the fence you live your life, and you will recognize your path. To remain faithful in your relationship, these elements must become a part of your life because they allow you to *be* for Him.

The next step to God (or a good renewal) is actually a matter of getting acquainted with Him. First, it indicates that you want a relationship with Him. If you have already taken the first steps, then build momentum by getting acquainted with the Father. I feel He is the best place to begin because He is the designer of the plan, the one who put it all together. Let's take a peek.

Do you know anyone who thinks of God as an old guy, an *ogre* who sits on His throne, sporting a long, white beard as He spends His days anxiously watching for someone He can zap? That depiction of Him is so far removed from His nature as to be ridiculous. We don't know a lot about His appearance, but we'll learn a lot about His nature, all of which contradicts such a characterization. Actually we have no physical description of God, which is just as well because we tend to place too much emphasis on appearances.

His Divinity

I don't know what this means to you, but to me it means He is perfect, so how can He be described? I have chosen three of His divine qualities that go beyond our human understanding. Possibly all of them fit into that category. It depends on the perspective by which they are examined. Nevertheless, it is impossible to aspire to these three qualities because they belong to God alone; however, perhaps they can help us understand who He is.

> *God is omnipotent.* This means that "nothing is impossible with God" (Luke 1:37). And another verse that brings all that power down to a level that is very personal is this: "For the Word of God is living and powerful, and sharper than any two-edged sword, piercing even to the division of soul and spirit, and of joints and marrow, and is a discerner of the thoughts and intents of the heart" (Hebrews 4:12 NKJV). He created worlds and stretched out the sky with His own hands, and He filled it with all that is in it. He formed light and created darkness (Isaiah 45). He not only sees into hearts but forgives the wickedness that is there, remembering it no more. These are a few of His powers. I repeat, "Nothing is impossible with God."

> *God is omniscient.* This means that He is all-knowing, "God is greater than our heart and knows all things" (1 John 3:20). What things does He know? He decides on a thing and causes it to happen (Matthew 1:18–25), He planned the justification of the Gentiles and brought it about, knowing it was a gift of grace equal to His gift to the Jews (Romans 3:19–26). He tells of end times forewarning while

He beseeches repentance and informs us of the result, "Blessed is he who reads and heeds" (Revelation 1:3). "Behold, the former things have come to pass, and new things I declare, before they spring forth I tell you of them," (Isaiah 42:9 NKJV). Was this *telling* a week or so prior to the new things? On the contrary, it was centuries prior, even hundreds of centuries in some instances.

God is omnipresent. This means that He is in all places at all times, "Am I a God who is near … and not a God far off? Can a man hide himself in hiding places so I do not see him? Do I not fill the heavens and the earth?" (Jeremiah 23:23–4). This aspect of omnipresence baffles me because God is not only here and now but in all past periods of time and all future periods of time at the same time. Jonah thought he was hidden from the Lord while he was in a boat running away from the Lord, but God caused a wave to flip him out of the boat and into a whale. It is impossible to hide from God (Jonah 1). Moses ran away from Egypt to a place called Midian, but God knew where he was and called him to bring His people out of the bondage of slavery. Moses did not run from God physically. However, he did not want the job God had for him, and he claimed incompetence (Exodus 3). We cannot hide from God's knowledge. Nor can we hide from His purpose for us.

We respond with awe to the descriptions of omnipotence, omnipresence, and omniscience, yet can we really comprehend these qualities? How can we when there is nothing to which we can compare them? They are literally characteristics that belong to Him alone. There are other qualities of His nature that seem less daunting on the surface. These qualities, while they allow a measure of duplication, cannot be duplicated. Therefore, as with His other divine qualities, we will assume they are unattainable as well, but we can aspire to learn a measure of each.

His Nature

For the purpose of better understanding, I give a perspective for each of these qualities. While this perspective is not the only one from which one may observe these qualities, perhaps it will help to grasp His infinite nature.

He is light. "This is the message which we have heard from Him and declare to you, that God is light, and in Him there is no darkness at all" (1 John 1:5 NKJV). It is logical that God is said to be light because of His purity. There can be no purity in darkness. His light is not a weak light like a battery almost spent but a strong floodlight capable of penetrating darkness to reveal its shameful secrets and capable of penetrating the darkness of each soul to reveal that which it has hidden.

Perspective: "Can I become light? No, I can't, but I can reflect His light, and as I gaze continually at His presence, I will gradually be transformed into His image" (2 Corinthians 3:18).

He is perfect. Qualities of perfection are found in His presence, goodness, justice, *mercy, and compassion.*

Perspective: We are given encouragement to reach for the goal of perfection, "leaving the elementary principles of Christ, let us go on to perfection" (Hebrews 6:1 NKJV). It is true that in this life we cannot be perfect; however, He challenges us to try, and He will reward the effort by giving us perfection in eternity so "that we may present every man perfect in Christ" (Colossians 1:28 NKJV). It will never be the same as His perfection, but with our steadfast focus on goodness, mercy, and compassion, it can be a reasonable facsimile.

He is faithful. Patient, understanding, forgiving, "Know therefore that your God, He is God, the faithful God, who keeps covenant and mercy for a thousand generations with those who love Him and keep His commandments" (Deuteronomy 7:9 NKJV). In our society a covenant is actually a contract between two or more. God is saying that His contract with us is permanent, provided that our love and obedience is maintained. He will not break His promises with you, but you can break them if that is your choice.

Perspective: Considering the scope of His faithfulness, our hope to match His seems limited. I would say that a good beginning is to focus on the commandments to love the Lord, your God, with all your heart, with all of your soul, and with your entire mind and to love your neighbor as yourself. Additionally in the words of Jesus, "Everyone who confesses me before men, I will also confess him before my Father who is in heaven. But whoever denies me before men, I will also deny him before my Father who is in heaven" (Matthew 10:32). Love and obedience are great starters that will produce great faithfulness.

He is righteous. "The Lord is righteous in all His ways and gracious in all His works" (Psalm 145:17). This word *righteous* is interesting because its definition means *to do right*, and in Romans 3:10, Paul tells us that "none are righteous." Paul is obviously referring to those who claim righteousness on the basis of following Christ, whereas the text from the Psalm refers to God. We must strive to be righteous; however, our efforts are but a poor replica of His holy righteousness.

Perspective: The writer of the Hebrew letter lists men of old who were triumphant in their faith. He begins by saying, "Faith is the substance of things hoped for, the evidence of things not seen" (Hebrews 11:1 NKJV). What is it that you hope for? I hope for the eternal home in heaven. If that is your hope, then we are speaking the same language. What about the evidence part? What do we look for that we've never seen? God is the evidence, never seen but believed. How can we achieve both? It can only be done by believing in the Son, that He came to the earth in the flesh (the incarnation), that He died and arose from the grave on the third day, and ascended back to heaven, where He sits at the right hand of God with all things in subjection to Him as head over all things to the church, which is His body, the fullness of Him who fills all in all (Ephesians 2:22).

He is impartial. "For He causes His sun to rise on the evil and the good and sends rain on the righteous and the unrighteous" (Matthew 5:45). Imagine that! You would think that such blessings would be withheld from the unrighteous, but God uses such blessings as a way of showing His love and His yearning that all men be reconciled to Him.

<u>Perspective</u>: To be impartial is undoubtedly difficult. It is probably a gift on the order of those listed in 1 Corinthians 12. Sometimes even families can't achieve it with their children or siblings, much less with other people. It is a gift on the order of God's love because the plan He devised maintains the integrity of His love for all people. Because peace is one of His objectives for the world, I would say that the ability to be impartial ranks right up there with love, something for which we should definitely strive.

He is wise. "Oh, the depth of the riches both of the wisdom and knowledge of God! How unsearchable are His judgments and His ways past finding out!" (Romans 11:33 NKJV). God tell us, "If any of you lacks wisdom, let him ask of God, who gives to all liberally and without reproach, and it will be given to him" (James 1:5 NKJV).

<u>Perspective</u>: That second verse really says it all. All we have to do is ask. Whoa! There is another necessity, and that is to recognize that we are lacking. Sometimes that's the hardest part. Consider God's wisdom: "Who created the heavens and stretched them out, who spread out the earth and its offspring, who gives breath to the people on it and spirit to those who walk on it. I am the Lord, I have called you in righteousness, and I will also hold you by the hand and watch over you" (Isaiah 42:5–6). He has all knowledge. The issue is this: Do we trust Him?

He is love. "The one who does not love does not know God, for God is love" (1 John 4:8). That is a nice, clear statement that should be very easy to understand. And I feel compelled to add, "Now abides faith, hope, love, these three; but the greatest of these is love" (1 Corinthians 13:13 NKJV).

<u>Perspective</u>: An entire book could be written on love. We have so much to learn about love, and like the idea of studying, all we have to do is start. Jesus told us that love is how we are known as belonging to Him. Love God, love your neighbor, and love your enemy. We have lots of material to work on, so I challenge us, you and me and anyone else who can be engaged in this project, *let's begin!* Let's take one day at a time.

It is fascinating to me that what we know of His nature describes the nature He wants for us. We will be judged by our nature (our motivations and our hearts). How closely did we follow His? Did we hurt someone deliberately and then rejoice in the hurt, or did we suffer in sorrow for what we had done? He will give justice for the one (what is deserved) but mercy for the other (compassion). It seems that mercy from within your heart is necessary in order to receive mercy from His heart. That is more than a fair exchange, as it rewards the spiritual yearnings of the heart just as His yearning is that we be reconciled to Him.

As for the specifics of God's nature, which is demonstrated in His actions, they are best known by the gift of His Son. We can see His actions both by faith and by the experience of living (Matthew 5:3–11 NKJV), but it is impossible to understand His agony in giving the Son or His love for mankind, for whom His Son was sacrificed. One might sum it up by saying He offered His perfection as a gift of one for the need of the many who are called mankind. I doubt we could have given such a gift had it been our own decision.

His Divine Roles

God's roles are quite different than His nature as they define what He does rather than what He is. They do resemble His qualities that are unattainable in that there is little to which we are able to relate. In that sense it is all rather incomprehensible as far as we can know by experience. However, as an example, consider yourself and try to name the things that you are. I, for instance, am quiet, curious, often moody, compassionate, and old. (Denying doesn't change it.) Now what do I do? (This list has changed considerably since I had five children in the house, all wanting the same thing at the same time!) Now I spend my time writing, sketching, and putting albums together for my children, grandchildren, and great-grandchildren. I also eat and sleep and try to avoid overt exercise if I can get away with it. Does this help at all to tell the difference between what our Savior is and what He does? Let's take a look.

Creator

It boggles the imagination that something can be made from nothing, and yet He did that. All the arguments in the whole of existed time cannot alter what He did. Some do not believe because they do not have faith, but among those who do believe, knowing should be enough. There should be no quibbling about the how. The how belongs to Him. Faith understands with the heart. If we had all knowledge, where would our faith be? God, as we know, was not created. He has always been "without beginning and without end" (Revelation 1:8). Would we understand it any better if we broke it down in parts? Let's give it a try.

- Bara[1] (Strong 2001) means "to create from nothing." There are three times in the Bible where the Hebrew word bara is used. In all three instances the definition is "to create from nothing." They are as follows:

  "In the beginning God created the heavens and the earth" (Genesis 1:1).

  "Thus says the Lord who created the heavens, (He is the God who formed the earth and made it), He established it and did not create it a waste place, but formed it to be inhabited" (Isaiah 45:1).

  Isaiah 45:18 is interesting because all of the forms of creation are in the same verse.

Here are the other three methods of creation used fifty-one times with other verbs that have broader meanings. These verbs include the following:

- Yatsar[2] (Strong 2001) means *to* form. Actually, this is a potter's word, and its literal meaning is to squeeze into shape, to shape, or to mold[3] into a form. Man was formed from dust (Genesis 2:7) as were the beasts of the field and the birds of the air (Genesis 2:19). Man is formed in the womb (Jeremiah 1:5). God also formed the earth after it was created.

---

1 Strong's Expanded Exhaustive Concordance, copyright 2001 by Thomas Nelson, (publisher Thomas Nelson Publishers, Nashville), Hebrew & Aramaic, 1254.

2 Strong's Expanded Exhaustive Concordance, copyright 2001 by Thomas Nelson, (publisher Thomas Nelson Publishers, Nashville), Hebrew & Aramaic, 3335.

3 Strong's Expanded Exhaustive Concordance, copyright 2001 by Thomas Nelson, (publisher Thomas Nelson Publishers, Nashville), Hebrew & Aramaic, 6213.

- Asah[4] (Strong 2001) means to do or to make. In the usage above, we learned that God both created and made the earth. I admit I had never considered that there were different functions in the creation process but I find it very interesting. Asah is used 2,633 times in a broad range of contexts and specific interpretations.

- Kun (kuwn)[5] (Strong 2001) means to be established on the order of to be prepared, be ready, be certain, and this word is used in a variety of ways. Samson requested that he be able to feel the pillars that held the roof so he could lean on them (Judges 16:26). In a similar sense the earth is firmly established, immovable (Psalm 93:1). And about the first creation, "He established it and did not create it for a waste place but formed it to be inhabited" (Isaiah 45:18).

As my mind tries to put God's role as Creator into perspective, I find that I can't. I think about the specifics of each animal, each bird, each creature of the sea, not to mention the human race and the world He created, formed, made, and established for us, and I am suddenly overwhelmed. Our God is amazing, isn't He? Not only is He amazing, but He is incredible. Each of us as humans of the species is unique. Our cellular makeup is similar but not the same. Our DNA and our fingerprints attest to our individuality. He finished the creative process by establishing us for a purpose. Have you found your purpose? If you have not, it is waiting for you somewhere. It would not be right for anyone else. It is just for you.

King

Does eternity have a definition? If it does, do we comprehend forever or endless or infinite? Not to have a beginning or an end boggles the imagination and tests faith. His eternal reign is an instrument of peace to the believer who knows he or she will be rewarded for the struggles in this life. More than rewarded for His eternal reign will allow for our participation in His very nature as we live with Him forever. Can we even envision it? There will be none of the problems that accompany our

---

4   Strong's Expanded Exhaustive Concordance, copyright 2001 by Thomas Nelson, (publisher Thomas Nelson Publishers, Nashville), Hebrew & Aramaic, 6213.

5   Strong's Expanded, Exhaustive Concordance, copyright 2001 by Thomas Nelson, (published by Thomas Nelson Publishers, Nashville), Hebrew & Aramaic, 3559 1b, 3. 6, 9.

relationships on earth. There will be no envy, misunderstanding, enmity, or strife. Instead, there will be an abundance of love and fellowship with the Father and those who are allowed to dwell in peace in the eternal home. "Now to the King eternal, immortal, invisible, the only God, be honor and glory forever and ever" (1 Timothy 1:17). To many people the fact that He is invisible is a stumbling block. Visibility is a matter of the mind. When loved ones are away from you, it doesn't make them invisible. My point is that much of our seeing is with the heart. As you become acquainted with God, His image becomes a part of your mind and your heart, and it becomes easier to talk with Him as we seek guidance in everyday life.

Judge

The facades we wear will not dupe this judge. He sees all the hiding places of our hearts and understands every motivation no matter how deeply it is buried. It won't work to say to Him, "But I meant to obey. I just didn't have enough time. Honestly, I meant no harm." He knows the hypocrisy of false piety and recognizes the absence of love. He knows all the heart's desires. With this judge, desiring to do right and failing is not the same as failing without that desire. He will judge both the righteous and the wicked, and there will be no appeal to a higher court. In Ecclesiastes the preacher comments that everything God has done is permanent. This can only be understood by knowing that He is perfect. He doesn't make mistakes. Because this is so, we are to fear God because we will be held accountable of all we have done. The preacher also saw that the evil man is filled with wickedness and the righteous man is filled with iniquity, so both will be judged. "God will judge both the righteous man and the wicked man" (Ecclesiastes 3:17).This is compatible with God's sameness, His impartiality. Of course He will judge both. Anything less would not be justice. "In accordance with your hardness and your impenitent heart you are treasuring up for yourself wrath in the day of wrath and revelation of the righteous judgment of God, (who will render to each one according to his deeds" (Romans2:5–6). "He has fixed a day in which He will judge the world in righteousness through a Man whom He has appointed, having furnished proof to all men by raising Him from the dead" (Acts 17:31).

"God will judge the secrets of men through Christ Jesus" (Romans 2:16.)

This is more than a bit scary, isn't it? We work so hard in life to bury the secrets we don't want anyone to know, and we are almost sure they will never surface. Confess them now and quit worrying because God is already aware of all we do and think. I promise you that our God does not give us what we deserve to receive for our sins, but He does judge us by the motivation of our hearts. Did we intend to do what we did? Did we want to hurt? Are you sorry for your actions, or do you harbor satisfaction? Confess now and experience His peace.

Savior

God the Father is more easily understood, but is the Savior the same as God the Father? I am far from being a theologian, but my theory has always been to use a lot of common sense in dealing with thorny issues. I started with what I know about each, and I have found that there is not even an ounce of difference in them. Jesus repeated over and over, "I do the will of the Father." He further said that He is a witness for the Father, and "if you have seen me, you have seen the Father." Titus tells us that it is by the grace of God that we have salvation (Titus 2:11), and God Himself created the plan before the foundation of the world. It was His grace that took the gospel to the Gentiles; the apostle Paul attests to His grace for what he became and through which he was empowered to serve. Is God the Father our Savior? How can He not be when the whole thing of salvation was His? This is like saying a house isn't the architect's because another was the builder. Paul reveals further that it is God's grace that leads us to repentance, and without repentance, there is no salvation (John 3:16). The love of God is the reason the Son was sent to man. From the *no* perspective, the plan from the beginning was that anyone who came to the Father would come through the Son, who willingly agreed and gave His blood. You might say that He was the only one who bore the pain and the suffering, but fundamentally this is not true. If you have children, you know what I mean. Jesus bore the weight not only of the sins of the world but the grief and sorrows of the world in order that we would not have to remain in a world of evil but that we could be redeemed by His blood. If you really stop and think about it, the Father was also wrapped in pain.

> They are one. There is no other way to express it. Try separating them, and nothing makes sense about the war we are in, about God's desire for reconciliation, about creation or salvation itself. My conclusion is that God is Savior by all of the things that make Him God. He shares the role. Isaiah 12:2 says, "Behold the Lord

is my salvation, I will trust and not be afraid; for the Lord God is my strength and song, and He has become my salvation." Isaiah is thanking God for both his own salvation and that of the remnant on the basis of the promised Messiah (the root of Jesse.) Of course, this is a prophetic utterance by Isaiah many centuries prior to the coming of the Messiah, but note that he understands that the promised salvation will be realized *because* of this Messiah who will come. His comment of *unafraid trust* shows powerful faith in God.

"For God, so loved the world that He gave His only begotten Son, that whoever believes in Him should not perish, but have eternal life" (John3:16 NKJV). The love of God is the beginning of salvation. Without God the Father we would not have a Savior. "For the law made nothing perfect; on the other hand, there is the bringing in of a better hope, through which we draw near to God" (Hebrews 7:19 NKJV). God the Son did not give the Law of Moses to the Israelites; it was given by God the Father for the purpose of bringing them to Christ. Why was this necessary? The law was an instructor, a teacher; it was a tool of preparation. Just as Adam and Eve were not ready for a more complicated list of what they could do and could not do, the Israelites were not ready for a law of the heart. The law preserved a route through which the Son would come—else the world might have been destroyed again. You might say that the law kept holiness alive in a path through which the Messiah would come to the world.

Christ was the better hope. Why? Because with the passing of the law and the shed blood of the Christ, forgiveness entered the picture, making the frequent offerings of blood unnecessary. Now the sacrifice is of one's self. We are to live for Him, or as I prefer to say, we can now *be* for Him.

As this chapter ends, I have a thought to leave with you. Think about His nature and question how it correlates to His magnificent qualities. They seem to go together, don't you think? Then I think of the fruits of the Spirit of Galatians 5:22 and the admonition that follows in verse 25, namely to live and walk by the Spirit, and it occurs to me that God is what He does. That's why He is all those wonderful things. Would He have been like Satan if He had not? I don't know, but I do know that if we don't try to be like Him, we will fail to achieve our greatest hopes. As we strive for those unseen things of Hebrews 11:1, we will learn many things that will help us in our walk with God. The Spirit I speak of is the one our Lord Jesus asked the Father to leave with us when He ascended back into heaven. He is a tremendous help in all things spiritual, and we will talk about Him before too long.

I take away from this lesson (and hope that you will too) a powerful realization of God's divinity, but I also understand that in order to approach Him we must know that He is a loving and compassionate Father and that in order to worship Him we must recognize the very qualities that are incomprehensible. Does that sound confusing? Here is a suggestion: Think of Him as your Abba Father, your loving daddy; however when it comes to obedience, think of Him as the King and the Judge. But always remember that He is the Creator of all there is and the Savior for all that will be. Why? Because if you recognize those two qualities, you will praise Him and love Him for what He is, not just for what He can do for you.

How can man relate to this perfection? In my opinion it can be done only by emulation. While we cannot copy His divine description or His divine roles, we can mold goals and ideals after His divine nature. Can I become light? No, but I can reflect His light. Is it possible to have all wisdom and knowledge? No, but I can devote myself to study and prayer, and He will grant me understanding and wisdom. In short by looking to Him as our pattern, we do become like Him, not by our own power but by His. Consider 2 Corinthians 3:18: "With unveiled face beholding as in a mirror the glory of the Lord (we) are being transformed into the same image from glory to glory." What is the meaning of *glory to glory*? It is simply saying that *we* (you and I) are changed (transformed) from His glory to a new glory that will be our own. What a promise!

Study Guide—Chapter 1

Q. What does eternal mean to you? (Please write your thoughts below).
A.

Q. Give three descriptions of God and define each.
A. God is omnipotent. As the Creator He made all things. As the Savior He gave His Son's life for yours. He is all-powerful. God is omniscient, which means He is all-knowing. God is omnipresent, which means He is everywhere.

Q. Think about it and write down in the space below one way (just one) that you recognize God's omnipotence in your life. (Remember omnipotence is power).
A.

Q. Write down how your nature differs from God's nature (This is a thought question).
A.

Q. Using the list below, mark in the order that you perceive them as incomprehensible from most to least, four being the most incomprehensible, one the least.

o   As the Creator He made something from nothing.

o   As the King His reign is eternal.

o   As the Judge He knows the secrets of your heart.

o   As the Savior He gave His Son's life for yours.

Q. Please explain how God the Father is your Savior, even though it was the Son's life that was taken.

A. God was the author of the plan for salvation, who foresaw the necessity for forgiveness and created the plan with the approval of Jesus, the Son, who volunteered to be the sacrificial Lamb. In addition God suffered the pain of the parent when He had to turn His back on Jesus, who carried the load of the world's sin. Further, God gave grace to the Gentiles through Paul and grace to the Jews through the law. In the analogy of those who build, we can with conviction say that God was the architect, Jesus was the builder, and the Holy Spirit dwells within us as the perpetual caretaker.

Chapter 2: Satan

What do we know about Satan? Is he just the Halloween caricature seen in comics and movies? Does he actually have horns and a tail and red coloration? You may be surprised to know that John's vision in Revelation 12:3–4 describes him in a very similar way. Don't expect him to appear to you in that fashion though. He is too subtle to make that kind of appearance. It is more in his nature to appear to you as having the voice, mannerisms, and looks of someone you know well, someone you like, perhaps even someone you love. Satan uses people and opportunities. Remember the snake in the garden of Eden? Why should we study him? We do so for the purpose of knowing and recognizing his strategies and avoiding the methods he uses against us.

We really do need to know the extent of his power because we are often his enablers. Does that surprise you? He can't make us do his will. It is our choice, and even though we made the choice in ignorance, we are still responsible for it. So what is Satan like? How is he different from other angels? Why was he thrown out of heaven? Does he have any authority? What does he do, and does he do it alone? How can we resist him? Do we want to? (We should!) How did he look before he was cast out of heaven? What do I need to know to protect myself from him? Are we really in a war now that is being fought on earth? By his own admission Satan roams about on the earth (Job 1:6–7). We are instructed by God to be alert because he prowls about seeking someone to devour (1 Peter 5:8).

His Description

In his comparison of Satan to the king of Tyre, who was a very prosperous seaman who was extremely puffed up by his successes to the extent that he said, "I am a god. I sit in the seat of gods in the heart of the seas. God told him he would die the death of a seaman at the hands of ruthless strangers in the same manner he had killed others." Then he told

Ezekiel to take up a lament over the King by comparing him to another who also considers himself a god. That being is Satan. "You had the seal of perfection, full of wisdom and perfect in beauty," Ezekiel said of him (Ezekiel 28:12) .Then he goes on to identity Satan. "You were in Eden, the garden of God, every precious stone was your covering, you were the cherub who covers and I placed you there, (Ezekiel 28:13–14). "Your heart was lifted up because of your beauty; you corrupted your wisdom by reason of your splendor," but "I cast you to the ground" (Ezekiel 17). This would be the king's fate as well.

I find a great deal of significance in the fact that Satan was beautiful because beauty so often corrupts. We know that he commanded a following among the angels and that he had ambition beyond his position. All of these characteristics seem to have evolved from his beauty. We know he was not content to serve but that he wanted to be served. Had he chosen to use whatever special qualities he had for God, his potential could have been fulfilled, but he wanted to be God. There is a paradox in contemplating the disposition of God-given blessings apart from God. In such situations a blessing can become a curse, and defeat is inevitable. Yet Satan was sure of victory. Nevertheless, his defeat came not from the power of his evil but from the weakness of his own nature. As an example of the poor direction he chose, consider the fact that he refused God's gift, the greatest manifestation of love the world has ever known. Though his final judgment has not been enacted, he was bound and limited in the damage he could do following the resurrection of Christ.

His Nature

What a dramatic change, from perfection and beauty to hatred and the use of others. Why do people murder and lie today? Don't they usually sin because of pride and greed? I want what you have, so I'm going to take it. You think you're better than I am, and I despise you. I'm not lying. I'm just looking out for myself. What's the difference if I do it? No one will know. Have you ever heard any of these excuses? They are common because they've been around since the rebellion of Satan began.

- "He was a murderer from the beginning, and does not stand in the truth, because there is no truth in him. Whenever he speaks a lie, he speaks from his own nature; for he is a liar, and the father of lies" (John 8:44). Does this mean he actually killed others? On the contrary, according to Matthew 5:21–2, anger (hate) is the equivalent of murder. It would be the same in any situation where one person degrades another by calling him or her worthless or no good. Punishment in such cases would be identical to punishment for the one who actually killed. This seems rather severe, doesn't it? The idea is that punishment is not only for deeds but for thoughts as well.

- "The one who practices sin is of the devil; for the devil has sinned from the beginning" (1 John 3:8). The thing to remember about sin is that it is depravity and therefore darkness. "God is love" (1 John 4:16), and in order to abide in Him (John 15:10), we, too, are to love (Galatians 5:13) because it is impossible for hate and love to dwell together. Love is the opposite of hate in the same way that God is the opposite of Satan. God speaks only truth (John 8:32), whereas Satan speaks only lies. It is important to know that lies are not only deception but excuses Satan plants within us to get us to do or not to do something.

His Ambition

It is too bad that ambition often gets in the way of spirituality. This is true not only of the age in which we live but of ages past. Satan is a good example. Isaiah 14:13–14 records the ambitions of Satan's heart. We have absolutely no idea how long God tolerated Satan's ambitions before the battle in heaven got him thrown out of heaven. I visualize God's tolerance in much the same way he tolerates our sin. One day, there will be a reckoning just as there will be for Satan. The following statements, God said, came from the heart of Satan (Isaiah 14:13–14): "I will ascend to heaven; I will raise my throne above the stars of God, I will sit on the mount of assembly in the recesses of the north. I will ascend above the heights of the clouds; I will make myself like the Most High." (The Most High refers to God.)

The ultimate corruption is that Satan wants to be God, but this verse says that instead he will be revealed as the son of destruction. God says of these ambitions that "the one who boasts of them will be revealed as the son of destruction who exalts himself above every type of worship and takes his seat in the temple of God, displaying himself as being God" (2 Thessalonians 2:3–4). God goes on to say that although he is restrained, he will be revealed until he is taken out of the way. This speaks of the end of time when everyone, righteous and evil, will stand before the throne of God. This comment obviously speaks of Satan as the one who is destructive. The man of lawlessness seems a title made especially for him. Some believe this refers to another being or person, but it seems unlikely to me because Isaiah 14:13–15 clearly identifies him as Satan. "How you have fallen from heaven, O star of the morning, son of the dawn! You have been cut down to the earth, you who have weakened the nations" (Isaiah 14:12). Satan is identified by God, not only by the title *star of morning*, which is a title that belongs to God the Son, but by the verse quoted earlier that placed him in the garden, a place the king of Babylon never had opportunity to visit. This liar, this murderer who corrupted himself now wants what can never be his. He is so wrapped up in how wonderful he is that he mistakenly assumes that he is not only God's equal but better. He experienced jealousy and envy.

You would think that perfection would be enough for him, but it wasn't. He was obviously aware that God was more than he was, and just as some humans behave he wanted what God had. I think he actually felt cheated. Was this the seed that corrupted his being? We don't know, of course, but it is an interesting thought to contemplate. Did Satan's ambition cause his corrupt nature, or did his corrupt nature produce his ambition? It is an ageless question, but I believe his nature came first because James 1:15 tells us, "When lust has conceived, it gives birth to sin." He chose wickedness. He cultivated wickedness, and it was wickedness that led to his ambition to be God. Is it not a warning to us? If degradation could claim this angel of beauty and wisdom, could it also happen to us? We need to examine ourselves to be sure we don't think of ourselves more highly than we ought. God loves the heart that is humble.

Satan's actions give us an unchanging principle around which his entire war revolves, and that is the principle of sin. By definition sin is separation from God, though it also means *missing the mark of perfection*. This rebellion by Satan is its first demonstration. Can you appreciate the significance of Satan's eventual punishment?

It is only common sense to assume Satan thought he would win the battle he had started. After all who goes to war without a conviction of victory? Nevertheless Satan and his angels did not win the most important battle for his cause, and that was the battle in heaven against Michael and the archangels (Revelation 12:8). With that loss he and his angels were cast out of heaven to earth. The earth was (and is) a place with which he was already familiar (Job 1:7), as he had won many souls to his warped cause while he was roaming the earth.

We are very much aware of some of those victories. His first battle was in the garden of Eden, where Adam and Eve resided in Paradise. He won that battle in a significant way, thus introducing sin into the world God had made for man. Eve was quick to involve Adam in her sin. As a result they lost their home in Paradise, and they would have to work the rest of their lives in an environment that reflected sin. At a later time Job could not be convinced to "curse God and die" as his wife suggested (Job 2:9), and Satan lost that battle. I hope you can see that both Adam's battle and Job's battle were over issues of belief. Eve chose to believe Satan's perverted version of the truth, and Adam chose to believe Eve; whereas Job's belief in God never wavered.

To sum up the comparisons made between Satan and the two kings, we learn that prior to his rebellion, Satan was a model of perfection, full of wisdom and beauty, a guardian angel ordained (chosen) by God. At the time of his creation he was blameless until his wisdom was corrupted by his beauty. Sadly he forgot that the image he reflected was just an image and that God was the light that provided the image. Without light there could be no reflection. As corruption continued in the path of evil, not only would Satan's beauty disappear, but his desire for evil would increase until he was no longer what he had once been. His pride probably came first in his fall, and it was pride that distorted his vision and his understanding and caused him to deny his Maker. Satan's sin is no different than ours, but he failed to learn that in the absence of spiritual enrichment, degradation is all that is left.

His Authority

We are often misled to believe one of two untruths—either Satan has no control over lives or he can do whatever he wishes. Both statements are false. He does not have unlimited authority, but we must not overlook the fact that he was given some authority for reasons God alone knows. It has always been Satan's viewpoint to search out ways that will be advantageous for his purposes. He does not seek fairness or equality. His basic motivation is that given opportunity man will choose to serve him. After all the evil he practices is exactly what he wanted, so why would it not be what others want? More difficult to assess is why he was give this freedom. I can only say that my trust is in God. Human reasoning might surmise that His decision had something to do with His sameness, His continuity, but I feel quite sure it isn't that simple. I know that He will not force obedience on anyone, so I'm willing to leave it there.

Let's take a look at the activities of demons in connection with Satan's right of choice. You'll notice that their power was often ineffectual in Jesus' presence. They also seem to have come and gone pretty much at will except in His presence. The demons were fearful of Jesus and recognized who He was. Consequently their power was diminished. We may not understand God's purpose, but I believe we can see that it demanded that Satan have some power, if he was to do battle with God. His limitations are clearly outlined in Scripture.

- He has power over the spirit of disobedience (Ephesians 2:2).

- He has power over pride (Luke 4:5–6).

- He has power over the whole world (1 John 5:19).

- He has power over darkness (Acts 26:18).

- He had power over death (Hebrews 2:14). (Please notice that the power over death is no longer in effect, having been removed by Jesus' resurrection.)

Wow! That's quite a list, isn't it? He is the one who challenges us to disobedience and pride, while he exercises his power over the world and death. He believes that when he causes you to sin, you are automatically his. In the meantime he has no concept of how far God will go to accomplish reconciliation. Scripture tells us he is depicted in 1 Peter 5:8 "as walking about" (KJV) or as he "prowls around like" (NAS) a roaring lion[6] (Zodahiates 1992). A beast that is bound would move in this manner, able to go only so far from his stake or tether before he is yanked back to the reality of his limitations.

---

6   Zodahiates, *The Complete Word Study, New Testament,* KJV, copyright second ed. 1992, Spiros Zodhiates (published by AMG International., Chattanooga), 1 Peter 5:8 "walketh 4043."

His Limitations

We are fortunate that God placed limitations on Satan. The more our faith grows, the stronger our resistance will be. James 4:7 tells us that when we resist him, he actually runs from us. What an amazing thought! Wouldn't you like to have a picture of that? Create one in your mind and then watch him as he scrambles away from you in fear! That is an empowering thought to keep in mind! These are the ways in which his limitations are effective:

- His power is limited by our individual faith (James 4:7).

- His power is limited by our resistance (James 4:7).

- His power is limited by our humility (1 Corinthians 10:13).

- His power is limited by God's grace (Job 1:12).

- His power is limited by our love (Revelation 12:12).

- His power is limited by God's blessing to Abraham (Genesis 12:3).

- His power is limited because his time is limited (Revelation 12:12). (There will be an end just as there was a beginning.)

Don't fool yourself that these limitations have incapacitated him. They have only made him angrier and more dangerous. He will go to any length within his power to win your soul. It is probable that Satan's powers were not limited until after the resurrection and ascension. Because Satan is now depicted as being on the prowl here on earth, it says to me that we can avoid him or that we can run from him as Joseph did. As you strengthen your faith don't forget the tethering pole because staying out of Satan's way makes it easier to resist him.

Satan does not accomplish his work alone. Scripture tells us that he has many helpers, but lacking from his list are angels who, we are told, are "in eternal bonds under darkness" reserved for judgment (Jude 6). First Peter 2:4 gives us a bit of additional information, "God did not spare angels when they sinned, but cast them into hell and committed them to pits of darkness, reserved for judgment." Perhaps this is one of the ways in which the Holy Spirit restrains evil as in 2 Thessalonians 2:6–7. It is wise to remember that Satan uses you and me whenever and by whatever methods he is able. How may we recognize these coworkers of Satan?

- In His reply to His apostles, Jesus instructs regarding those who claim to be Christ. "Recognize there will be some who will make the claim, He says, but do not believe, because He has already told us how He will return in the clouds" (Thessalonians 4:16). Whether those who would make such a claim are deluded by an illness of the mind or are instruments of Satan, Jesus seems to be saying that knowing is enough, leave it alone (Mark 13:22).

- As for false prophets, they will be showing signs and wonders. Jesus says to beware because they are wolves in sheep's clothing. They can be known by their fruit (Matthew 7:15).

- Did you think demons were a thing of the past? (Timothy 4:1). Don't expect them to look or act like demons. How will you recognize them? "Search the scriptures daily" (John 5:39).

His Work

Satan's work on earth began in the garden with Adam and Eve. His great deception was in the statement, "You shall not surely die." Whether or not he was aware of spiritual death, I'm not sure. God's plan had been hidden all those years since creation, so how would the Devil have known? In the garden, Satan knew that the death that follows disobedience would not be immediate. That may have been all he knew at that time. He was looking to score a point against God, and he was successful. Having been driven from the garden, without access to the tree of life, Adam and Eve would have died eventually, and although they didn't know it, their disobedience had already separated them from God. There was no hope for their salvation except for the plan God had created.

Satan may or may not have known there was a plan, but I don't believe he did, first because of the secrecy with which the plan had been protected and second because Satan was egotistically confident in his own power. I am convinced that His power over death was not an immediate thing, but whether or not he already had that power, we have no way of knowing.

He was still unaware of God's plan when the way it was would change to the way it will be!

Of course there would be other battles. Among those Job would defeat Satan, and that great warrior Paul would realize the error of his ways and join the battle for God. It is probable that Satan exulted at the time of Jesus' crucifixion, feeling confident the victory was his. By now he had the keys of death, and even though he had been unsuccessful in having Jesus destroyed at birth or during the temptation, the Jews and the Romans had now taken care of it for him. I do not believe he even imagined the extent to which God would go to achieve reconciliation, but even if he had, did not death still belong to him? It was the resurrection that purchased victory over both physical and spiritual death. Jesus paid the price that none of us could pay, paving the way for reconciliation. Satan, angry, defiant, and bitter to the end, continues to inflict as much damage as possible in the time that is left to him.

The methods he uses are predictable but deceptive.

- He lies (Genesis 3:4–5).

- He deceives (Corinthians 11:3).

- He inflicts disease (Job 2:7).

- He performs signs and wonders (2 Thessalonians 2:8–9).

- He changes his appearance (2 Corinthians 11:14).

- He distorts Scripture (Matthew 22:29).

- *He tempted Christ.* "And the tempter came and said to Him, 'If you are the Son of God, command that these stones become bread'" (Matthew 4:3). Can you imagine that Jesus would actually do such a thing? I am convinced that Satan used this approach because he wouldn't have dreamed of doing without anything he wanted, much less needed. Surely he knew that Jesus could feed an entire village if the need arose, so I'm wondering if this reveals Satan's jealousy of the Son of God. Actually Jesus answered Satan by quoting Scripture, which was His means of refusal. When I have considered the temptation of Jesus in the wilderness, I have felt quite certain that Satan judged our Lord by his own standards. Food, power, and wealth are likely things Satan would have coveted, had he been of human flesh. Surely he knew that God is omnipotent and that Jesus has "all the fullness of the Father," meaning that He could have provided food for Himself. Has he forgotten that Jesus created the world and all that's in it? That is power. There is always the possibility that Satan may have considered our Lord's powers suspended while He was on earth. If this was so, he obviously didn't understand the relationship between God the Father, the Son, and the Holy Spirit. Satan could do nothing to harm God or the angels who were under His protection, so if he had had the power to deal in the spiritual realm, he would have done it without qualms, for he possessed no compassion, no empathy, and certainly no conscience.

- "For this reason, when I could endure it no longer, I also sent to find out about your faith, for fear that the tempter might have *tempted you*, and our labor should be in vain" (1 Thessalonians 3:5). What is Paul saying here? He is telling the Thessalonians that following Satan can undo all that has been learned.

- *He tests man.* "Simon, Simon, behold, Satan demanded permission to sift you like wheat" (Luke 22:31). Satan not only tempts us but also puts obstacles in our way to test our strength. Remember that if you resist him, he will run from you! He accuses man before God. "Then Satan answered the Lord, 'Does Job fear God for nothing? Hast Thou not made a hedge about him and his house and all that he has, on every side? Thou hast blessed the work of his hands, and his possessions have increased in the land. But put forth Thy hand now and touch all he has; he will surely curse Thee to Thy face'" (Job 1:9–11). Why does Satan suppose that this is what Job would do? I think it is because it is what he would have done.

- *He wages war.* "Be of sober spirit, be on the alert. Your adversary, the devil, prowls about like a roaring lion, seeking someone to devour" (1 Peter 5:8). Satan is always quick to sense a weakness, a pain to turn to his advantage, fears to put insidiously into your heart, depression to control your mind. Therefore, remember to continually strengthen your faith and your spiritual growth, and also keep in your heart and mind that unless things go his way, he fears you. Why? Because you have the tools to resist him.

Would it surprise you to know that the war in which we are engaged is already won? We don't feel as if it is won because it continues on the battlefields right inside of us. The proof, however, came with the resurrection. Satan has been defeated, judged, and condemned by God (Hebrews 2:14), so what's the deal? There are two possibilities. One is that God and Satan fought phase one of the battle and Satan was defeated. I suggest this because his defeat with Michael got him thrown out of heaven, and as a consequence he is no longer welcome in heaven; however, it was a blessing for us in that he can no longer play the advocate against us in God's presence. It is also true as evidenced from his wrath at the time he was thrown down that fighting man alone was not of his liking. Remember his ambition? He had some bizarre plans for himself in the heavenly realm. So my guess is that we are in phase two of this battle now because we are the ones he came to when he hit the ground running.

Let's take a look at the other possibility. From God's perspective He is interested in saving as many souls as possible. Only He will know when no more good can come from continuing the battle, and when that time comes, He will declare the victory by sending His Son for those who belong to Him. First Thessalonians 4:16–18 says, "For the Lord Himself will descend from heaven with a shout, with the voice of the archangel and with the trumpet of God, and the dead in Christ will rise first. Then we who are alive and remain will be caught up together with them in the clouds to meet the Lord in the air, and so we shall always be with the Lord." Jesus paid the blood price for the salvation of souls and for the forgiveness of the sins of all, including all who lived by faith both before and after this age in which we live. Perhaps you hadn't thought about it in this particular light, but the principle of choice given to us by God gives us an edge on salvation. Why? Because it puts the responsibility for choices made right on our own two shoulders. Choose wisely. God did His part, and Jesus did His. Now it is our time to choose. Matthew 12:30 says if we are not for Him, we are against Him. Have you decided yet? It is the most important question of your life.

When God says, "I am the Alpha and the Omega," He is reminding us that just as there was a beginning, there will be an end (Revelation 1:8). Neither victory nor defeat will be complete until that end is manifest to us. Even though Satan knows he is defeated and knows the punishment that awaits him, I believe when that punishment comes it will be beyond anything he could have imagined. In the meantime he continues to do his prowl, hoping to take lots of us with him to whatever God has provided for those who rejected His Son.

His Defeat

There are numerous reasons for Satan's defeat, but here are three that are recorded in Revelation. These particular reasons apply just as well to our own battles. We are not currently suffering the persecution that was going on in the first century, but this doesn't mean that it will never be in our future. In addition to the fact that Satan and his angels were not strong enough to defeat Michael, here is what God had to say, "They lost because of the blood of the Lamb. They lost because of the testimony (in support of Jesus) of those who gave their lives (the martyrs). They didn't love their lives (more than they loved God) when they were faced with death" (Revelation 12:11).

The prayers of the saints are another contribution to Satan's defeat. This example is a heavenly scene demonstrated for the strengthening of those under assault on earth by Satan.

As prayers go up to God they are placed on an altar before God and covered with much incense. The smoke of the incense with the prayers of the saints (that's you and me) goes up before Him, and the angel takes the censer that held the incense and fills it with fire from the altar and throws it to earth as an act of cleansing in response to the prayers on the altar (Revelation 8:3–4). I realize this may be metaphorical, but it coincides with other teachings, such as the one that says that through us, the sweet aroma of the knowledge of Him is manifest in every place (2 Corinthians 2:15). And with even greater similarity there is the ritual cleansing of Isaiah's mouth (Isaiah 6:5–7). My response to the example of the altar and incense is shame that more of my own prayers are not on that altar.

The example that follows from Revelation reveals Satan on earth, which may or may not be an indication of a step in his actual fall. It is my belief based on God's statement that he was a liar from the beginning, that his fall occurred almost immediately after his creation. How long God tolerated this rebellious situation we have no idea. We do know that Satan spent time away from heaven based on God's question to Him in Job when the Lord asked where he had been, and Satan replied, "Oh, from roaming about on the earth." My conclusion from this is that he was not restricted from heaven but that he didn't spend much time there.

As for his actual fall I would say inappropriate behavior with God came first and then probably corruption of the angels followed by involving himself in the introduction of sin on earth, which prompted God to include him in the curse of Adam and Eve. These were all steps from which there was no return. His list is endless, however. He instigated the death of Abel by his brother, Cain, which temporarily eliminated a righteous line of descendants for Adam. He tried to kill or corrupt Moses. He attempted to do the same with Jesus at birth and thus eliminate Him as a competitor. I surmise he hoped beyond reason that Jesus would not make it through the temptation. The curse pronounced on Satan after sin was introduced to the world was that there would always be enmity between Satan and the seed of woman, which in its singular form applies to Jesus. The outcome of his rebellion is that he would be punished eternally. Jesus, on the other hand, would be victorious (Genesis 3:14–15). He really should have listened to what God said, which implies he wasn't as wise as he thought he was. We must be careful that we don't make the same mistake that he made.

Summary

It has been difficult for me to write about Satan. The more I learn about him, the more I am appalled that such a beautiful being that was created so lovingly and perfect could turn out the way he has. Were he a person of my acquaintance, I'm sure I would weep for him, but because he is Satan, I am very angry that he chose such a decadent, self-absorbed path. He had God. He had the beauty of the heavenly home. He had the blessed task of being with God as a covering cherub, and he was perfect in beauty and wisdom. I'm not sure I know exactly what a covering cherub was supposed to do, but I do know that the position was an honor. My question is this: How could anyone throw away such an existence to live in hate for the sake of evil? There is no sense to it, and I hate for decisions to be senseless.

In retrospect I would say he is a person (or being) who doesn't care about anyone except himself. We call that ego or narcissism. It means to be totally self-absorbed. He lies and cheats, and he is a murderer. He has sinned since his beginning. God did not make him that way.

This raised the question in my mind about where evil comes from, and I am of the conclusion that the possibility for evil is in all of us. It is a matter of choice to decide which we will follow, goodness or evil. That makes choice an eternal principle, one that has always been a part of the heavenly sphere. You need to know that principles are unchanging. Instructions on how to do almost anything can change over time, but the principle remains the same. When choice was added to each individual's determination, evil became a part of the equation. Can evil be changed? I rather doubt it, but I do know that the inclination to do evil changes with some people as they are taught.

We learned that Satan has certain authority but that the extent of it is limited. Quite unexpectedly we learned that the individual is in control of his limitations. How is this possible? It is only possible through Christ by the increase of faith allowed within the heart. It is faith that enables our resistance to evil.

Outside of human resistance to his temptations and the testing of individuals, Satan is limited by controls that come from God. These are focused on God's grace and the fact that only God knows when the war will be complete, so Satan understands his time is short. He doesn't have any idea when the end will come, and that bothers him. One thing we must keep in mind is that he has no guilt or sorrow. He is perverted in his thinking, and he will cause you all the trouble he can command. He doesn't care about you or me or anyone. He seeks only things that are advantageous to him. He knows that he is defeated and knows the fate that awaits him, but he is still delusional because he has not yet experienced that punishment. He still hopes for something to break in his favor. He is a gambler.

Study Guide—Chapter 2

Q. When Scripture says that Satan is a murderer, does this mean he kills? Explain.
A. Probably not. We are of no benefit to him dead. However, the New Testament teaches that he is a *murderer*, meaning he lies, and Jesus teaches that the thought is the same as the act.

Q. Define sin as it relates to death.

A. Sin separates us from God, and without God there is no life. The more complicated answer is that God is light and without light it is impossible for anything to live.

Q. Why do you think Satan rebelled against God?

A. I think Satan rebelled because of jealousy, greed, and hatred. Now why he harbored those destructive attitudes would be a hard one to answer. He had everything—beauty, intelligence, even wisdom. The answer lies in the fact that both angels and humans are *capable* of evil. You might need another question if you seriously start thinking about it and begin to realize that the capability to do evil is the reason we have choice.

Q. Name four ways in which Satan's power is limited.

A. I think we'll start with grace. By God's grace Satan was created and given choice for the path he would take. When God saw which path he chose, the Lord had to put limits on what Satan could do. My opinion is that had Satan not chosen as he did, he would have had the same power that God and Jesus have. Then God allowed him to have some power to tempt and test man; however, those powers are controlled by the one he has chosen as his victim. The victim can rebuff Satan depending on his or her own faith and spiritual growth, or he or she can join Satan in what he or she is tempted to do. His power is also limited by our humility and by our love.

Q. What happened to the angels who followed Satan's lead and rebelled?

A. The angels who chose to follow Satan's lead in rebellion are in chains confined to darkness awaiting judgment.

Q. Why was Satan freed from his restrictions after the thousand year reign? Do you think he was confined to the abyss during that time?

A. Scripture reveals that he would be released from his prison and that he would again go about deceiving nations. As for the second part of my question, we're getting into some opinions here. I don't agree with a lot of what is said about the end of time—that there will be a thousand years of Armageddon and rapture. I have studied it carefully, and we will get to that in the nineteenth and twentieth chapters; however, for now just let me say that it is an interesting subject and one in which many people are very interested. I'm not sure that it makes a whole lot of difference which side of the fence you are on, and I will explain why I believe that when we get to that part of our study. I would urge you to do your own studying because in the end it is each person's own individual responsibility to understand what God is saying to us about the *end times*.

Q. Name three categories of coworkers who are active in aiding Satan's cause.

A. Strangely, as we saw in regard to the angels who followed Satan, they are no longer of benefit to him. He still has demons and false prophets on his team, and though much smaller in number, I would imagine, we hear occasionally about those who claim to be Christ. Scripture calls them *false Christs* and says they should be recognized as such but left alone.

Q. Name the moment of Satan's defeat.

A. The resurrection marked the time when Satan was defeated, and his defeat was solidified when Jesus ascended back to heaven and was exalted where He sits at the right hand of God.

Q. Which of Satan's methods is most effective with you? (This is another thought question. Write your answer in the space below.)

A.

Chapter 3: The Dilemma: Sin v. Salvation

The Preliminaries

Satan introduced sin in heaven by rebelling against the Creator (Isaiah 14:12–17; Ezekiel 28:11–19), by taking angels with him in his rebellion (Matthew 25:41 and Revelation 12:1–14), and by introducing sin into the human race by his temptation of Eve (Genesis 3:1–15).

What is the other side of this situation with which God was suddenly confronted? To begin with, it was not a surprise because He knew it would happen. That is why He created the plan before the foundation of the world. That way He would be prepared. We can't get into His mind and find out why he wanted to create man or for that matter why he wanted to create Satan. But for whatever reason it seemed good to Him, and I suspect that He did it with the same love and care with which He did all of creation.

We are incapable of changing what occurred with the result that we are in darkness, separated from God. We are fortunate that God wants reconciliation with us. If we fail to accept His offer, our lives will be lost in eternal punishment without access to God, who created us and loves us. In my mind I would think that the agony and regret of not accepting His offer could bring insanity to anyone.

Sin is universal. It is a part of every person's life that has ever lived or ever will live, and as with everything God did there is a reason. The ability to sin is within us, and God knew that we would sin. Therefore, according to Paul, He "shut up all in disobedience so that He may show mercy to all" (Romans 11:32). In other words there will be no partiality. There is another little quirk here that is most intriguing. The fact that we will sin puts the responsibility for sin on us because the choice is ours. Sin is the reason we have choice.

This is a marvelous example of God's sameness. Mercy has many motivations, but this one puts us all on an even playing field. People have to choose which sides of themselves they will follow. The decision is up to the individual. No wonder it was inevitable that there would be universal war between man and Satan with the heavenly host participating on our behalf as they keep Satan in check to prevent his going beyond limitations. The dilemma that faced God was not whether or not to grant reconciliation but how to bridge the gap in such a way that there would be no partiality.

The principle presented to Adam was one of belief. Now God didn't say it quite that way. Instead He told them something they must not do and why. When they did what He told them not to do, it demonstrated that they had not believed Him when He had said they "would surely die."

The dilemma would have to be solved by finding a way in which the principle of belief would be developed in order that its integrity would be the same for all people of all time. The question, though hypothetical, would hinge on a single premise of belief in order to fill that qualification. The purchase price (when paid with the blood of Jesus) would apply equally to faithful believers of all ages, past, present, and future. Inherent in the plan would be the concept of obedience, which preceded Adam's sin and takes us back to Satan's sin of unbelief.

As indicated earlier, principles don't change, but instructions do. Never again would a potential believer be instructed not eat of the tree of good and evil. Nor would a potential believer ever again be told to build an ark. Situations change, making it necessary for different instructions, but principles never change

We'll learn that no man is without an avenue of belief, so there will be no excuse for those who choose not to believe. God has provided us with different avenues through which we may come to believe. The Israelites were entrusted with what is referred to as "the oracles of God" (Romans 3:2). In this age we have the Scripture (2 Timothy 2:15), but what of those who had neither? Paul tells us, "That which is known about God is evident within them; for God made it evident to them ... since the creation of the world His invisible attributes, His eternal power and divine nature, have been clearly seen, being understood through what has been made, so that they are without excuse" (Romans 1:19–20).

The Foundation

Actually beginning with Adam and Eve, God began to lay a foundation for His plan. I like to think of it as analogous to our lives on earth. As infants we are totally dependent, but eventually we do become aware of things greater than ourselves. Why? It is because God placed the desire to know Him within our hearts. He allows us the choice about what we'll do with the knowledge we learn and the time in which to demonstrate it. In his spiritual infancy man was unable to comprehend all that God required of him, so he needed time in which to learn both God's requirements and obedience. Keep that in mind during the centuries that follow as man is learning. No man is without an avenue of belief.

Let's compare resolving the dilemma to something we can understand. If man were to build a magnificent cathedral, he would not start with breathtaking arches that are so beautiful and that make the vast open spaces possible. No, he would begin with a foundation, something that is not of itself a thing of beauty but is a practical necessity for the beauty and magnificence to come. So it is with God. His plan was ready, but man was not yet ready for the plan.

God's foundation is a building block that builds on the solution God devised. It would accomplish several things.

- It would help man know God.

- It would help him develop his own conscience toward the ends of obedience.

- It would prepare the way for the completion of God's plan.

- It would preserve holiness in a line through which Jesus would come.

The world became very wicked, and God saw "that the wickedness of man was great … and that the intent of man's heart was only evil continually and the Lord was sorry that He had made man on the earth" (Genesis 6:5–6). God was so grieved over this situation that He asked a man named Noah to build an ark. He would destroy the earth and all that was in it. Noah and his family were the only righteous people on the earth, and his obedience allowed them to be saved from the flood that resulted. Let me point out that up until that time it had never rained because God had caused a mist to rise up from the earth to water things. Noah's obedience required tremendous faith as he constructed the ark and was harassed and ridiculed by his neighbors.

This example shows clearly that faith begins with belief that produces obedience.

A man by the name of Abram, who lived in the land of Ur, was told by God to leave his country and go to a land He would be shown. Abram didn't ask God why. He just got things together and went. In time God told him he would be blessed by becoming a great nation of people and that all people of the earth would be blessed through him and that he would have a son who would be his heir. Abram was one hundred years old when Isaac was born.

In addition God told Abraham (whose name had been changed by God) that his descendants would be in bondage in another land, but after four hundred years, they would return and possess the land in which Abraham was a sojourner. And God said of Abraham, "I have chosen him so that he may command his children and his household after him to keep the way of the Lord by doing righteousness and justice, so that the Lord may bring upon Abraham what He has spoken about him" (Genesis 18:19). So now we understand the purpose for which God directed Abraham to leave Ur and go the land of Canaan, namely to provide a place for the Israelites to begin their existence as a new nation, which would be the fulfillment of part of God's promise to Abraham. God is faithful.

These events all became a part of God's foundation, and eventually, the foundation itself would be finished after the resurrection and ascension. Then God the Holy Spirit would come to Jerusalem on the day of the Pentecost, and His church would have its beginning.

Eventually the Law of Moses would become the guideline by which the Israelites lived. It contained particular instructions for a particular time, as did instructions given individually to those who lived before the law was given. With the giving of the law God's method of communication changed, and He spoke to His people through the law. After the day of Pentecost and the establishment of His church, the law was no longer an active law to be obeyed; however, this does not mean it would be thrown away as something with no value. As God's Word it must be studied but not used as law.

Hebrews 10:1 tells us that the law was a shadow of the good things to come and Jesus would be the guarantee for those good things. Forgiveness is the new principle. It seems strange to us that there was no forgiveness under the law, but because there was no forgiveness, animal sacrifices had to be made every day as an act of faith so that their forgiveness would eventually be a reality. This promise would be fulfilled through the shed blood of Jesus, but His blood would grant forgiveness for not only their sins but for all sin, past, present, and future.

One of the ways God helped His people to understand His will was through prophets, who were called by God and instructed in what to say. This, too, was a part of His foundation.

Summary

The principle of belief coupled with obedience is a vital part of God's foundations. We saw it in the examples of Noah and Abraham, and in chapter 1, we saw it by its absence with Eve. It is not exaggerating to say that next to the incarnation, crucifixion, and ascension, it is the *key* principle of salvation. Of course the reason it is key is that God established it. But to help understand its importance, let's look at the why.

To understand the why, we need to point out that God is not partial to any man. He treats all people the same, no matter in what age he lives. That seems to have created a lot of division in the Christian world over the years because we didn't understand. Today we seem to interpret His Word by our backgrounds, our current understanding, and our attitudes instead of following God's plan. I'm sure none of us wants to cause dissension, but it happens. The solution God established can eliminate all division if we comprehend the significance as well as its beauty and simplicity. Eve chose to believe Satan rather than God, and that was all God had instructed her regarding salvation. We can easily see that it was a simple request, but to Eve it had no significance because of her naivety as well as her spiritual immaturity. God provides a way to overcome even that situation, and we will get to that soon; however, for now it's important that we understand this requirement: Believe and obey. If that's all you know, that's all that's required, and in some parts of the world today that's about all that's known before individuals become martyrs.

In the case of Noah he heard and obeyed. It is the same with Abraham, who heard and obeyed. This doesn't mean that they were perfect men or that their belief and obedience was all they accomplished spiritually during very long lives. But it does mean that faith followed by obedience put them in touch with God's grace and that in time they would learn of other things God wanted of them. It would be time then for other acts of obedience. God tells us at a later time of their ongoing imperfections. This is why it seems obvious to me that belief coupled with obedience achieves the reconciliation God so desires. Circumstances change. Situations change. Instructions change. But throughout the ages, the one thing that is unchanging regarding salvation is the necessity to believe and obey. God's sameness requires that we be in touch with His grace by the same method.

But what do we obey, and when do we do it? Obedience is required when you learn what God wants you to do. It's that simple. It is not a huge package of do's and don'ts. It is a gradual process of learning. Of course as you learn to study and pray, you will learn at a faster pace. Your heart also plays a big part. While God will judge you by the fact that you try and that you want to obey, it is not the same as not wanting and not trying. He wants to be in your heart.

God's dilemma was augmented by the fact that He still wants us back. He has honored us with a means to achieve the fellowship that He so desires, but we must want it as well.

Study Guide—Chapter 3

Q. What was God's dilemma? (I hope you recognize that the word *dilemma* doesn't apply to any of His qualities, so when it is used here it is in what is euphemistically called the *editorial sense*.)
A. His *dilemma* was how to make salvation available to people of all generations so that is was completely impartial.

Q. What purpose did God wish to achieve?
A. Firstly I believe he wanted to achieve reconciliation, which would put each individual in touch with His grace and which would make repentance and forgiveness available for all.

Q. What is the fundamental principle of reconciliation and salvation?
A. It is quite interesting how this has developed while we are maintaining God's principles of sameness and impartiality, but as each new principle is added it is easy to see that without belief that principle itself would be useless. Of course, as one develops in maturity he or she is capable of

handling other principles as well, but *belief* has to be the beginning. It was the beginning for the first man and woman, and it will continue to be for all humanity.

Q. How do we know that obedience is inherent in belief?
A. Forgive me for saying so, but belief alone has weak legs. Look for example at Satan and the demons that believed and trembled. *Belief* has to be like a two-sided coin with the flip side the principle of obedience. To be of benefit both sides are necessary. Satan wouldn't dream of letting his belief develop into faith. That's why he only has one side.

Q. Why was it necessary for God to lay a foundation? Why didn't He just send Jesus to redeem mankind immediately instead of spending time on a foundation? These are the foundation bones, even for a spiritual building.
A. How many buildings have you seen that have no foundation? To take the analogy further, how many successful businesses do you suppose have made it without goals and plans to get there? A foundation is the strength of any building.

Q. God's foundation would continue to be laid until what event would transpire?
A. God's foundation began with Adam and Eve and will continue until the resurrection when it will be complete. After the ascension it will be solidified because Jesus would be sitting at the right hand of God.

Chapter 4: Sin and the Promise

Sin is the action exhibited in man that originates in evil. The possibility to participate in evil exists in all men, but Satan cannot force such action. It is a choice. James, the brother of our Lord, tells us, "Each one is tempted when he is carried away and enticed by his own lust. Then when lust has conceived, it gives birth to sin; and when sin is accomplished, it brings forth death" (James 1:15). James also tells us God cannot be tempted by evil because of His holy nature and that He Himself does not tempt anyone but each one is tempted when he is carried away with his own lust.

Sin begins with desire, and when that desire is accomplished, it becomes sin. Sin is often defined as the lust of the eye, the lust of the flesh, and the pride of life. Peter refers to it from God's perspective, "Do not be conformed to the former lusts which were yours in your ignorance, but like the Holy One who called you, be holy yourselves also in all your behavior; because it is written, 'You shall be holy, for I am holy'" (1 Peter 1:14). His appeal is addressed to obedient believers.

The promise God made to Abraham seems ahead of its historical time slot, but I guess that, too, is to establish the need for the plan. It is necessary for us, therefore, to grasp that the part after the crucifixion could not have happened without the foundation that came first. God was preparing the way for His Son's entrance into the world as a human. Without the foundation, which provided the criteria by which to identify Jesus, He would not have been their Messiah. This information would come through the teaching of the law and the knowledge of the prophets, whose information came from God. The fact that many Jews did not accept the reality of their Messiah is addressed in Romans. "If some did not believe, their unbelief will not nullify the faithfulness of God ... let God be found true, though every man be found a liar" (Romans 3:3).

God's lack of partiality was demonstrated by the gift of Jesus' blood, which was publicly displayed as propitiation by faith. I realize that's a big word, but it simply means that Jesus' blood is the reason for man's justification. "Abraham believed God, and it was credited to him as righteousness" (Romans 3:25). God goes on to say that if a man works, his wage is not a favor but what is due him. If he does not work (in this instance, "does not work" simply refers to the fact nothing has been done that deserves a wage) but believes anyway, he is justified by God and credited with righteousness (Romans 4:5).

Of righteousness apart from works, David is quoted as saying, "Blessed are those whose lawless deeds have been forgiven, and whose sins have been covered, blessed is the man whose sin the Lord will not take into account" (Romans 4:7).

This discussion in Romans leads to the reason for Abraham's circumcision before the law and why it was counted as righteousness. The seal of circumcision was later established as a seal of the covenant while it remained a seal of righteousness (because he had not worked for it) "in order to be the father of all who believe, both of the circumcision and the uncircumcised" (Romans 4:10–12).

And here is the final word from God: "For the promise to Abraham that he would be the heir of the world was not through the law, but through the righteousness of faith" (Romans 4:13). "That it may be in accordance with grace" (Romans 4:16). This may also help to explain righteousness versus unrighteousness: "Take care, brethren, that there not be in any one of you an evil, unbelieving heart" (Hebrews 3:12). And also consider this passage: "That there be no immoral or godless person like Esau, who sold his own birthright for a single meal. For you know that even afterwards, when he desired to inherit the blessing, he was rejected for he found no place for repentance, though he sought for it with tears" (Hebrews 12:16–17). Nonbelief, according to God, is evil. I know our generation doesn't see it in that way, but God says it is so. It can be compared to a bad apple in a basket of fruit; it contaminates those with whom it comes in contact.

God's Plan

At this point in the history of the children of Israel simplicity has been the key. However, God repeats to Abram, "This is my covenant which you shall keep, between me and you and your descendants after you" (Genesis 17:9). The covenant was conditional on obedience. Though the nation as a whole was apostate, there was always an obedient remnant of faithful Israelites (Zephaniah 3:12-13). And God chose to continue with the covenant for the sake of those who were obedient as well as for the lineage that would come from within the remnant.

How does that affect the plan? The one who believes in God grows in faith, and the one who grows in faith develops the desire to obey God. It is the same today. Faith produces faith. We are to walk by faith. We are justified by faith. There is one Lord, one faith, one hope, one baptism, one God and Father of all, and it all works by love. These are all qualities that we must grow in. None is accomplished immediately, but with consistency we gain in abilities as we move forward in faith and obedience. In addition it is faith that draws us closer to God and to His plan. Because of sin God has introduced the principles of repentance, mercy, and justice. Repentance puts us in contact with God's mercy and His grace. Consequently man learns (or should learn) from his disobedience that God exacts justice and that every decision carries with it a consequence, but when man chooses to obey God, then God is merciful. Expulsion from the garden was both justice and mercy in that Adam no longer had all his needs met and would have to work by the sweat of his brow, with all its trials and worries. However, God could have exacted his life without hope of reconciliation.

A Promise Given

It should be noted that God didn't *have* to continue with His plan. Only His love for man compelled Him to go forward. In the midst of sin, God gave man a promise of hope. Speaking to the Devil in the garden after the fall, He said, "I will put enmity between you and the woman, and between your seed and her seed (singular) He, shall bruise you on the head and you shall bruise him on the heel" (Genesis 3:15). The implication is of hate that develops into constant warfare between Satan and the seed. An additional reference to the seed of woman being singular is found in Galatians 3:16, "Now the promises were spoken to Abraham and to his seed." He does not say, "And to seeds," as referring to many, but as to one, "And to your seed, that is Christ." The phrase "He shall bruise you on the head" means that Satan will die from the conflict as we can see from this text that comes from the close of the warfare. "And the devil who deceived them, was thrown into the lake of fire and brimstone" (Revelation 20:10).

Genesis 22:18 repeats the promise to Abraham and adds, "Because you have obeyed my voice" (Romans 9:7–8), which refers back to Abraham's obedience in offering his son, Isaac, as a sacrifice. Of course, we know that

God halted the knife in Abraham's hand and Isaac was not offered, but God knew by Abraham's obedience the strength of his faith.

The promise is now defined between a spiritual and a physical blessing of all nations, and the two verses connect in understanding in Galatians 3:8, where it says, "The Scripture, foreseeing that God would justify the Gentiles by faith, preached the gospel beforehand to Abraham, saying, 'All the nations will be blessed in you.'" Thus, we are able to see that Satan does not have free reign. Quite the contrary, there is *hope*.

It is clear from the following two passages that the blessing was not to be limited to Abraham's physical descendants. "All the families of the earth" and "all the nations of the earth" go beyond the familial bond.

"Now the Lord said to Abram, go forth from your country, and from your relatives and from your father's house, to the land which I will show you; and I will make you a great nation, and I will bless you, and make your name great; and so you shall be a blessing; and I will bless those who bless you, and the one who curses you I will curse. And in your all the families of the earth shall be blessed" (Genesis 12:1–3). To sum it up Abraham and his *physical descendants* (plural) were the means through which Jesus (descendant in the singular) would come, and the blessing He would bring (salvation) would encompass not only the Jews (physical descendants) but *all nations* (spiritual descendants by faith) (Genesis 12:1–3).

These verses speak of several facts:

- God would justify the Gentiles in His own time.

- It would be essential at that time to know that the blessing given to Abraham was given to him before he was circumcised, specifically before the law was given.

- Abraham would have two sets of descendants, those of his flesh and those of the spirit.

- His descendants of the flesh would inherit the first part of the blessing stating that Abraham will be a great nation (the physical part of the blessing).

- His other descendants will be spiritual descendants by reason of faith (children of promise), which would make them children of God. Their blessing will be of the spirit.

To facilitate this happening God says to Abraham, "I want you to pack up everything and go to a place I'll show you, and Abraham went." Then a good while later when he was on his way, God met him at a place called Haran, where Abraham had just buried his father along the road to Canaan, and God said again, "I'm going to make a great nation out of you, and I will bless anyone who blesses you and curse anyone who curses you." And again Abraham did as the Lord directed. He was seventy-five years old. And then the Lord came to him this time in a vision and said, "Abraham, your reward will be great. Don't be afraid." And this time Abraham reminded the Lord that he had no children, and God took him outside to show him the stars and told him to count them if he could because "so shall your descendants be" (Genesis 15:1–6). Later after Sarai had taken things into her own hands and decided they would have their son by means of Hagar, the handmaiden, things got a bit sticky, and when that son (Ishmael) was born, God appeared again. After He repeated the blessing, God told Abraham what his future would be. He began by changing Abram's name to Abraham and Sarai's name to Sarah. To Abraham's physical descendants He would give all the land of Canaan, the land where Abraham had sojourned since leaving his home in Ur.

Then God gave Abraham the commandment for circumcision and told Abraham he would have a son, and this time Abraham fell on his face and laughed because by now he was ninety-nine years old. After this event, God offered burnt sacrifices to seal the arrangement and told him he would have a son within the year. Though Abraham was ninety-nine years old, he believed what God said and continued to believe even when God told him to offer that son as a sacrifice to God.

God's Choice of Israel

God tells us that He didn't choose Israel to be His people because they were a great nation but because they were a "nation fewest of all peoples" (Deuteronomy 7:7). Remember how the nation started out? Abram, Sarai (his wife), Terah (his father), and Lot (his nephew) made up that first group that would eventually become the nation of Israel. It was Israel's lack of size that caught God's interest. Other nations that were larger might have claimed credit for the seemingly impossible victories won by Israel. In the process of observing the Israelites, those other nations would learn of the God of Israel.

Through weakness, God told them, His power is perfected (2 Corinthians 12:9). It is also how other nations would learn of Him in awe or in fear. Have you considered that it is the same relationship that man has with Him today? We are His ambassadors to proclaim His message through example and by teaching. Is man then the source of salvation? Not at all, but the power of God's Word is demonstrated and perfected through the messenger.

The fact that Abraham and the nation of Israel were chosen as the vehicles through which the blessing would come did not mean God was playing favorites. On the contrary, with greater blessings there are always greater responsibilities. Whatever there was about Abraham that caused God to choose him as the recipient of His plan, it was a responsibility and would continue to be a responsibility to Israel even after Abraham's death. It would take 430 years before the law was given to Moses on Mount Sinai, a period of time when they were slaves to a king in Egypt who didn't remember Joseph and how he had saved the country from starvation by God's grace.

Abraham's physical descendants would be known generically as Hebrews. Later a grandson named Jacob would come to be known as Israel, and the descendants would then be called Israelites. Still later corruption of the name Judah, a son of Jacob, would give us the designation Jew. These were all descendants of Abraham, which were by blood. The spiritual descendants would follow a different requirement.

Though the Israelites were a small nation, they were very important because God had entrusted the oracles (Word) of God to them (Romans 3:2), through which sin was identified (Romans 3:20). For this reason we owe a great debt to the nation of Israel and to the law, from which we have so richly benefited. Jesus has paid that debt for us also by His crucifixion and resurrection, which now forgives the sins incurred under that law.

Our Lineage

It is interesting to me—and very much a shadow of God's plan of reconciliation—that biblically these two words bond and free represent slavery and salvation. But what does our lineage have to do with it? Keep in mind that keeping track of one's ancestral lineage was very important during the time period at which we are looking because it was one of two reasons for taking a census of the people periodically. Let's take a look.

Jesus descended (in the flesh) from Mary, who was a descendant of King David by his son Nathan (Luke 3:31). Of Jesus, the angel Gabriel told Mary, "He will be called the Son of the Most High; and the Lord God will give Him the throne of His father David; and He will reign in the house of Jacob forever and His kingdom will have no end" (Luke 1:31–2). The word *father* in reference to David is an example of the necessity to keep track of your ancestors. When the Messiah (Jesus) was born, we recall the blessing given to Abraham. "In your seed all the nations of the earth shall be blessed" (Genesis 22:18). From that moment on Jesus' lineage was of monumental importance. But we aren't of Abraham's seed! Don't worry because God has taken care of it.

The Seed of Blessing

"For they are not all Israel who descended from Israel; nor are they all children because they are Abraham's descendants … that is, it is not the children of the flesh who are children of God, but the children of the promise are regarded as descendants" (Romans 9:6–8). We have already established that Abraham would have two different lines of descendants. As an illustration I have selected an example from the first century—John, the apostle. Jewish by birth he saw Jesus and followed Him. He is a follower, a disciple, a believer. Therefore, he is also a descendant of Abraham. In the same time period another Jew by the name of Judas, who was also an apostle, saw Jesus and followed Him, but because his heart wasn't right he probably followed for what he could get out of the relationship. Although he was a Jew, it could not be said that he was a descendant of Abraham because he was not a believer. However, his physical connection ensured that he would be counted as a descendant of Isaac (Abraham's son), which would make him a participant in the physical blessing, but he did not receive the blessing of which the promise speaks. For our third example, we will use Cornelius as our non-Jewish example. He was a military man, a leader of an Italian Cohort, which meant that he had one hundred men under his command. He was a Gentile of Italian birth and was a devout man. He was led to God by prayer and was sent to a town named Joppa to be told about God. As a believer the Gentile Cornelius was a descendant by faith of Abraham and one who had been blessed through the resurrected Jesus.

These are the reasons Abraham was called righteous. He believed and obeyed what he was told to do. Is that all there is to salvation? No. One needs to continually grow, and in the process God leads him or her to new growth, new faith, more love, and more service. It is a growth process, one that must <u>continue</u> for the remainder of physical life because sin doesn't end and neither should worship and praise for the one who made salvation possible. Everyone sins, and contrary to opinion there is no such thing as a big sin or a little sin. "God shut up everyone under sin, so that the promise by faith in Jesus Christ might be given to those who believe" (Galatians 3:22). Now this verse is a prime example of God's impartiality. Knowing that everyone would sin because we all have the ability to follow evil, God didn't pick out certain *big sins* by which we would no longer belong to Him. Instead, He "shut up everyone under sin," meaning that missing the mark of perfection was all it required. Our Lord Jesus is the only one who has measured up to that mark of perfection, so the playing field is level. We all begin from the same spot.

When a follower by the name of Nicodemus asked the Lord how he could be born again at his advanced age, Jesus said to him, "Unless one is born again, he cannot see the Kingdom of God," and continued by saying this new birth is of both water and the Holy Spirit and essential for entering the kingdom (John 1:3–5). I believe this reference to the water baptism facilitates the indwelling spirit. It is as if one is saying, "Yes, Lord! What a wonderful idea, let me be baptized immediately." This is my definition. Others have different definitions. However you interpret it, God's helper will be within you to assist in living the Christian life. It also means that one's life must be not only immersed in water at the appropriate time, but immersed in the message of the Holy Spirit. One can confirm this fact by reading His Word. It is not a life devoid of imperfections, and yes, there will still be sin. However, your purpose, our goal is to live for Him, and in the trying, it becomes a spiritual life one dedicated to Him and to becoming like Him. The difference lies within the intent of the heart, trying, succeeding more than you fail. That is what our Father looks for. "As Moses lifted up the serpent in the wilderness, even so must the Son of Man be lifted up; so that whoever believes will in Him have eternal life" (John 3:14–15). So we have come full circle to belief, but this time our Lord has added that He must be lifted up and that we must be born of the water and the Spirit.

Having identified Jesus' physical lineage, how does it apply to us as children of faith? Let's look again at Jesus' statement in regard to Himself. "The Son of Man must be lifted up." What do you think He means? To me it refers to the priority we give Him in our lives, and thereby it is His life that should be exemplified. We lift Him up by living for Him. We show the world by example what it means to be a follower of Christ. Living for Him is a life of attitudes, of incorporating the fruits of the Spirit in a way that makes others wonder how it can be. Love, of course, is the key, and guidance comes from the Holy Spirit who lives within.

As the Spirit within guides you into knowledge and truth, your life changes by the power of God, and you become more like Him as the Corinthian letter explains "from glory to glory." It is our aim for daily living and our goal for the future.

Life cannot be just about one's self. This takes us to the final aspect of Jesus' statement, "So that whoever believes will in Him have eternal life." How do others learn of our Lord? Ideally, they learn from our lives. Fundamentally they don't because we forget that "we are a letter" to the world. What Jesus is saying is that when we live for Him, we bring others to Him, which makes us in a very real sense, the gospel message.

This is our lineage—children of God made possible by the sacrifice of His Son and through the guidance of the Holy Spirit within. This automatically put us in the free category of *bond* or *free* where the guidance of the Holy Spirit is ignored, if we still live by the lust of the flesh, illicit desire, and the pride of life, we can slip back into bondage. The decision is always up to the individual.

Summary

This will probably come as a shock to some, but we learn that unbelief is considered evil by our God. The definition supports this finding in saying sin, which has been characterized as unbelief, is synonymous with evil. The finding also explains that sin dwells in all people and begins in the mind with unlawful desire, which becomes lust and then sin. Sin evolves from the eyes, the flesh, and the mind in the form of pride. Because we are called to be holy, this information places us in severe conflict with God.

Fortunately for man God has brought to us three new principles that will help alleviate the eternal consequences of sinful action, while man must still take responsibility for the human consequences of sin. Those principles are repentance, mercy, and justice. Just as redemption is a gift, so will justification be a gift dependent on God's mercy, but we need to avoid justice because it is rendered without mercy. Though man does not deserve such gifts of love, they are granted to us by grace.

At first, it seemed a strange way to choose a nation of people, but God chose Israel because she was the smallest of all nations and would therefore not be credited with the power of battles won against all odds. God says that this is how His power is perfected through weakness, and it was also how nations learned of the God of Israel. As His ambassadors today we carry this tradition on as we demonstrate His message with our words and our lives. The message of salvation is certainly not of us, but we should count it a privilege to bear the role of messenger. Praise God.

We see the promise to Abraham defined between the physical and spiritual blessings, and we learn that because of disobedience God could have chosen to give up on the covenant. He didn't, probably for many reasons, but love for mankind comes to mind, along with the fact that there was always a believing remnant for which He persevered.

By looking at our spiritual lineage we find that we are children of God by purchase with the blood of Christ and the adoption by faith through Abraham, and we find that we are enabled in the Christian life by the Holy Spirit that dwells within us. The justifiable conclusion is that our lineage by adoption through Abraham makes us a part of the family of God, and as such we have been purchased from bondage and have freedom.

Study Guide—Chapter 4

Q. From Genesis 3:5 who does the term *her seed* in its singular form refer?
A. The singular form of this noun refers to Jesus; in its plural form it refers to all mankind.

Q. God promised a twofold blessing to Abraham directly related to that seed. Name the blessings and explain why each was considered a blessing.
A. Abraham's twofold blessing is hypothetically his will to God's descendants. It is divided between his physical and his spiritual descendants. His physical descendants were those who were of his physical body. They would receive his physical inheritance—goods, property, land,

protection—whereas his spiritual descendants were heirs by reason of having the same faith as Abraham in God and the Messiah God would send through whom the blessing would come. Those people could be from any people, tribe, or nation, and they would receive some of their blessings in this life and more in the next life, which would be eternal.

Q. By what measure are non-Jews descendants of Abraham?
A. Abraham believed God when he was told he would be blessed; therefore, God counted that as righteousness for him because he believed it by faith. According to the Hebrew letter faith is the evidence of what we believe but can't see. Because he believed by faith, God told him he would be the father of all the faithful.

Q. Can you think of a reason why God would choose a specific nation in which to fulfill His promises?
A. God's plan always included a nation through which He would teach about holiness, discipline, obedience, and the Messiah that He would send. Keep in mind that the world had already been destroyed by water because of evil and the corruption it had spawned. Teaching about sin was necessary if any were to be saved to complete His plan. Toward that end He called Abram, as he was then called, and sent him to *sojourn* in the land called Canaan, which would one day become the land for the nation that would come from Abraham. Before Abraham died God told him that his descendants would go to a land where they would stay for more than four hundred years in slavery but would be brought out with many goods by God Himself, who would lead them to the land of their inheritance. And then they would take the land of their inheritance. The underlying reason for all this activity was to prepare a land for the nation that would be coming. After that God prepared a law for them, instructed them on how to build a tabernacle and how to worship Him, and finally told them about the one who would come. This is the thread that winds throughout Scripture. It is more than a church in the making, it is the heritage of a people, actually of all people, and it shows the connectivity from Adam to the end of time. There is no way it can be separated.

51

Chapter 5: The Law

As we study the law and the books of law, we must keep in mind a major concept of the Mosaic Law. The law was supposed to teach things that the Israelites (and all people) needed to know about sin and holiness. Initially the law was supposed to identify sin so that it could be avoided. It raises an interesting question that I don't have an answer for: Would Satan have sinned if he had possessed such definitions? My own answer would be yes, but it is a theory, not a fact. Did all of Israel learn all that could be learned about sin, or do we? Of course we do not. The point is however that the knowledge is available, and we can choose to learn and choose to heed the teaching or not. God does not force obedience.

The second concept is that by learning about sin God was teaching people about the need for the Messiah. Had the lesson been well learned I suspect there would have been more acceptance of Jesus both then and now. My conclusion is that knowledge is wisdom, and the choice is still ours.

In general a law book is a system of rules and regulations that outlines how a people will be governed. This law differs from others of the same era because it was given by direct revelation of God, and it is therefore righteous, holy, and good. Most ancient laws were about the ruler and were often kept secret so the ruler could do as he pleased as he punished those who followed his example.

In contrast biblical law came from God's nature, and in that sense all of its laws are religious as they were based on God's moral principles and were the expectations of His wishes.

Violations of the law were considered to go against God and were disciplined accordingly. Turning after idols and away from God (Samuel 12:9–10) received severe punishment as did the act of empty worship (Amos 5:21–4). However, because God considers life valuable, His laws are humane, protective of the defenseless, and are applied to all equally.

Laws were grouped into categories that basically included violations that went specifically against Him, discipline, holiness, corruption, boundaries, prophets, judges, personal issues (e.g., marriage, children, etc.), servants, slaves, property, and as you would expect, civil and religious matters. It was interesting to me that lawsuits were heard by different judges who were divided into those who heard religious trials (priests) and civil trials (not priestly). I suppose it was a sensible solution because priests were the most knowledgeable regarding God's laws. Judges were also military leaders as in the case of Deborah (Judges 4–5).

Why should we study this ancient law? Study is always presupposed for learning. Why do I believe the Mosaic law is an inactive law? Because there are two specifics missing that would indicate that God's law would be violated. They are the laws regarding the sacrifice for sin to be made only by the high priests and the fact that the genealogies that would have identified those who could make those sacrifices are unavailable. God's commands regarding the sin sacrifice and the priesthood make it impossible to follow the law as commanded by God. Anything else would be considered abhorrent, a sacrilege.

I don't know what the Jewish people have done to compensate for this lack, but I do know that God did not leave them destitute. His sacrifice was not for one race of people but for all people. I also know that it was specifically intended to bring the Jewish people and the Gentile people together by fulfilling the law through the blood sacrifice provided by Jesus. His sacrifice granted forgiveness for all people of faith, and the ability to follow the Mosaic law was an act of faith that their sins would be forgiven in time. The law taught people about sin, but it didn't forgive sin. Forgiveness required the blood price be paid, at which time it covered all sin, past, present, and future. Our cost is negligible as we are required to believe and obey as we learn His requirements. We are expected to grow. It is comforting to know that this new commandment is called the law of love, indicating that we are to love God and each other.

Our courts all over the world have laws archived that are no longer active laws. They are kept for a number of reasons, but primarily we store them for referral. They are also studied, compared, and evaluated. I see this as an act of wisdom and prudence. Studying the past has always had its advantages for the future.

What about the Mosaic law? How is it useful? Above all other considerations, it is God's Word, and it should be studied for its varied and beneficial offerings. As I've mentioned before principles don't change, and many are offered in the old covenant. The law, however, is obsolete (Hebrews 8:7–13) and has been replaced.

Secondly there is much to gain from this section on law as we attempt to understand God's judgments. Why does He allow evil in the world? In what ways does He use evil in punishment of His people? What will their end be? Why does He allow Satan to persecute good people? These are all human things that Satan loves to prey upon, and so we have battles with Satan in our lives. We can study the battles of the past and learn a bit about one-upmanship regarding our adversary, the Devil. On God's side sometimes His punishments bring repentance, which is His goal, but these are not always understood as such among His people. It is the same today. Disasters plague us on every side, but we fail to see them as messages from God. Both the books of law and the books of history illustrate that though situations and circumstances are different. Life is basically the same, so we study to learn. At any point in Scripture, if we search for God's wisdom, it is evident as examples to emulate. At times He demonstrates pieces of our future through prophetic warnings or predictions, and these speak of how time will end. I have heard it said repeatedly from people of historical backgrounds that the only way to avoid mistakes of the past is to study the past. Sounds like good advice to me.

Specifically how does our study of this section of the Law of Moses contribute to our knowledge of Satan and the war he began? The only complete answer is that through knowledge we gain wisdom. It's hard to express exactly how I feel about it except to say that by putting all these pieces together from before the creation to the end of time, anyone who reads this book will have a greater understanding of God, Satan, the war, and our own ability to be prepared for the future, whatever it brings. This is my prayer.

The Purpose of the Law

The most important aspect of the law is that it was preparing the people for their Messiah. It was teaching them to recognize sin. It was teaching them discipline. It was teaching them holiness. I heard a minister recently who said that all teaching is hostility in the absence of love. God's teaching itself was an act of love. The Israelites were most fortunate in that God's message, His teaching, was an act of patience and love and that the information He shared is eternal. Why study it? Because He is God, and we are not.

This law God gave to the Israelites is remarkable because of its love. While they didn't all respond the way He would have liked, it achieved its purposes. In identifying sin we are able to avoid it. That wasn't possible prior to the law. Love was emphasized in the Ten Commandments and was later recognized as the most important of all the laws. When they were in the wilderness, they built the tabernacle and learned to worship God. These were all qualities that prepared them for the coming of Christ (Galatians 3:24). Did you know that Moses would gather the people to him and they would listen to him read? The entire law was read to them twice before their entry into Canaan to begin the conquest of that land. This used to be the way knowledge was gained. Most new knowledge is acquired by some sort of teaching.

My guess is that the tutors of the first century, especially in the Greek civilization, taught their charges about life in addition to more academic types of lessons. They would have taught all things that pertained to maturity. The child and his tutor would have wanted him to be fully responsible when he joined the father because he would by then be considered an adult. Even though he was a child under the rule of a tutor and the father's heir, he was in bondage just as a slave. The assumption was that the father would decide on a date when the boy would return to him, and from that time forward the child would be responsible to the father for mistakes or omissions in what he had learned (Galatians 4:1–3).

Here is the comparison: "Until Christ came, the law confined us and kept us in custody" (Nelson Bible Dictionary 1995). The quotation goes on to say, "But when Christ came, we attained the freedom and maturity of faith."[7] This is such a perfect description of the bondage of the law and the freedom from bondage that we are granted through Christ. The apostle John is quoted as giving the difference between the two (John 1:17), for the law was given through Moses but grace and truth came through Jesus Christ.

There is one important thing that the law didn't do. The law can't invalidate the promise because it did not precede the promise. This is important because the blessing promised to Abraham for all people was the forgiveness of sin, which was not available under to law (Romans 4:13).

7　Nelson's New Illustrated Bible Dictionary, copyright 1995 by Thomas Nelson Publishers, (published by Thomas Nelson, Nashville), Law.

The Covenant

God said to Moses, "Write down these words, for in accordance with these words I have made a covenant with you and with Israel" (Exodus 34:27). Moses was with God on the mountain for forty days and forty nights as he wrote down the Ten Commandments.

What does God mean when He says He has made a covenant with Israel? A covenant is a legal document between two or more people. It told of what God would do for them and what would be required of them. It promised His faithfulness in exchange for their obedience. There were two things that were nonnegotiable in my opinion. They must remain faithful to Him and not worship the gods their neighbors worshipped, which were idols. Unfortunately that is exactly what they did (Judges 2:17), and in doing so they broke the other commandment, "You shall love the Lord your God with all your heart and with all your soul, and with all your might" (Deuteronomy 6:5).

On their way to Canaan, the future nation of Israel camped at Mount Sinai, where God gave them the law. Commonly called the Law of Moses, it became part of the foundation. Before Abraham died, God repeated the promise of the blessings that would be bestowed upon him, but He also told him that his descendants would be strangers in a land where they would be enslaved and oppressed for about four hundred years. God told them that when they came out from that land, they would have many possessions, which I see as punishment for the Egyptians for their treatment of His people (Genesis 12:3). God delivered them from that bondage after 430 years, and He recognized that after they had endured these experiences and learned to discipline themselves under great hardship, they were again ready to learn.

He has not been inactive. He has prepared for this day over many years through circumstances and people. All of the preceding years have been years of learning for the nation of Israel. However, though we didn't realize what God was doing at the time, in retrospect we are able to view the results of His work. The Israelites learned a lot about worship and praise when the tabernacle and the ark were finished. They also learned what God expected in the way of obedience. Sadly they disregarded God's instructions most of the time, so God continued to teach them about consequences. He even destroyed the world and all that He had put in it. He raised judges for the people to get them out of their problems and instead they did what they pleased rather than profit from their mistakes. Was God busy? Yes, I would say He was more than busy.

He did many other things, all of which became parts of His foundation, which was designed as the solidity of its plan and its integrity to ensure there would be no partiality.

In the meantime He manipulated behind-the-scenes circumstances to either teach His people or prepare them for the future. He sent prophets to both sides of the divided kingdoms to bring them back to His love for them. He took Elijah to heaven with him, possibly as an example to His people, and when the time had come, He gave a law in order that His people could recognize sin and thus avoid it. It would be a very specific law where the penalty for "stumbling in one point is to be guilty of all" (James 2:10). They will show their faith by obedience to the law. It was by their obedience that they would show their faith.

Think for a minute about all the Bible stories you learned as a child. Eve and others didn't have the desire to please. We don't know why, but we can see that she didn't grant the proper importance to what God had said. We all do it at times, but when we practice turning our desire to Him, He helps us as He helped Daniel stand against the king of Babylon and survive a night in a lion's den, as He helped Esther listen to Mordachai's advice and become a queen, and as He helped Abraham when God told him to sacrifice the son He had given him. As a result Abraham's descendants are now on their way to Canaan to possess the land God promised to them. Of even greater importance he was chosen by God to be the one through whom all nations would be blessed—that is, all people, each possessing the same method by which to bridge the gap of separation between man and God.

It has been His purpose in all of those stories that we understand not only His principles but the necessity for teaching holiness, and that is what the covenant is about. Specifically it will be in preparation for the coming of His Son. God says it will be a Covenant in which He will do certain things in return for things that they will do. It will then be sealed to signify its legality. The seal would be the act of circumcision.

Circumcision was not only the seal of the Covenant. It was a tenet of the law. It was an ongoing commandment that all male children were to be circumcised when they were eight days old. It would serve as an identifying mark to the Jews, and it would be divine proof of their connection to Abraham as well as to God. That Abraham was circumcised 430 years before the law was given was the connective proof that demonstrated the spiritual aspect of God's promise.

In addition to this great nation of people through whom the seed would come, there would also be other descendants who would not be of blood descent. These descendants like Abraham would be heirs of the promise by reason of faith instead of blood (Galatians 3:26–9).

Abraham was circumcised before the law was given, so he could be the father of the uncircumcised (the Gentiles, who had no command for circumcision) and the father of the circumcised while they were as yet uncircumcised. This would demonstrate that his faith preceded both the law and circumcision (Romans 4:11).

As we see the covenant take its place in the history of the Jewish people, we are enabled to see more clearly the common thread that holds their stories together. It has been spun by God Himself through His love for man, which creates within us the desire to do His will. Did any one of our characters ask God, "Why me?" Not a single one. Well, I didn't mention Moses, who gave every conceivable excuse, but without avail. God wanted Moses, and eventually Moses agreed. I want to mention that Moses really had (by our standards) a pretty good reason for not wanting to go back to Egypt. He was actually a wanted man. What he failed to understand was that God's protection was so much greater than his fear. Do you ever use fear as an excuse? I have, and it is not a good feeling to live with.

We are more often like Jonah, who complained so much that he ended up inside a whale (Jonah 1:17). Was there a purpose behind that? Of course there was. Jonah didn't trust God, and his attitude was bad. He didn't want the Assyrians (Gentiles), to whom he was to preach repentance, to be forgiven. After all Mosaic law was not for Assyrians. It was for Israel. God's message, I think, was two-pronged: "Forgiveness is for all people" and, "Clean up your act, Jonah. Where is your love?" Let me also say that we should beware of excuses because they are addictive and because it could be said that God's whales are everywhere.

We really need to remember that sin is not always an overt act. One can sin by attitudes or by thoughts. God knows we will not be perfect, but He wants us to aim for perfection. And when we stay the course and don't give up, He will reward us as if we achieved the goal. Isn't that marvelous? Our God is more interested in the condition of our hearts than in the fact that we make mistakes. For that reason alone it is imperative that we want to please Him. Without that desire we are in effect asking for justice rather than mercy, and I really don't think we want to go there. Desire for God therefore can be said to lead to obedience.

The law was both complex and detailed. It taught people about matters of health, hygiene, warfare, government, marriage, and even matters of relationship; how to worship, how he felt about divorce, one's personal rights, and responsibilities, and the weightier matters of justice and mercy. These teachings went beyond mere instruction and prepared the Israelites for the greater law of love, which was yet to come. The fact that the law would be impossible to keep perfectly would also begin to teach people about grace.

These were the mechanics of how the law would work. The mechanics, however, were no more sufficient then than they are now. Just as God looks at hearts today He looked at the hearts of those who were under the law, and what He looked to find was faith.

Shortcomings of the Law

In excess of 430 years have elapsed. It's been a busy time for our God as He continued to prepare the foundation so necessary for the future strength of the new covenant. The following verses will help readers understand why the old covenant (called the Law of Moses) was destined by God to be replaced with the new covenant, which would eventually come to be called the covenant of love. The law would last a little less than 1,500 years.

The law, according to Hebrews 10:1 NKJV, was but "a shadow of the good things to come," and it's many sacrifices, "which they offer continually year by year," can never make sinners perfect. The sacrifices referred to were animal sacrifices that could not take away sin. *Perfect* refers to man's perfection through the forgiveness of sin, which is granted at the end of our struggle on this earth by the grace of God.

God was not pleased with the animal sacrifices and offerings (burnt offerings for sin), but Jesus is quoted by inspiration in Psalm 40:6–8 NAS, "Behold, I have come … in the scroll of the book it is written of me I delight do your will, O my God." I believe this is our Lord volunteering to be the sacrifice that would take away sin.

"For by one offering He has perfected forever those who are being sanctified" (Hebrews 10:14 NKJV). This refers to the sacrifice of the Son of God for the sins of all mankind.

One of Jesus' roles following the resurrection made Him a high priest forever to take the place of the Aaronic priesthood who lived and died and had to be replaced. The eternal nature of Jesus would mean that this priest would never be in need of replacement. The writer of Hebrews quotes the Psalm (Hebrews 10:5–10) and adds, "He takes away the first in order to establish the second." By this we will have been sanctified through the offering of the body of Jesus Christ once for all. "For the priesthood being changed, of necessity there is also change of the law" (Hebrews 7:12 NKJV).

And this same Jesus would be the guarantee of this new covenant. "Jesus has become a surety of a better covenant" (Hebrews 7:22 NKJV).

Why is it a better covenant? It is enacted on better promises, "For if that first covenant had been faultless, then no place would have been sought for a second"; (Hebrews 8:6 NKJV). "Behold, the days are coming, says the Lord, when I will make a new covenant with the house of Israel and with the house of Judah" (Hebrews 8:8). "I will put my laws into their minds, and I will write them on their hearts, and I will be their God, and they shall be my people" (Hebrews 8:10) "when He said, 'a new covenant', He has made the first obsolete" (Hebrews 8:13).

In the first part of this quotation, the referral to faultless has reference to the lack of forgiveness under the law. They were promised forgiveness in the expectation of the Messiah.

In Romans 3:31 NKJV, Paul asks the question, "Do we nullify the law through faith? May it never be! On the contrary, we establish the law." He is saying that the faith of those under the new covenant will validate the faith of those under the old covenant by the fact of forgiveness, for those under the old has been granted because of acceptance of the sacrifice by those under the new.

This is what our Lord referred to when He said all of the law and the prophets hang on love. Both covenants were established by the power of love, God's love (who gave His Son), the Son's love (by becoming a sacrifice), and the dedication of the Holy Spirit (who dwells within us each). But the chain of love can't stop there. It depends on our love for the Father, the Son, and the Holy Spirit and the faithfulness to what has been done for us. I hope we can grasp that without our part the years of preparation, the sacrifice, the dedication, and the wisdom of the Holy Spirit would be of no effect. Compiling his great list of the faithful, the writer of Hebrews 10:40 sums it up nicely, "Having gained approval through their faith they did not receive what was promised, because God had provided something better for us, so that apart from us they would not be made perfect."

Summary

God's agreement with Abraham and his descendants by faith is called the Covenant and was validated by the circumcision of males at the age of eight days. Abraham's circumcision came at the age of ninety-nine when the Covenant was given.

The Mosaic law, commonly called the Law of Moses, is both complex and detailed. Man was introduced to so much material at this point in his physical and spiritual development that he must have been overwhelmed. Fortunately because they could not perfectly keep the law, they were also learning about the grace of God. It may have been about this time that some began to realize their great dependency on Him as a result of the teachings of the law, which would have eased their burdens. Gradually in those who took to heart God's message, obedience and belief would have intertwined, never perfectly, never universally, and not without hindrance but with some realization of purpose.

The law was defined as a system of rules and regulations that outlined how a people would be governed. Inspired by God, the law reflects God's justice and His holy nature. Because of God's respect for life, His laws are humane, protective of the defenseless, and applied equally to all. The laws are categorized in groups that cover everything from legal matters, both civil and religious, to property, from personal matters of family to characteristics of good health and to the protection of society from greed and corruption. It is more than a book of law. It is a reflection of God, His love, His will, and His nature. The Bible stories that have entertained children for centuries have been proven to connect to His overall purposes and design as they have taught children and adults the principles that guide His decisions.

The status of the promise to Abraham remains the same. Because the promise came first, it is not under the authority of the law and cannot be invalidated.

Abraham's descendants are divided by those who come to Jesus by faith and those who came to Him through faith (Romans 29-30). If that sounds confusing, look at it closely. God justifies the Jew by the faith they had under the law and the Gentile through faith in the Son of God.

Abraham's blood descendants are also divided by the faith they have or do not have. Romans 9:6–8 explains that not all his physical descendants are children of the promise, but only those who are both believers and descendants by blood. The principle of forgiveness for which Jesus died establishes that salvation is dependent on coming to the Father through the Son. This principle was one of the "stumbling blocks" for the Jewish leaders, and as time passed, more and more of the people began to reject that He was the Son of God. The antagonism of the leaders can be explained by their apprehension of losing their positions and the power that came with it. I believe however that the rational of the people was quite different. Perhaps their reaction was fear. I believe the Mosaic law lasted for fifteen hundred years, which is more than a lifetime. The law would have been all they knew. Those Israelites who struggled to remain faithful would in a lot of circumstances have felt such apprehension and would most likely have been influenced by their leader's hatred for Jesus.

In regard to the matter of sin we must educate ourselves to awareness of those who are not overtly committed. Such sin is like a disease hidden from awareness. Its damage is insidious, taking a toll unknown by the one who sinned. Such sins are overtly committed but remain hidden within the individual. Such sins are found in the mind and in attitudes and are sores that fester and sicken within a person in a spiritual sense. One must be on guard against these sins and pray for God's help in eliminating them from one's life. It should be noted that two commands of the law were nonnegotiable, the worship of idols and failing to love God.

Scripture points out the failure of the law to grant forgiveness but with assurance that the situation is taken care of for the forgiveness of all repentant sinners. Illustration is given to verify that God repeatedly forgave the Jews for idol worship and the failure to love Him, while He retained the right to deny salvation in the absence of repentance.

Study Guide—Chapter 5

Q. According to Galatians 3:24, for what purpose did God give the law?
A. The law known as the Mosaic law was given for two purposes. The first was to reveal sin in order to be able to avoid it. The second was to serve as a tutor (teacher) to bring people to Christ through the knowledge of the blessing He would bring.

Q. Give several ways in which the law fulfilled that purpose.
A. The law taught about sin but was unable to forgive sin by the blood of animals, so as they began to understand the importance of that missing factor (the lack of forgiveness), they could better see their need of the promised Messiah. He would bring forgiveness, and that element of faith

would be added to what they had learned in regard to grace. So as you can see it required faith to live by the law, and faith would be supplemented with grace.

Q. Explain how the same principle restrains sin today, thus illustrating God's continuity.
A. Sin is restrained by knowledge. Does that surprise you? Think about how you learned from your parents. Knowledge is not only a teacher but also the forerunner of wisdom.

Q. Was the law a shift of emphasis from God's prior dealings with man?
A. Yes, it was. In the new shift of emphasis God speaks to man through the law instead of to individual patriarchs who spoke to their families.

Q. Why is it important that God's promise to bless all people preceded the law?
A. The blessing came through the promise to Abraham, which was given four hundred years before the law was given, so it had no control over the promise, which meant it couldn't be compromised.

Chapter 6: Books of Law

The following five books of law, called the Pentateuch or Torah, record the history of early man and their collective relationship with God. Keep in mind that God continues to lay His foundation in preparation for a complete revelation of His plan, which will culminate with Christ. To this end watch for the principles we've emphasized but also keep an eye out for new ones as they manifest themselves. And do keep in mind that principles do not change.

I urge you to look beyond the fundamentals of any story or lesson for evidence of God's unchanging nature and for the consistency of His actions as He interacts with His people. How He acted then is identical to how He deals with us today. As an example the concept of the deliverance of the Israelites from bondage relates to our own deliverance from the bondage of sin. God continues to lay His foundation in the books of law, and we will witness Him from a slightly different perspective.

The Books

Genesis is a book of beginnings and is therefore termed a book of origins. Those origins are the key not only of the book but the history of the human race. In this book God begins to reveal himself to man. Central to the revelation is the fact that all life came from God, to whom man is accountable both now and in the future of judgment. The principle of belief is introduced to Adam and Eve in the garden as a form of choice. Consequently sin enters the world, and the beginnings of God's foundation are laid.

God talked with Adam in the garden directly or as we might say, face-to-face. When Adam was cast out of the garden, he no longer had his evening walks with the Father, but God still communicated with him as a patriarch (head of family). It is important that you understand that God did not cut Himself off from Adam. Nor are we cut off when we sin.

God and Adam no longer had their face-to-face relationship, but there is no doubt that He continued to instruct him in the same way that He later communicated when there were numerous patriarchs. Because this was a change from a face-to-face relationship, it can be said that the new method in the age of the patriarchs was from God to heads of families and for the most part was carried out by dreams or visions and by angels, who were the messengers. This change in the method of communication would occur again in about fifteen hundred years, but for now it is perfect for teaching what they have most need of knowing, how to recognize sin, and what to do about it. The Messiah who would complete this law they were struggling with and make it all worthwhile by bringing the forgiveness of sin they are promised by means of the blessing to Abraham.

At about this time Moses began to record the history written after the Exodus. It might be interesting to recall that only four people left the land of Ur by God's command to go to Canaan, and seventy went down to seek help because of the famine where they were *sojourning*. In addition there were five relatives already in Egypt (Joseph and his family who had been sold by his brothers, which was quite unknown by their father). By the time of the exodus about 430 years later, God delivered 630,000 males twenty years or older, not counting women and children, allowing by estimate a population of about two million.

These figures really speak of population growth, don't they? God told Abraham 430 years prior to this happening exactly what would happen as well as what would happen after the exodus. This is just one example of His omnipotence, omniscience, and omnipresence. It is easy to grasp that we are unable to attain these three descriptions of His divinity by any measure.

It is evident that His own faithfulness is of paramount importance to the accomplishment of His plan. When God says something will be, it is the same as knowing that it has already happened. You can go back to the previous chapter and reread the section on shortcomings and gain a better grasp of what is to come now for the Israelites and for us as a part of our future. That there will be another shift (the third) in communication with the coming of the predicted new covenant is obvious, but for now knowledge to be gained from the law necessitates that communication remain through the law. This new learning curve will bring remarkable changes to the Israelites' lifestyle.

To begin with, the law will identify sin. At this point in the triumph of civilization that sounds a bit odd to me, but if you think seriously about it, our generation could benefit from reading and assimilating God's law. I think we still know the meaning of sin but have forgotten the importance of avoiding it. This presents a major challenge for civilization because God has set forth a new principle that will make all the difference in coping with sin, and that is repentance. It can also be called godly sorrow. Because the act of repentance under the old law required continual animal sacrifice, it would eventually be replaced with the blood of Jesus, which would grant forgiveness. Under the law the animal sacrifice represented the *promise* of forgiveness on God's part, and it represented *faith* in the promise by the penitent heart.

Exodus begins with Israel in Egypt and the birth of Moses. Then it moves to the plagues God placed upon Egypt and chronicles the Israelites' departure from Egypt and their deliverance by God's hand. It is in this book that Moses was raised to prominence. As with Abraham we are shown that Moses was not a perfect man. Because of his lack of confidence in his own ability and his failure to trust God, he begged to be excused from the work God had for him. "Who am I," he said, "that I should go to Pharaoh, and that I should bring the sons of Israel out of Egypt?" (Exodus 3:11). We wouldn't dream of speaking to God in that way, would we? I can only speak from experience, but I'm afraid we would do exactly as Moses did because we are unable to see the insight God has for us and we don't have sufficient trust.

Exodus leads us through the ten plagues, the exodus, forty years in the wilderness, the building of the tabernacle, the preparation to enter Canaan, and the death of Moses. It is so evident that when God punishes, He also teaches. There probably is no better example of it than the wilderness deaths of those who didn't believe. Of the group who came out of Egypt, the ones who had seen miracle after miracle were the ones who failed to believe they could conquer the land of Canaan, the older generation. Their punishment was to wander in the wilderness for forty years. Have you thought about all the others who weren't guilty of unbelief? They were sort of trapped, weren't they? My point is that even today when God punishes, the innocent may be in proximity and suffer as well. This happens in natural disasters like hurricanes and tornadoes and all sorts of other tragedies. What we have to remember is that death is not the end for those who believe. The other thing to remember is that God made good use of those forty years by teaching the younger generation the law and by preparing them for the conquest of Canaan.

Proximity to any kind of disaster is a factor that isn't always possible to avoid; however, I want to put an idea in your head (if it's not already there) and that is that physical death is not our enemy. God's people have nothing to fear from death. No matter how or when it comes, it is usually unexpected, so it's our responsibility to be prepared. This doesn't mean that we should seek death. Only God knows when our time is up. On the other hand, we should not be inordinately fearful, but we should be able to stand fast even as temptation threatens death or physical harm.

Have you considered that the deliverance of Israel from Egypt was a miraculous event? The most common definition for exodus is exit, but there is another quite astounding definition in the Greek that connects three of the great men of the Bible—Moses, Elijah, and Christ—and that is departure[8]. In fact, Joseph on his death bed spoke of the *departure* or *exiting* of the sons of Israel, which was 350 years in the future (Hebrews 11:22) and is commended for it as a great act of faith. The word *departure* is the entire concept of the book and presents the miraculous intervention and deliverance. Luke 9:28–31 gives additional background for the connection of this word as a description of the Exodus when he tells of Peter, James, and John, who went up the mountain with Jesus for the Lord to find a place to pray. While our Lord was praying, they noticed that the appearance of His face changed as His face and clothing became white and gleaming. And then they noticed two men were standing with Him, and the two men were Moses and Elijah, who were also in glory and were speaking to Jesus of His departure, which He would soon accomplish at Jerusalem. Now Peter and his companions had gone to sleep while the Lord prayed, but now they were fully awake. They saw the glory before them and Peter said to Jesus, "Master, it is good for us to be here; let us make three tabernacles: one for you, and one for Moses, and one for Elijah."

Not realizing what he was saying, they became frightened as a cloud formed over them. They entered the cloud, and a voice came out of the cloud and said, "This is my Son, My chosen one. Listen to Him!" And when the voice had spoken, Jesus was found alone. And they kept silent and reported to no one in those days any of the things which they had seen.

---

8   *The New Strong's Expanded Exhaustive Concordance of the Bible*, Red letter ed., copyright by Thomas Nelson Publishers 2001 (Nashville) 1841, (1b).

Now the departure of which they were speaking was the imminent death of Jesus. Why did Moses and Elijah come? All we can do is make an educated guess, but I am thinking they came to encourage Him. If you consider their lives, there probably were no two who had more right to spend some time with Him. Elijah spent his life preaching to the Assyrians of the Northern Kingdom evidently with little or no results as he was constantly rejected, and Moses spent his life leading the Israelites out of Egypt with all of their stubbornness and disobedience and in the end didn't get to go in to the Promised Land because he lost his cool over their hardheadedness. I hope they were a comfort to Jesus before he was arrested and crucified. Actually they had another similarity between them. Elijah was taken to heaven in a flaming chariot, and God carried Moses down Mount Nebo and buried Him so no one could find him. Jesus' exit would be different. He had a heavy load to carry as He left this world, and He had to do it alone; however, it, too, would be a unique exit. No one before or since would ever carry the world's sin upon his or her shoulders and in the process provide forgiveness for all of humanity who wanted to be forgiven. Like I said, my reasoning is pure speculation, but the facts are a matter of record.

Leviticus is a book of worship and communication. After the fall of Abraham's descendants from having *some* holiness to sin and the degradation of slavery, Leviticus as a book that takes us back to the holiness of God. This combination of deliverance and holiness allows us to understand that it is our redemption from the slavery of sin that is now offered by God to humanity. It would seem that the physical deliverance of the Israelites was a shadow of the deliverance of believers from the bondage of sin. God's requirement for this era of the law was for absolute obedience, so it wasn't going to be easy. If you recall in the chapter on law, to be guilty of one part of the law was to be guilty of the whole law. In the second year of Darius and the eighth month, the word of the Lord came to Zechariah with a message for Israel. It is in my opinion one of the most beautiful calls to repentance of the entire Bible. Found in Zechariah 1:3, this is His message: "Return to me … that I may return to you." God doesn't leave man, but man can leave God. It's hard to understand why anyone would want to.

Another illustration I would like to make is that nothing is ever asked of us that has not first been done as an example for us by God. To my heart this gives new meaning to another of my favorite verses, "Be holy, for I the Lord your God am holy" (Leviticus 11:44).

The laws of Leviticus are a fulfilled law, and it is therefore no longer binding; however, the concepts and principles as well as the moral values remain for our learning and observance, and these are unchanging. We can also read and study some of these from Jesus' Sermon on the Mount (Matthew 5:1–7:29).

At the time when Jesus was on earth in the first century the law was in its last days. As soon as Jesus was crucified, the last requirement of the law (for a blood sacrifice) would be furnished by Jesus on the cross. Jesus said about this, "Do not think that I came to abolish the Law or the Prophets; I did not come to abolish but to fulfill" (Matthew 5:17).

After His temptation our Lord was preaching in Galilee. John the Baptist had been taken into custody, and soon it would be our Lord's time. As He preached He said, "The time is fulfilled, and the kingdom of God is at hand; repent and believe in the gospel" (Mark 1:15). And finally as they were gathered for the Passover meal, Jesus said to the apostles, "I have earnestly desired to eat this Passover with you before I suffer, for I say to you, I shall never again eat it until it is fulfilled in the kingdom of God" (Luke 22:16). These texts all speak of the crucifixion that was imminent, and they also say that after His resurrection His kingdom on earth would begin.

After the resurrection God says of it that it was impossible that he be held in death's power (Acts 2:24). Do you remember that the power of death was Satan's? God also says that He has appointed a day in which the world will be judged through a man He has appointed because proof has been established by the resurrection that Jesus is the Son of God (Acts 17:31).

The setting in which Leviticus was written occurred at the foot of Mount Sinai[9], where God gave the Law to Moses (Nelson 1995). It was written the year following by Moses, but was not revealed until 1447[10]" (MacArthur 2005).

Numbers records the experience of a spiritually lost people as they wander in the wilderness. We learn an important lesson about God from the behavior of the Israelites not only in the wilderness wanderings but from the

---

9   *Nelson's New Illustrated Bible Dictionary*, copyright 1995 by Thomas Nelson Publishers, general editor Youngblood, Ronald F., (Nashville), Leviticus (Historical Setting).

10 MacArthur, John, *MacArthur Bible Commentary*, copyright 2005 by John MacArthur, (Thomas Nelson Publishers Leviticus, (Author and Date).

time of their deliverance. Our God despises murmuring and disobedience. It is a lesson well worth remembering. The wanderings not only served as punishment for the older generations but also as a time of preparation for the conquest of Canaan by the younger generation. In a lot of ways Numbers is a sad book. It is sad for a number of reasons but primarily because of the disobedience of the older generation. After all the miracles they witnessed from the deliverance itself, but to have manna and meat and water as needed and God's guidance and protection not even counting their freedom from slavery. I wonder what could have turned them into such self-centered, selfish people, and there is only one answer. They left God. Moses' death would have been sad at any time, but it was unusually sad to me because his temper caused him to sin and in the process he brought dishonor on the God he loved more than he loved life. It is said in the last chapter of Deuteronomy that God knew him "face-to-face" (Deuteronomy 34:10).

Numbers is actually a sequel to the book of Exodus as it follows the escape from slavery, the journey across the wilderness to Mount Sinai, the forty years of wandering, which ended at Moab on the eastern side of the Jordan River, and finally their readiness to occupy the land of Canaan. It also picks up where Leviticus left off by continuing to teach the Israelites about God and worship.

I think we have to mention that the core of this book illustrates God's wrath, which was precipitated by disobedience by the people brought out of Egypt. As Leviticus indicated God expected exact obedience, and even Moses was not immune from punishment. However, even in His wrath, which was brought about by the Hebrews' refusal to enter Canaan, He did not give up on them[11] (Nelson 1995). The punishment in the wilderness for forty years took two generations of the oldest people. These were the ones who had seen the miracle after miracle and yet they didn't trust him. I don't know how you feel about it, but it does a good job of witnessing for us the extent of God's wrath and the knowledge that His patience does run out. Do you think we try His patience in this way? I expect we do but probably don't think about it at the time. Maybe we should begin to examine our attitudes, our reactions when we don't get what we want. I hope you noticed how He turned that catastrophe into a blessing by training the next generation for the conquest of Canaan.

---

11   *Nelson's New Illustrated Bible Dictionary,* copyright 1995 by Thomas Nelson Publishers, general editor, Youngblood, Ronald F., (published by Nelson Publishers, Nashville), Numbers, (Theological Contribution).

Besides picking up from where Leviticus left off, we learn more about another major character in God's story, a warrior by the name of Joshua, who led the Israelites after Moses' death. One of Moses' last acts was to commission Joshua to take the place that had been Moses' for so long. But Moses had reached the end of the life God had for him. Although he wouldn't be allowed to enter the Promised Land, God would take him to "Mount Nebo the top of the Pisgah mountain range which is opposite Jericho and the Lord showed him all the land that had been promised to Abraham for his descendants." And Moses died there in the land of Moab, and God buried him in the valley. But no man knows his burial place. That brings up an interesting piece of information I had never realized before, and that is that Moses wasn't buried on top of the mountain as I had always assumed. What a wonderful picture that brings to my mind as I envision God carrying Moses in His arms down the mountain (Numbers 34:6). It is an image I plan to keep as a reminder of God's love. Moses was 120.

Numbers received its name from the numbering of the tribes as preparation was made for war.

Deuteronomy actually means second law and refers to the second reading, which occurred after the death of Moses. This reading was for the benefit of the next generation of adults, who had been children when the law was originally read. It was important that they hear the law read and probably explained to a certain extent. It seemed that they were excited about what they were doing and were anxious to please Moses and thus God. The emphasis of the book is the covenant relationship between God and the Israelites, which assures God's love in return for their obedience. Please notice that this is the same requirement expected of Adam and Eve and everyone else since time began. Joshua and Caleb would be the only men who would be from the original group who came out of Egypt. They were probably older than sixty and the only two spies who did not rebel against God.

Moses wrote the speeches he made to the people prior to being taken up Mount Nebo to view the Canaan land the Israelites would be taking over after his death. He was 120 years old, but God said his eyes had not dimmed nor had his vigor. Moses gave his farewell messages to Israel, beginning on the first day of the fortieth year after the exodus from Egypt. He wrote the speeches down and gave them to the priests and elders to keep for future generations[12] (Deuteronomy 31:9, 24–6). After all the grumbling and complaining it is like a breath of fresh air that the focus of this book is trust.

Deuteronomy takes place in one location called the plains of Moab in Numbers 36:13 and the "central rift valley east of the Jordan River" in Deuteronomy 1:1. It had been forty years since the Israelites left Egypt. Moses read the divine revelation, recorded the law in a book, and commissioned Joshua as the new leader. Moses was allowed to view Canaan from the top of Mount Nebo, and then he died at the "command of the Lord" (Deuteronomy 34:5), which according to one interpretation meant "not from old age or illness, but at a kiss of God" and was interpreted midrashically to mean that Moses died "of God's mouth"[13] and was buried by God (Tigay, 2012).

While Leviticus' emphasis was on the priests, Deuteronomy focused on the people. Perhaps of even greater importance was that Moses called the people together before he died and encouraged them to take the land God had promised by oath to their forefathers. It is said that Moses not only looked back but forward and saw Israel's future disobedience (MacArthur 2005).

Summary

It is generally conceded—and supported by Christ—that all five books of law were written by Moses (Mark 12:26 and John 7:23) during the same time period, roughly 1445–05 BC. I believe it is divine inspiration rather than coincidence that they parallel the progression of human life as it moves toward life in Christ. The themes of these books move from the bondage of sin to deliverance by and accessibility to a Holy God, followed by death as a result of unbelief or victory as a result of obedience. All of these five books are rich in history as well as law, but they are primarily considered a part of the law.

12　*MacArthur, John, MacArthur Bible Commentary,* copyright 2005 by John MacArthur, (Thomas Nelson Publishers, Nashville), Deuteronomy, (Author and Date).

13　Moore, Beth, *Deuteronomy, (The Law of Love),* copyright 2012 by Crossway, a publishing ministry by Good News, 6, II, quote: Dr. J H. Tigay, (JAS Torah Commentary, p. 337), (published by Jewish Publication Society, 1996,, Philadelphia)

Study Guide—Chapter 6

Q. Name the five books of law.

A. These five books give us the beginnings of the people of the world. God built a heritage for us in these books, some of it good and some of it bad, which is a fair representation of who we are. The fact that God calls us to excellence while He extends endless patience with our imperfections provides opportunity for unlimited progress if we care to take it. The names of the books are Genesis, Exodus, Leviticus, Numbers, and Deuteronomy.

Q. If Genesis is a book of beginnings and Exodus is a book of deliverance, of what significance is the book of Leviticus?

A. God has taken us back to the principle of holiness in Leviticus and shows us the beauty and the joy that can be had in worship.

Q. How does God's miraculous deliverance of His people from oppression correlate to our own deliverance from sin?

A. One could say it is an exact replica. They were delivered from the bondage of slavery. We are delivered from the bondage of sin, which is slavery. Only in God is there either freedom or life.

Chapter 7: Books of History

The historical books record the conquest of Canaan, the period of the judges, the rise and fall of the monarchy, the captivities of Israel (the Northern Kingdom) and Judah (the Southern Kingdom), the return to the Promised Land, and the restoration of the temple and walls. God continues to reveal Himself in these historical accounts. The patience with which He deals with a disobedient people is amazing and shows His great love. His severity for disobedience is a reminder for us that consequences for sin will be terrible beyond what we can imagine, while reward will also be beyond imagination. Be certain to choose well.

The Books

There are twelve books of history that begin with the conquest and possession of Canaan. After Joshua's death Israel began to wallow in confusion with every person doing as he liked. These historical books mark both the rise of Israel under the military power of King David and the United Kingdom and her decline after the kingdom divided. God allows Israel to be taken into exile. Their history under the leadership of Joshua ends with the Israelites living in the Promised Land again but no longer in possession.

Joshua

The book of Joshua picks up where Deuteronomy ended. Joshua, the person, was handpicked by God to continue Moses' work. He had been an assistant to Moses, who took him when he went into the mountain to meet God at Sinai. He was also one of the scouts picked by Moses to spy out the land of Canaan. Joshua died at the age of 110 and was buried in the land of his inheritance.

Joshua is *the* book of victory for the Old Testament. It records what can be accomplished when one works in tandem with God instead of against Him. It records the history of the numerous victories under Joshua's leadership plus the division of the land by tribes.

Canaan was a wicked, idolatrous nation that had totally failed to follow God in His commandments. The fact that the Canaanites would lose their country for lack of repentance is a vivid example of where disobedience leads. Joshua's failure to utterly destroy the Canaanites as commanded would sow dreadful circumstances regarding idolatry for the Israelites that would lead to their exile. We need to keep in mind that God's timing is always perfect. He understands many things of which we have no knowledge. The message for us about war is to be prepared for whatever His decisions may be. This is never easy as it demonstrate for us that nothing is permanent in this temporary world. We need to remember God's qualities of compassion, patience, and love as we take in the significance of these wars just as we also need to remember that the Israelites, American, and the citizens of all countries have ample opportunity to follow what He would have us do and be. He has shown us both His patience and His wrath. I believe wisdom advises us to be prepared for whatever comes and the only way to accomplish that is through obedience to Him.

Judges

Judges is a history of alternating rebellion and repentance and shows Israel's trials under the leadership of fifteen judges. Their confusion seems to have been brought about in part by Joshua's death as they didn't seem capable of doing their own thinking. Left basically without a ruler the result was that every man did as he pleased (Judges 21:25). There is no other book that shows the alternating phases of worship and idolatry quite like this one does. Disobedience was followed by idolatry, intermarriage with Canaanites, and disobeying the judges. This would be followed by rejecting God, chastisement by military defeat, and subjugation, after which Israel would pray for deliverance, prompting God to raise up another judge to guide them. They followed this pattern time and again, demonstrating the confusion of living without God's guidance. Judges was written about 1051 BC, probably by Samuel. Judges focuses briefly on the closing days of Joshua, and it is grouped around themes rather than employing a chronological pattern. It was a time of turmoil brought about by ungodly leadership not only of judges but by priests and parents, and the problem was nationwide. This was a new generation, one that hadn't experienced God's work, and their trust was almost nonexistent. It seems when Joshua died, confusion descended, and the people did as they liked, disregarding laws and consequences.

God was faithful throughout this cycle that lasted over three hundred years. It was a cycle that included rebellion, oppression, forgiveness, and deliverance, and it was during this time that the people began to beg for a king. They wanted a king because it was what their neighbors had. In doing so they ignored the fact that God was their king. They were warned of the difficulties and problems of having a king; however, eventually their wish was granted, and the period of the judges ended. Their attitude can be summed up by this verse at the end of Judges: "In those days, Israel had no king; everyone did as he saw fit" (Judges 21–5).

There are many stories you would recognize from the book of Judges, such as those about Samson, Gideon, and Deborah. I believe God shared these trials with us to show the futility of living without Him.

Samson was a man known for his great strength and bad morals. Though he was the son of godly parents, you would not have recognized it. After a life of immorality he was able to call on God, who returned his strength so that he could fulfill what had been his purpose in life. Samson's life demonstrates for us that it is never too late to show repentance.

Deborah was the only woman judge, a wife, and a prophetess.

Ruth

Ruth gives us the story of how a Gentile woman became an ancestor to Christ. Her story shows the life history of the Israelites in its greatest simplicity and success, and in the process it reveals the identity of the Gentile woman who became Christ's ancestor. The book of Ruth proves beyond a doubt at least two truths: (1) God is not partial, and (2) circumstances neither make nor break belief. Belief comes from the heart. Ruth's choice to stay with her mother-in-law was a choice that stemmed from the heart. God shows us the far-reaching results that come from a good choice. In many ways Ruth is an exemplary character in the Bible. We should admire her love and loyalty. Don't miss the fact that she is a foreigner (a Gentile) and not a Jewish woman, and yet she is an ancestor to Christ.

In many ways Ruth was a perfect example of spirituality. She lived in obedience and faith and became the Lord's ancestor, yet she was an uncomplicated person whose heart yearned for God as she illustrated the love she felt for Naomi. Though her mother-in-law was not the main character of this story, she somehow remains the heroine in my mind. If you question how Ruth, a Gentile woman, came to think so highly of her Jewess mother-in-law, even after the death of her husband, your mind has to go back to Naomi as the key. It is obvious that Naomi loved Ruth, had Ruth's best interests at heart, and beyond the obvious, loved God so much that she was an inspiration to Ruth.

The book of Ruth demonstrates God's manipulation of behind-the-scenes facts that control the purpose for which the foundation is laid. It begins with the kindness of Naomi to her daughters-in-law after her sons are deceased, her faithfulness to God as she determined to return to God's people, and the obedience that follows. Perhaps the most outstanding factor of the book is that we needed to know of God's acceptance of this Gentile woman. It proves the promise to Abraham that the blessing through Jesus would be for people of all nations, doesn't it? What requirement did God have for His acceptance of Ruth? It was the same requirement Adam and Eve were offered—belief coupled with obedience. This is a beautiful example of God's impartiality. This book also demonstrates our own responsibility to provide loving examples to those with whom we are associated.

The book of Ruth closes with the genealogy of Jesus, descendant of Ruth, the Gentile ancestor.

This part of Samuel begins with Samuel's birth and training for the priesthood. After Eli's death Samuel became a judge as a permanent position and was recognized as the new leader of Israel. In that position judges became more than military leaders, and he was called on in times of national crises. He was reluctant to grant the people's request for a king, but God helped him to understand that they were not rejecting Him, "for they have not rejected you, they have rejected me" (1 Samuel 8:7 NKJV). It was Samuel who anointed both Saul and David to the kingship. When God rejected Saul as king, it was Samuel who made the announcement, and when David committed adultery with Bathsheba and then had Uriah killed in battle, it was again Samuel who was in the leadership position.

First Samuel

First Samuel gives us about 135 years of history. During these years there was a complete transformation from a tribal people under judges to a united kingdom ruled by a monarchy. Invasions by the Philistines with their advanced weaponry fueled the people's demand for a king. This transition from a tribal people provides the key for 1 Samuel.

Theologically the country was a mess. The priesthood was corrupt. The

Ark of the Covenant was not at the tabernacle. People practiced idolatry, and the judges were dishonest. Through the influence of Samuel, these conditions were reversed. The book of 2 Samuel ends with God's anger withdrawn from Israel (2 Samuel 24:25 NKJV). First Samuel was written before the exile to Babylon. (Information for this paragraph can be found in 1 Samuel 2:12–17, 22–6; 1 Samuel 4:3–7:2; 1 Samuel 7:3–4; 1 Samuel 12:23; 1 Samuel 13:14).

David's loyalty to King Saul is one of the highlights of character in the Old Testament and illustrates God's love for obedience. It also shows David's patience and loyalty that preceded his kingship. Another example of loyalty is the friendship between Jonathon and David, an unlikely friend who, except for David, would probably have been the successor of his father as the next king.

The attitudes of these central characters are as important for us today as they were at the time when they lived. In fact this may have been one of the reasons these particular stories are parts of God's foundation. We've emphasized the heart, but the attitude is what comes from the heart, so these stories demonstrate the desires of the heart. I would urge you to pray often regarding the attitudes of your heart. Remember Ruth, Naomi, David, and Jonathon and study their lives.

(To learn more about the period of judges, read Judges, Ruth, and 1 Samuel 1:1 to 10:16.)

Second Samuel

Second Samuel shows the glory of the Jewish monarchy under King David. It would seem from David's life that we need to learn that when things start going really well it is time to be on guard because Satan uses those times to place temptations before you. David was faithful throughout his difficult times, but when he became king and everything was going smoothly, he relaxed his guard and was caught up in sexual temptation. This book reveals both David's high point (his ascension) and his low point (the adultery with Bathsheba and murder of her husband, Uriah). We need to note that in spite of God's forgiveness, David was still responsible for the consequences of his sins. Even though God's forgiveness was immediate, the consequences were severe with both personal disasters and how they affected his kingdom and his family. Nevertheless the covenant God made with him in 2 Samuel 7:12 to make his dynasty an everlasting one was fulfilled in Jesus and shows God's faithfulness and His love for repentant sinners. I would say that 2 Samuel demonstrates all of that . We need to remember that all things are known of by God. Nothing is hidden from His knowledge and His grasp of every situation.

Samuel was originally one book in the Hebrew language but was divided by the Greek translators as they began work on the Septuagint version because the book was too large for their scrolls. It is assumed that Samuel wrote both sections since it was originally one book and was written before the exile to Babylon.

First Kings

David wasn't the first king, but he was the one God picked. What an honor! His would also be the kingdom that would be eternal. How is this possible? It is possible through the unbroken line of his descendants who sat on the throne following his death and his lineage (through Mary). Both Mary and her husband, Joseph, were descendants of David.

During the four centuries covered by Kings nineteen different kings ruled the nation of Israel, and twenty-two kings ruled Judah. Israel was the first nation to collapse under the weight of disobedience and depravity. It fell with the loss of its capital city, Samaria, to the Assyrians. The nation of Judah carried on for another 136 years when they were overrun by the Babylonians in 86 BC. It was just a little over twenty years later that 1 Kings was written (538–536 BC).

There were many things achieved during Solomon's reign, but the most striking difference between Solomon and David was that David increased the Israelite territory by warfare, while Solomon's contribution came by means of building activity. During his forty year reign he is best known for the magnificent temple he built, but aside from the building itself, he was also remembered for the administrative and cultural transition that he enabled along with great prosperity that followed.

In spite of the prosperity of the period, obedience to God was largely lacking. It has always seemed strange to me that Solomon's wisdom didn't result in a righteous reign. He was allowed to build the temple because there was no blood on his hands, and yet he did not have a heart that yearned for God. His request of God for wisdom seemed promising for his future, which is interesting as we consider the type of person he became. Sadly he did not have the nature of his father, David. Nor did he love the Lord as David did. I believe this illustrates that hardships strengthen the desire for God, whereas luxuries can make one dependent on the self.

The example David set by taking so many wives undoubtedly influenced Solomon to follow in his father's footsteps. Bathsheba exacted a promise from David that their first son (actually their second son) would succeed him on the throne. Of course there was much rivalry involved among the mothers and their sons, and one of the sons took matters into his own hands and proclaimed himself king. In order to keep his promise to Bathsheba, David sent armed forces to prevent this act of arrogance and immediately made Solomon his successor. However, Adonijay continued to plot against the royal command and died by Solomon's hand as a result (1 Kings 1:17–26). It seems a sad happening that to gain one son, he had to lose another. I wonder if David understood that this whole problem lay at his feet. Nevertheless, Kings is a good example of God's choice to combine punishment with mercy. Both the first and second books were written around 450–430 BC, having been originally one book.

By the end of Solomon's life his extravagant spending and huge harem caused division in the kingdom. It had almost seemed inevitable, considering the decline in obedience and the lack of trust that existed amongst the people and the rulers. God allowed the tribe of Judah to be captured and taken into captivity by the Babylonians. The Northern Kingdom had been in exile since 930 BC and continued their fall into apostasy. They were basically absorbed into the Assyrian culture and society; however, the Southern Kingdom was returned to Jerusalem, and the people were allowed to rebuild the temple.

First and Second Chronicles

If you keep in mind that both 1 and 2 Chronicles are considered the official histories of the Israelite kingdoms, it is easier to understand that they carry the message of faith and hope, largely maintained by Ezekiel, the prophet who was in exile as both priest and prophet. It was his responsibility to remind the Israelites while in captivity of their sin and of all that God had done for them. Can you imagine their joy when they actually got back to Jerusalem? Unfortunately their joy was limited to the fact that they were in their own land. Through selective memory this book presents only the good times, the glory of the past, which was intended to give hope for the future.

As mentioned the writer "left out what was negative or anything that was in opposition to the Davidic kingship. On the other hand he made unique contributions in validating temple worship and the line of David."

And finally he concludes in the second half of Chronicles in a hopeful tone for the future because of the release and their return to Jerusalem. You might call this approach the power of positive thinking! The conclusion is that the selective genealogy plus the fact that they were a united kingdom under Saul and David, and that they had come home to Jerusalem all meant that God still had future blessings in store for them[14] (MacArthur 2005). Ezekiel's purpose in his positive storytelling was to remind them of their spiritual heritage in the difficult times that they faced.

Both sections of Chronicles were originally one book like Kings and the two sections of Samuel. With no Hebrew king and still ruled by a Persian king, although they were back in Jerusalem, with no security making it necessary to rebuild the walls as quickly as possible, no temple in which to worship, and no longer dominant in the area in which they lived. The Jews faced a bleak future. Essentially a message by way of reminder of God's past and present blessings. First and second Chronicles show by illustration God's intentions for their lives in the future and the restoration rests in the new covenant. With no king (although the promise of a king was valid for the future), no temple worship that included the land, the nation, the priests, or animal sacrifice, it was obvious that their hope for restoration lay in the new covenant (Jeremiah 31:31–34).

(To learn about the united kingdom, read 1 Samuel 10:17–31:13, 1 Chronicles 10:1–2 Chronicles 9:31, 1 Kings 1:1–11:43, and all the books of poetry, including Job, Psalms, Proverbs, Ecclesiastes, and Song of Solomon.)

Second Chronicles begins with Solomon's reign and the building and furnishing of the temple. When the preparation of the temple was completed, worship began again, which was an indication to the people that God's presence was once again with them. This also signaled God's forgiveness. The book traces the apostasy of Judah (the Southern Kingdom) and her kings, who make up the line of David. It's rendition of Jewish history is accurate but not balanced for lack of those things that were displeasing to God.

Do you see God's faithfulness to forgive and His continuity in rescuing the people after they repent? Please note again that the Northern Kingdom was not rescued, indicating their lack of godly sorrow.

It should be noted that God always left the Israelites with hope, no

---

14 MacArthur, John, *MacArthur Bible Commentary*, copyright 2005 by John MacArthur, (published by Thomas Nelson Publishers, Nashville), 1Chronicles, Background and Setting

matter how bad their situation appeared. He does the same for us because as part of spiritual Israel we are part of His people.

Second Kings

Second Kings is a history of corruption of both kingdoms, which resulted in slavery. Prominent in both 1 and 2 Kings (which were also originally one book) are the prophets Elijah and Elisha. From the concept of what He is revealing to the Israelites regarding sin, as He also reveals to us, is He telling them that sin and depravity were the reason for their captivity? Of course He is, but he is also speaking of slavery to sin. Elijah and Elisha are the dominant characters of this book. However, their efforts didn't bring repentance from the Assyrians (Northern Kingdom) but did result in an amazing miracle. Elijah was translated (taken) to heaven without dying. This reminds me of the martyrs in Revelation who were evidentially translated directly to heaven.

(To learn about the divided kingdom, read 1 Kings 12:1–2 Kings 17:47 and 2 Chronicles 10:1–28:26. You can also read the prophets Hosea, Joel, Amos, Jonah, Micah and Isaiah.)

(To learn about the kingdom of Judah alone, read 2 Kings 18:1–25:30 and 2 Chronicles 29:1–36:23. You can also read the prophet Zephaniah.)

(To learn about the Babylonian captivity, read 1 Chronicles 1:1–9:44. You can also read the prophets Daniel, Ezekiel, Lamentations, Jeremiah, Obediah, Nahum, and Habakkuk.)

Ezra

Ezra was a priest, and he was also a scribe who copied Scripture. He also demonstrated a responsibility for the encouragement of the Israelite captives. He did this as an exile himself by repeating the events of their history while reminding them of the power and love of God. He recorded the return of the Jews from captivity and the rebuilding of the temple, emphasizing their need of God to accomplish the enormous task ahead; he encouraged their adherence to spirituality and the necessity of returning to God's commandments regarding their homes and their relationships with the Canaanites. Ezra was trusted by the king of Persia to the extent that he was given access to the king's records. Because of his faithfulness, the king gave him privileges he would not have had otherwise[15] (MacArthur 2005).

---

15 MacArthur, John, *MacArthur Bible Commentary, copyright* 2005 by Thomas Nelson, (published by Thomas Nelson Publishers, Nashville), Ezra, Author and Date

As restoration of the temple progressed and the hope in their hearts grew, there was renewal to some extent among the people. Ezra dedicated himself to God and God's cause and gained the respect of the king of Persia, who as a result returned goods that had been taken in the captivity and released all the captives who wanted to return home. This illustrates God's power, His omnipotence while it also shows how He used those in power to implement His purposes. This is an example of how His hand was the motivating factor behind certain accomplishments. God used those who were rulers to implement His purposes (the hand of the Lord).

I tend to think of this period of time in regard to restoration alone, but as difficult as restoration was, it is likely to have been the easier part of what faced the people. Few, if any of the spiritual rituals and practices of the nation were allowed them while they were in captivity. They were not allowed to maintain the separate status God had required of them with the result that there was intermarriage and heathen customs were adopted. They would have to relearn God's commandments. It would not be easy to organize communities around the information within the law. Habits learned in captivity would have to be totally removed from their lives in order to regain covenant relationship with God. They had neighbors who were none too happy to see them return and who would be a moral and idolatrous temptation. It would be a difficult time, for undoing is always much harder than doing. I see this as a depressing example of the extent of consequences. We must learn from their example and from David's example that sin is spiritually life-threatening. The consequences of David's sin with Bathsheba and the murder of Uriah followed him the rest of his life, and they were still with him on his deathbed.

Nehemiah

Nehemiah is a history of the Jewish post-exile from Persia (formerly Babylon), and it speaks mainly of rebuilding the walls and the restitution of worship. It is book of renewal. Since Nehemiah was an eyewitness to much of the material covered in this book, information was drawn from his personal diaries, but both Jewish and Christian traditions recognize Ezra as the author[16] (MacArthur 2005).

Nehemiah was taken to Babylon in one of three captivities and had gained a significant role in the palace. Elevated to the position of cupbearer

---

16   MacArthur, John, *MacArthur Bible Commentary*, copyright 2005 by Thomas Nelson, (published by Thomas Nelson Publishers, Nashville), Nehemiah, Author and Date.

and confidant to the king, he was both admired and trusted. In 445 BC, he was returned to Jerusalem, where he led the people in rebuilding the walls. Elevated by the Persians to cupbearer and confidant to the king, he was both admired and trusted. Rebuilding the walls could have been considered a threat to the Persian government without such trust.

Both Ezra and Nehemiah were concerned for the people as they realized more fully what they were returning to. It would not be the same as it had been. In addition to rebuilding the walls of the city they would be faced with regaining a covenant relationship with God. While they needed to know what had happened to Jerusalem during their absence, they also needed to recognize what had changed them during their years of captivity. The problems would be immense. Nehemiah and Ezra's work was similar in that they had to reteach what had been lost. Nehemiah went to God continually on their behalf, and he was their example. When Ezra returned, he confronted the people with their sins and taught them the law, which had basically been forgotten during their captivity (Nehemiah 8–9). The significance of this teaching was a renewed ability to recognize sin and repent.

For our benefit it is good to remember that Ezra and Nehemiah's faith were contributing factors in influencing King Cyrus to hear God as He prompted the king to release the captives. You and I have the same responsibility today to live lives of example and responsibility in order to demonstrate God's principles.

Esther

The book of Esther "shows how God preserved His Chosen People by her courage and quick thinking"[17] (Nelson 1995). I would add that this also applies to Mordecai, her uncle, who had raised her. Though the book reports actual events, it is written like a story and shows God's providential help to Jews who chose to remain in Babylon. Not too long after the Persians captured Babylon, Jewish captives were allowed to return to Jerusalem, but thousands chose to remain in Persia. The events of Esther occurred about a hundred years after the captivity.

With the exception of the book of Esther the narratives of the post-exile period dealt exclusively with those who returned to Jerusalem. Esther's challenges were quite different in part because they are in a royal setting but

---

17   Nelson's New Illustrated Bible Dictionary, copyright 1995 by Thomas Nelson Publishers, (published by Thomas Nelson, Nashville), Esther, Introduction.

also because that setting is the royal palace, which is the seat of power. It is possible that the returned captives could have read this account of Esther. If so, it must have been quite a shock. Although Esther became a queen, the book is about ordinary people who accomplished extraordinary things under difficult circumstances through God. And that, I think, is the whole point for us today. God would be pleased if we would learn from it.

It does occur to me that this type of service to God requires an enormous amount of confidence not in one's self necessarily but in God and in His providential care.

Esther's story also illustrates the Jewish struggle to survive in the midst of a hostile world, even with God's protective intervention. Considering that her life was on the line, she displayed amazing faith and courage. To me this indicates that despite captivity Mordecai had taught her about God. It was obvious by her attitudes and her overall ability that she was well trained in how to respond to those around her with a gracious spirit that demonstrated her concern for their well-being. Mordecai was a blessing in her life because he prepared her for an unknown future. Such principles as respect for others in harmony with her faith made her a perfect choice to achieve the protection necessary for her people.

Haman was the evil person of this narrative, and if it were possible to choose only one word to describe him, I would choose the word *pride*. It fits Haman in just the same way it fits Satan. For Esther many words could describe her nature, and I have chosen four: obedience, faith, humility, and service. You notice, I hope, that I do not consider beauty her primary description, and I'm sure God didn't either. God would not have chosen her for this role if beauty had been even her main attraction. She was undoubtedly attractive, but her inner beauty and strength and her faith above all made her outstanding. The king got more than he was looking for I expect. When I think of Mordecai, Esther's uncle, I would describe him as one who regularly worshipped. (He stayed in touch with God.) He was wise (He knew how to apply what he learned.). He was obedient (He knew who to obey.) And he was courageous. (He took risks to accomplish God's Word). Used by God, Esther and Mordecai were amazing ambassadors for His purposes. All in all Esther is a fascinating book with an impressive view of God's behind-the-scenes role.

Summary

Although the book of Esther is a short account of a major event, one is able to read between the lines to gauge the depth of a situation that could have destroyed God's people. That God's protection to a scattered people proves His continuing love is apparent, while His manipulation of events is fascinating. As we have progressed through God's work since the creation, His behind-the-scenes activity is more evident. I suggest to you that He has not altered in this regard. He continues to work in each of our lives as well as in governments to achieve His purposes.

As we complete the historical books of the Old Testament we've seen both God's patience and His wrath. We've seen failures as well as successes and find that each is related to trust. We've learned that God uses people and events and nations and tribes to achieve His purposes, and we've seen how He works behind the scenes. Finally we've experienced God's faithfulness and his continuity as well as His love and His mercy, and the transition to the law has enabled preparation for the coming of the Messiah through prophecy. Much of the information contained in these books is validated in contemporary historical recordings. Archeology contradicts many contemporary historians' arguments against the biblical records of Solomon's reign as either exaggeration or complete fiction. However, archeological excavation of the cities of 1 Kings 9:15 helps to demonstrate that the Bible account is precisely as described therein[18] (Archeology Study Bible, The Zondervan Corp., 2005, NIV 1984, publisher Zondervan, Grand Rapids, Michigan pg. 497).

---

18   Archaeology Study Bible, NIV, copyright 2005 by Zondervan, (published by Zondervan, Grand Rapids), Building Activity of Solomon, p. 497).

Study Guide—Chapter 7

Q. How many books are in the division of history?
A. There are twelve books in this division.

Q. Why was the conquest of Canaan a milestone event?
A. This was a huge event in the history of the Israelites because it was proof that God kept His promises. Of course He had done so continually, but this was an event that they knew was to happen. It is important to us as well because it shows us His faithfulness over a long period of time, His continuity, and His love in spite of the necessity of dealing with a grumbling and complaining people. We are not that way, are we? You would have to be kidding if you were to say that! We can't say it of our selves any more than they did, but I know that we do the same thing from time to time.

Q. Israel's many relapses into idolatry belied their miraculous deliverance by the hand of a loving God. Do you see those relapses as unfeeling, uncaring denials of God, or do you see them as the undisciplined naughtiness of the adolescents (that they were) of God's continuum, struggling with their carnal nature?
A. I hope that it can be seen as the learning of adolescents because we all go through that even as adults at times. For us it is an indication that we need to spend more time in study and in prayer. There is another aspect I would like you to consider and that is how critical attitudes creep into our thinking quite unknowingly. I challenge you to monitor your attitudes on a day-by-day basis to see if some critical attitudes need to be excised. You'll be happier with yourself if you do this self-examination, and God will be pleased with you.

Q. The divided kingdom refers to the separation of the twelve tribes of Israel into two kingdoms. The apostasy of both kingdoms and their resultant captivities illustrated that without God their government could not stand. In light of the fact that the people had desired a king in disobedience to

God's will, what more basic meaning, intrinsic to their relationship to God, can you draw?

A. Their basic problem seemed always to be a lack of belief that God could do what He said He would do. This translates into lack of trust.

Q. Because we as Christians have not attained perfection, would you rather God judge relapses as the acts of those struggling to overcome or as denial of Him?

A. This is a dumb question, but in many ways it's an important one. It's dumb because there can only be one answer, but it's important because attitudes are so important. I have to poke a hole in our balloons here because any disobedience is lack of belief and trust, so we're going to have to admit that we often deny Him. As soon as you realize, you have repent by talking with Him about it and ask for His forgiveness.

Chapter 8: Books of Prophets

The prophets were men who were raised up by God in times of apostasy, who spoke for God to the conscience of the nation. They were God's messengers. They usually had two purposes. First, they spoke to whatever physical need confronted the nation at the time, and second, they spoke to the divine purpose of the future, which was the promised coming of the Messiah. Both purposes dealt with the nation as God's covenant people who had failed by sin to keep their side of the contract. Because the contract had been broken, God could have rejected them, but He chose to continue in order to redeem and forgive. This shows His patience and His love as well as the mercy of His forgiveness.

All of the prophets delivered basically the same warnings against sin, upcoming destruction, exile, and restoration along with the hope of a coming Messiah. The message was at times primarily to Israel and at other times primarily to Judah, but it was often directed to both nations. The people were rebuked, warned of national vulnerability, and encouraged to pray, fast, and repent in order to stay judgment. In spite of their many transgressions they were always given hope for the future.

The Messiah

The term Messianic or *anointed one* refers to the coming Messiah. The word Messiah means *deliverer*, but when capitalized, it refers to Jesus Christ[19] (*New College A. H. Dictionary* 1980). The fact that the prophets told of His coming, His lineage, His suffering, and His crucifixion makes it difficult to understand His rejection. It is easy to say they should have known Him. After all they had been told of His coming for hundreds of years. In fact the people of the generation in which He came were actively

---

19 New College Edition, American Heritage Dictionary of the English Language, copyright 1980 by Houghten Mifflin ed., William Morris, (publisher, Houghten Mifflin, Boston), "M".

looking and hoping for Him; however, the reality was different from their expectations. If they should have recognized Him, what about us? Do we recognize Him for who He is? Our knowledge is even greater than theirs, our avenues of opportunity endless. Perhaps it isn't knowledge on which recognition hinges. If faith is missing, our knowledge will be insufficient, as was theirs.

He Was Forsaken

Isaiah 53:3 says, "He was despised and forsaken of men, a man of sorrow, and acquainted with grief; and like one from whom men hide their face, he was despised, and we did not esteem Him."

Why was such a good person so despised? The rabbis, who had largely replaced the priests by then were divided regarding the meaning of certain texts, and there were followers of each sect with the result that the people were also divided. The rejection by the religious leaders was easier to understand because they had positions and power they could foresee losing, and that was not to their liking. The message to some extent reflected the opinions of leadership, emphasizing a religion of works rather than one of faith. It was for this reason that their faith had weakened. Confronted with the Son of God, it seemed they could only defend their own opinions instead of seeing who stood before them. To what did a man of sorrow refer? I think it refers to two things: (1) His sorrow at the condition of man's heart in regard to sin and (2) the fact that He knows the outcome for those who reject reconciliation. I wonder at times if we are as off base as the Israelites were in the ways in which we misunderstand all sorts of spiritual admonitions in regard to the Messiah's role as the king. That their expectations were for an earthly king demonstrated their distress under the Roman rule, but it seems to me that it was also an attitude of superiority or ego because His coming was not as they expected. First Corinthians 1:23 reveals that a crucified *deliverer* or Messiah was a stumbling block to the Jews, while the cross itself was a sign of weakness and failure. This was especially so because they wanted an earthly king to deliver them from their distress and hardship and raise them to a position of power in the world. Instead Jesus message was one of love, humility, and service and was noticeably lacking in force.

Isaiah 53:5 says, "He was pierced through for our transgressions, He was crushed for our iniquities; the chastening for our well-being fell upon Him and by His scourging we are healed."

Why would He do such a thing for us, and what does it mean to be a man of sorrow? Because He sees our sin and has love and mercy in His heart He wants to reconcile us to the Father. So His sorrow probably refers both to the condition of man's heart and the outcome for those who reject reconciliation. I think He would also be sorrowful because He was rejected. Knowing the rejection that would come from the Father didn't make it any easier to bear. When Jesus prayed in the garden, "Let this cup pass from me," He was probably remembering that at the proper time when He carried the weight of the world's sin upon Him, the Father, knowing it had to be done for the sake of forgiveness, would turn away from Him. Nevertheless, He added, "Yet not as I will, but as you will" (Matthew 26:30).

While expectations for an earthly king demonstrated the stress of the people under Roman rule, it seems to me that it also exhibited an attitude of superiority or ego because He was an ordinary man and didn't come with pomp and ceremony. We need to recognize our Lord's humility when we begin to think how important we are, and we must pray with humility that acknowledges our unworthiness.

The angel who brought the news of the coming birth told Joseph He would be called Emmanuel, which means "God with us." His human name was Jesus.

Emmanuel

Oh, holy night
In shining splendor gleam
His birth the precious promise
For which we hoped and dreamed.
Oh, holy night the angels joyously sing
In chorus of our Savior
Prophet, Priest and King.
Shepherds bow in worship
In awe to see Him there
Nestled in a manger
Emmanuel, Son and Heir.
Holy, Holy, Holy!
My Lord, my God, my King!
Accept my adoration
As of you alone I sing.
Righteous Lord and Savior
In you my soul delights
To lay before your presence
My heart, my soul, my life.
All glory, praise and honor
To you alone I cling
As I humbly beg forgiveness
For what I cannot bring
—Marie Hunter Atwood, 2009

And so the tiny babe, the infant Jesus came. His incarnation is the most amazing thing that has ever happened. God with us, Emmanuel, imagine! His place of birth was as prophesied in the little town of Bethlehem. "But as for you, Bethlehem Ephrathah, too little to be among the clans of Judah, from you One will go forth for me to be ruler in Israel. His goings forth are from long ago, from the days of eternity" (Micah 2:6).

God's consistency shows even here in identifying the city in which He would be born. The city of His birth was said to be of little importance, so if He were to be judged by its size, He would already be condemned. His strength is from God and not the size of the city in which He would be born or reared.

Jesus' physical heritage would come from the line of David (through Mary, descendant of Nathan, son of David), and He is often referred to as a branch from that tree.

- "'Behold, the days are coming,' declares the Lord, 'when I shall raise up for David a righteous Branch; and He will reign as king and act wisely and do justice and righteousness in the land'" (Jeremiah 23:5).

- Isaiah 25:8 says, "He will swallow up death for all time, and the Lord God will wipe tears from all faces, and He will remove the reproach of His people from all the earth; for the Lord has spoken."

When Scripture uses a phrase like "the Lord has spoken," you can understand that it is as sure as if it has already happened. Isaiah was prophesying that Christ would do away with death as we know it. But why would he say, "He will swallow up death?" To swallow anything seems a strange metaphor for death. Let's see if we can understand it.

Physical death is a normal occurrence. One lives, and then one dies. I think most of us understand that life isn't over at that moment as we continue to live or die in another environment. This new place knows and remembers all that we've done and not done while we lived, but it's too late to do anything about it. So what happens? It depends. We are a sinful people, but too many of us don't really understand that. We live our lives in the happy ignorance that we are acceptable in God's light because we have not killed anyone among other deeds. That is spiritual death.

I'm sorry to tell you that nothing could be further from the truth. We live in our self-absorbed surroundings pleased (or unhappy as the case may be) by how well we've done in life or how miserably life has treated us, and we give ourselves credit for the first and blame others for failures. We dust off the Bible on Sunday, but we may have to look for it first. Our eyes and ears are dulled by mention of spiritual matters, and we can't wait to see the new movie that came out recently. Although we haven't committed any of the big sins, the Holy Spirit within us no longer has access to the heart. That's spiritual death.

This is not the life God wants for us. We must have God to be able to find the other life that is available, and if we choose that life and live it, we will have another after the physical body no longer lives. So as you can see, we have two lives, and without God, two deaths, the physical one and the spiritual one. We all die physically, but if we've lived for God instead of for ourselves, when we reach that point, we go on living for Him and with Him. The decision to live for Him comes from the mind of the physical body, but it is essentially a spiritual decision. What it means is that you want to follow the guidance of the spirit instead of the guidance of the flesh, so you are putting to death the old person of the flesh with your decision, which is followed by the act of baptism. Baptism is symbolic of Jesus, who Himself rose from the watery grave of baptism as an example for us. We rise from baptism to walk in newness of life. This is how it is a death of desire for sinful things but also a spiritual resurrection because it transforms one from death to life.

Eventually there will be death of the physical body, and for the one who has lived for Christ, this death is followed by living in Paradise to await the judgment. This is what Jesus refers to when He speaks to the thief on the cross, who will join Him in Paradise, but it also refers to the blessing that awaits the one who participated in that spiritual resurrection from death to life. That person will not be hurt by the second death, which is the punishment that follows judgment (Revelation 20:6). In both situations, at the moment of physical death, one knows his or her destiny, but the waiting place for eternity is separate. Both the reward for the obedient and the punishment for those who chose not to repent are still to come. So when Isaiah says that Christ will swallow death, he is simply saying that for the faithful believer, death from sin can no longer claim us because we belong to Christ.

Our intent to live spiritually is renewed on a day-to-day basis as we strive for the perfection that He wants for us. This is where the heart comes in. To desire (make the effort) and fail is different in our Lord's mind than to fail to make the effort. He says to us that if we seek Him, we will find Him. Seeking combined with belief is the key to salvation (Matthew 7:8).

To do away with the death that is a result of sin was the purpose of the incarnation, His ministry, the crucifixion, and the resurrection. This is why He gave Himself to us. By the crucifixion He suffered the death that should have been ours. By the resurrection He broke the bonds of death and Satan's power over death. We live because of His death.

Prophets and Prophecy

The prophets, although inspired by God, did not understand the messianic prophecies because it was still a hidden happening yet to come. First Peter 1:10–12 tells us that they "made careful search" of the Scriptures, hoping to learn the meaning of their prophetic words. Peter records that it was revealed to them that these things would come to pass at a later time. God's hidden plan gave new meaning to the designation hidden wisdom and mystery, didn't it? Why do you suppose even the prophets didn't know the meaning of the words they uttered? I can think of two reasons. Firstly they spoke as God had instructed whether they understood or not, and secondly because of angelic rebellion that Satan had begun, this would stay a very well-kept secret until the time was complete for revelation. Second Peter 1:21 gives the authority for prophecy. It does not come by an act of human will, but it is inspired by the Holy Spirit spoken from God. The prophets were the messengers of God's Word.

There were two things the Israelites were never to do. I call them nonnegotiable. Even though the law did not provide forgiveness of sin, God provided it for His people repeatedly when it came to rescuing them from their actions. Beyond His love for "this stubborn, stiff-necked people," as He often named them, His plan could not be dropped. There had to be a righteous line through which the sacrifice of his Son would accomplish the provision of forgiveness for all.

Repeatedly the Israelites broke the covenant by doing the very thing they had been told not to do. This is the sign of unbelief just as it was with Eve. So the punishment phase would begin until repentance came, and then they would sin again. God called those who remained faithful "the remnant," and it was on their shoulders that His plan rested. From the remnant there would come one who would be a descendant of King David of the tribe of Judah, so lineage was important just as it was with priests who offered sacrifice.

As the prophets shared God's will with the people they began to reveal the information needed for identification of the Messiah. It was important information, and some held it in their hearts and pondered its significance, as Mary did when told she would be the infant's mother. Others failed to recognize its importance, and in doing so they formed in their own minds what He would be like. Messianic prophecy provided hope for the future, and with some it encouraged faithfulness.

I have divided the seventeen books of prophecy into historical time periods. What had been a united kingdom under King Solomon was now divided into two factions under his sons. The two sides were called Israel (the Northern Kingdom) and Judah (the Southern Kingdom). In Judah there were only two nations that remained, whereas Israel carried away ten.

The Books, Pre-Exile

Joel

Joel tells of the devastation of Judah by locusts and gives a parallel warning of judgment to come. His message is repentance for the day of the Lord. An outstanding feature of this book is the demonstration that God's message can often come in the form of a natural disaster. Do we see disaster in this light today? God's sameness and His lack of partiality don't change. We need to understand that disasters serve the same purpose today that they have always served. It is through these incidents that God calls man to attention to the necessity of repentance.

The message of Joel as doctrine can be applied to any age. The key phrase is repeated nineteen times in a very short book. Its message has both a near fulfillment which is an historical event repeated nineteen times in a very short book, while at the same time it is an aid in understanding the distant one which is eschatological.

In the eschatological fulfillment Joel foresaw the work of the Holy Spirit at Pentecost and the beginning of the church. The historical outpouring of the Holy Spirit celebrates the delivery of the Hebrews from the bondage of slavery[20] (Nelson 1995); whereas the eschatological fulfillment celebrates the deliverance of man from the bondage of sin[21] (Nelson 1995). However, Pentecost also honors Passover because the memorial feast in our Lord's honor was established on Passover at the last supper[22] (*Archaeological Study Bible*, p. 1611). It might help if we understood that Pentecost is a harvest

---

20　Nelson's New Illustrated Bible Dictionary, copyright 1995 by Thomas Nelson Publishers, (Thomas Nelson Publisher, Nashville), Feasts and Festivals, (Passover – Egypt- slavery).

21　Nelson's New Illustrated Bible Dictionary, copyright 1995 by Thomas Nelson Publishers, (Thomas Nelson Publisher, Nashville), Feasts and Festivals, (Feast of Weeks -Harvest).

22　Nelson's New Illustrated Bible Dictionary, copyright 1995 by Thomas Nelson Publishers, (Thomas Nelson Publisher, Nashville), Feast and Festivals, (Pentecost – Sin).

festival based on the outpouring of blessing from God of sun and rain that made the harvest possible. The symbolism for us is the same. The outpouring of spiritual blessings at Pentecost allows a faith that grows from belief and obedience to reconciliation and salvation[23] (*Archaeological Study Bible*, p. 275).

Joel prophesied regarding Pentecost more than any other prophet. In addition he praised the joys that would be poured out on repentant believers.

Jonah

Jonah was a prophet to the Northern Kingdom, sharing that reputation with the prophet Isaiah. In his native language, Jonah's name means dove, and he was a reluctant messenger for God. The story of the whale is almost like the Israelites miraculous delivery from Egypt, which defies explanation. I would suggest that it is an expression of faith in God's power, omniscience, and omnipresence as in Psalm 139:7 when David asks of God, "Where can I go from your Spirit? Where can I flee from your presence? If I go up to the heavens, you are there; if I make my bed in the depths you are there. If I rise on the wings of the dawn, if I settle on the far side of the sea, even there your hand will guide me; your right hand will hold me fast."

This phenomenon of Jonah and the whale cannot be explained in a logical manner, so it must be accepted by faith. The Gentile nation of Assyria had enjoyed a time of peace and wealth during these years, but spiritually, they were bankrupt in morals, ethics, and spirit. God was ready to send punishment upon them, but He chose first to send Jonah as a missionary to the Gentile Assyrians. Jonah's reluctance to carry out God's command was compounded by the repentance of the people of Nineveh, to whom God extended His compassion. God's message is that His grace and concern are for all people and not just the Israelites. Jonah had a really bad attitude. He was actually angry because the Assyrians repented. Jonah wanted them punished … *now!* We should remember that His grace is for all people and His mercy extends to all those who repent. Be sure to look at the book of Nahum for the sequel of this story.

---

23   Archaeological Study Bible, NIV, copyright 2005 by Zondervan, (published by Zondervan, Grand Rapids), Cultural and Historical Notes, (Pentecost).

Amos

Amos is called the herdsman prophet in light of his simple background. He experienced great outrage for the Assyrians, who were diligent about making sacrificial offerings but refused both justice and mercy to the oppressed and needy. Because we will always have people who are needy, we must be cautious both personally and nationally that we do not forget those in need. It is a God-given responsibility. God's message through Amos and Hosea, prophets to the Northern Kingdom, was not received, and those ten tribes never went back to Jerusalem. Instead they continued to go downhill in their apostasy, and they were eventually absorbed into the Assyrian population. Do you see the difference the heart makes in being reconciled to God the Father? Because of idolatry and immorality, the desire to serve God was lost. Sadly it would be less than twenty-five years until the capitol of Assyria lay in ruins. Remember that this is a Gentile nation. Their rejection came at the eleventh hour so to speak when their time was almost up anyway, but God tried one more time to bring them to repentance. I hope you can see the extent of His love.

Hosea

Hosea used his own disastrous marriage to point out the comparison between his unfaithful wife and the unfaithfulness of Israel for God's love. Although God cannot condone sin and suffers as He punishes man, He is still willing to extend His mercy and loving kindness. Hosea's message demonstrates the pain that sometimes is a result of love, but I encourage you to think for a moment about God's pain. We sometimes feel that love is only sweetness and light, but this demonstration says, "Not so." Love demands but love also forgives. This is the love our Father gives, a forgiving love. It is also the painful love regarding His Son's time on earth. If there were no godly sorrow, there would be no forgiveness and no reconciliation.

From the time Jeroboam died, the country experienced anarchy for the next thirty years, during which time four of the last six kings were assassinated by their successors. Hosea is the first of the minor prophets so labeled because of the brevity of content of the book.

Isaiah

Probably the greatest of the prophets, his prophecies span the most comprehensive range of time reaching back to creation. He looks backward to the counsel of God and forward to the time when God will create the new heavens and a new earth. "No prophet is more fully occupied with the redemptive work of Christ. In no other place, in the Scriptures written under the law, is there so clear a view of grace"[24] (Scofield 1988).

In addition he prophesied regarding all the nations of the earth. His subjects ranged from empty worship and idolatry, oppression, immorality, and pride. He predicted the Babylonian captivity and the final day of the Lord when all people will face judgment. He looked forward to the coming Messiah, who would be the Redeemer from sin. One emphasis used by Isaiah was in regard to God's wrath. "The day of the Lord is coming, a cruel day, with wrath and fierce anger, to make the land desolate and destroy the sinners within it" (Isaiah 13:9). "I will punish the world for its evil, the wicked for their sins. I will put an end to the arrogance of the haughty and will humble the pride of the ruthless" (Isaiah 13:11). "I will make the heavens tremble; and the earth will shake from its place at the wrath of the Lord Almighty, in the day of his burning anger" (Isaiah 13:13).

Let's take a look at Isaiah's teaching in regard to our own lives:

1. *Empty worship.* We surely don't do this, do we? How often do we look around us to see who is or who isn't present for worship? How often do we do other things to occupy our minds instead of participating in the worship? Do we close our minds to the service and think of the meal to come or what we need to do as we wish things would move along a little faster? If so, our worship is empty, meaning nothing is gained toward our spirituality. Nor is anything given to God. Neither our minds nor our hearts were present. Our worship has been useless.

2. *Idolatry.* An idol is not necessarily an image. It can be a house, a car, clothes, a reputation, or a position. It can be power, or it can be the self. In the case of the Israelites these were foreign gods, idols made with hands. Today we create our own idols by placing any of these things above God in importance.

---

24 New Scofield Study System, copyright 1967 by Oxford University Press, ed., C. I. Scofield, rev., 1967, NAS ed., 1988 (published by Oxford University Press, New York, Iowa Falls World Bible Publishers), *Isaiah*, (Introduction).

3. *Oppression.* Can we oppress by neglect or by ignoring? Of course we do it all the time. Oppression can take many forms. How about the child who is always chosen last or the teen who isn't dressed quite like others and is ignored or the family down the block that doesn't have enough to eat or the husband who needs help finding a job or the family down the block that is a little different and doesn't quite fit in or the families who are the "survivors from earthquakes, hurricanes, floods or fires who need help in distant places." Opportunities are endless. Do we see them?

4. *Immorality.* We all know what immorality is, but it is usually the other person who is guilty. How about wicked and immoral thinking, cheating, or lying? (Big lies and little lies are the same in God's sight.) Sin is not always overt.

5. *Pride.* Wow! I'm afraid this one is of epidemic proportions. Ego, narcissism, putting others down to make ourselves feel better, ridicule, all of these are sins of pride.

Isaiah is able to comprehend what lies beyond the surface, isn't he? I hope we are able to see ourselves when we consider Isaiah's teaching of the Lord's will. It only does harm when we see these faults in someone else. Knowing ourselves is a great blessing toward our effort to change into people God wants us to be. If we lie to ourselves about what we are, we may not be able to change after a time.

Micah

Micah was a contemporary of Hosea in the north and Isaiah in the south. He was like Amos in that he lived in a country setting, removed from the political and religious turmoil of the time, and yet God chose Micah to prophesy to royalty of those houses and people of the two capital cities Samaria and Jerusalem.

His message was also similar to that of Amos, with indictments of social injustices, religious corruption, and justice to come. He predicted the fall of Israel and Judah, the destruction of Jerusalem and the temple, the return of Judah, and the coming of the Messiah, who would render mercy. It was to the "disintegration of personal and social values to which he delivered his most stinging rebukes and stern warnings"[25] (MacArthur 2005). As an indictment against the leaders in the two capital cities, Micah taught that a people will be like their rulers, giving a share of the responsibility to them for the sin of the people. We are always responsible for our own actions as they influence others around us. On the other hand, if it is a positive reaction, God gives us credit for the influence.

Nahum

Nahum takes place about a century after Jonah preached to the Ninevites. As such, his book is a sequel to Jonah's. This time the message was not received. Nahum is a good example of the fact that repentance and forgiveness last only as long as there is repentance in the heart. Repentant at one time, Nineveh had gone back to her evil ways. Repentance and its fruit must be ongoing because evil is ongoing.

Zephaniah

He is a great-great-grandson of King Hezekiah, the only prophet descended from a king. A contemporary of Jeremiah, he warned that their final day of the Lord was near through the hands of Nebuchadnezzar, implying that many would not survive. He also preached regarding the end time (judgment) by pronouncing judgment against immorality, injustice, and idolatry and by predicting that it would also come for the oppressors who prospered at the expense of the righteous. The day of the Lord refers to the time at which His wrath will be poured out against evildoers, and as he looked beyond to that final day he pleaded with the people to seek the Lord for shelter in the midst of the current judgment by the Babylonians and proclaimed eventual salvation for "God's remnant, the believers"[26] (MacArthur 2005).

Jeremiah

Jeremiah was the son of a priest who served as both a priest and a prophet. His ministry spanned five decades and records Judah's sins,

---

25 MacArthur, John, MacArthur Bible Commentary, copyright 2005 by John MacArthur, (published by Thomas Nelson, Nashville), Micah, Background and Setting.

26 MacArthur, John, MacArthur Bible Commentary, copyright 2005 by John MacArthur, (published by Thomas Nelson, Nashville), Zephaniah, Historical and Theological Themes.

their coming doom, the Messiah, and a new kingdom. As a result of the wickedness of King Ahaz the sacrifice of children was still a problem under Manasseh, son of King Hezikieh. Under Joash, who followed Manasseh, there were reforms, but not enough to make them long-lasting. There was much "religious insincerity, idol worship, dishonesty, adultery, and injustice that were practiced regularly in Judah." Eventually Judah would repent but the consequences of their sin would not be removed. Nor will it be with ours. The new kingdom, of which Jeremiah prophesied, refers to the new covenant and the forgiveness that would be bought at the cross. It would be the new covenant with Israel, a covenant of grace with Israel, referring to the new Israel, which includes the Israel with whom God had the old covenant and the Israel that now includes Jew and Gentile. The new kingdom of which Jeremiah prophesied refers to the new covenant and the forgiveness that would be bought at the cross. It would be a covenant of grace with Israel, referring to the new Israel, God's church.

Habakkuk

Contemporary to Jeremiah, Ezekiel, Daniel, and Zephaniah, Habakkuk questioned God's use of the wicked nation of Babylon to bring punishment against His own people. The reply he received was that evil men are used to accomplish God's purpose, but they also will be destroyed. While God is teaching Habakkuk that all evildoers will be brought to justice, He is also teaching him that God is not to be worshipped for what He does for man but because He is God. This is the greater lesson of Habakukk. It seems to me that God has always used wickedness to teach principles, although we all have a tendency to find reasons for excuse if we are involved.

Exile

During the time period just discussed Judah, under the leadership of King Uzziah, had enjoyed a prosperous existence both commercially and militarily with a port on the Red Sea and the construction of walls, towers, and fortifications, yet there was a marked decline in spirituality (MacArthur 2005).[27] This decline is the reason God allowed the Babylonians to take His people into captivity. As we consider the return of these captives, think also of the Israelites in the world today as they are scorned and persecuted and question whether God is using the evil of the world to bring His

---

27   MacArthur, John, MacArthur Bible Commentary, copyright by John MacArthur, (published by Thomas Nelson, Nashville), Isaiah, Background and Setting.

people back to Him. If so, our prayers for Israel will be a sweet aroma at the throne of God.

At least three of the exiles made strong impressions on the kings who reigned over them, resulting in benefits for God's people. Look for those benefits as we highlight each book.

Lamentations

Lamentations means *elegies* or *plaintive poems*. Jeremiah, who had so eloquently prophesied the capture and destruction of Jerusalem, now laments the fall and expresses hope for Judah's future restoration. Jeremiah realized God's harsh treatment of man will save him from eternal doom. This lesson is one that is continually necessary in all civilizations.

Daniel

Perhaps the most remembered story of the book of Daniel is the episode of the lion's den. An edict was issued by the king that stated anyone who made a petition of any god or man other than himself during a thirty-day period would be thrown in the lion's den. When Daniel learned the edict had been signed into law and could not be altered, he faced Jerusalem on his knees three times a day in prayer. The edict was carried out. He was thrown into the lion's den with two of his friends, and God protected them. The next day when they were found unharmed, the king had them removed and ordered that his advisors, who were the instigators of the plot against Daniel, be thrown into the den.

This story illustrates the key to the book, which is God's victory over all creations and kingdoms, and it is a lead-in to the primary subject of Daniel, which emphasizes the rise and fall of nations, each of which demonstrates God's control. With God victory is guaranteed and is accomplished when the time is right. Faithfulness and repentance are up to us.

Daniel was taken to Babylon in the first of the deportations. Exiled in 605, in the first deportation, like Joseph, he excelled in wisdom and gained favor with his captors.

Much of Daniel is in a veiled or hidden style, so it is said to be apocalyptic. Such writing reveals God's reality behind what man perceives as real.

Ezekiel

Ezekiel was both a prophet and priest, taken into exile along with his wife and about ten thousand others, which included King Jehoiachin. In exile his purpose seemed to be to keep before the people their national sins and to sustain their faith by keeping their national pride alive with expectation of justice. Please notice that this pride was pride in God and not in self. His reminders of their sin helped to balance out the situations they had reason to be proud of. With God's love evidenced they did repent and were brought back to Jerusalem after seventy years. This is typical of our constancy today, so I think we can't afford to be self-satisfied about the Israelites' cycles of falling away and coming back through repentance. It is a good idea not to judge situations like this. For one reason we are promised that we will be judged in the manner with which we judge others (Matthew 7:1–2). Besides judging others speaks of a haughty attitude instead of a humble spirit that says, "There but for the grace of God go I."

Ezekiel predicted the fall of Jerusalem, judgment against their oppressors, restoration, the new kingdom, the church, and Christ's kingdom on earth, which in time will be united with His kingdom in heaven. "Your kingdom come, your will be done on earth as it is in heaven" (Matthew 6:10).

Obadiah

Judgment is prophesied against Edom (descendant of Esau and twin brother of Jacob), who had given aid to Judah's enemies and who rejoiced over the capture of Jerusalem. Obadiah serves as a warning to those who would express joy over the misfortunes of others, even when that misfortune is justified. The point is that God Himself is sorrowful over any loss, and therefore it is an attitude we need to cultivate.

There is also the fact of God's promise to bless those who bless Abraham's descendants and curse those who curse them (Genesis 12:3), which would seem from this example to apply to fellow descendants. What a sad story of bitterness and hatred. According to history, the Edomites were never heard from again after the destruction of Jerusalem.

Post-Exile

Most of the exiles (except for those who chose to remain in Persia) are back in Jerusalem, and the message of these post-exile prophets is significantly different in regard to the present need of the people. As for the Israelites who remained in Persia, I read somewhere that it was the largest group lost to Israel of all the dispersions, but I don't have the specific number of people involved.

As for the other purpose of the prophets, the one that was to be a tutor for the coming of Christ the time is running short. You could almost say we are (historically speaking) to the countdown.

In the meantime the leaders who made it back to Jerusalem had their hands full. They encouraged those who worked on the temple and urged the people to do God's work before they turned to their own. In addition, the people began to hear more frequently about the promised Messiah and the coming doom of the heathen nations.

Zechariah

Zechariah was born in captivity and would have succeeded his father as a priest, but his father died before the transfer could be made. He was returned to Jerusalem (538 BC) in the first group released by Darius of Persia. Contemporary of Haggai, they began to work on the temple; however, the spirit to build didn't last, and the work was set aside for sixteen years. He continued to urge Judah to finish the temple work, pointing out that God helps those who help themselves. Zechariah's prophesies concerned the Messiah and His reign, His priesthood, His rejection and betrayal, and His second coming. The prophet begins with a plea from the Lord, "Return to me …that I may return to you" (Zechariah 1:3). What a vivid, beautiful plea for repentance that shows the intense love God has for Israel.

Malachi

About one hundred years had passed since the return from captivity, and the people had sunk to a level lower than when they had been taken into captivity. Malachi rebuked the Israelites for their worldliness and lack of spiritual discipline, and he encouraged them to lead lives that would make them fit for God's holy kingdom. His message was this: The day of the Lord is coming. Malachi "delivered God's message of judgment on Israel for their continuing sin and God's promise that one day in the future when the Jews were repentant the Messiah would be revealed and God's covenant promises would be fulfilled"[28] (MacArthur 2006). There would

---

28　MacArthur, John, MacArthur Bible Commentary, copyright 2005 by John MacArthur, (published by Thomas Nelson Publishers, Nashville), Malachi, (Background and Setting)

be over four hundred years of divine silence before the people would hear another prophet with God's message for them, and that message would come from John the Baptist as the forerunner to Jesus.

Summary

The prophets played a vital part in the foundation as God's messengers to the people. There has never been a more potent message to link the people to the actions of their rulers than the one that stems from the revolt of the northern tribe. Idolatry followed, instigated by the first king of the divided Israel, and from then on idolatry was a part of their national religion. All of the kings of Israel subsequent to that event were depraved, and the nation followed their example. As a result they ceased to be a nation and eventually became a part of the Assyrian nation.

In the divided nation of Judah there were twenty kings, all descendants of David who held the throne for almost four hundred years. Six of them were highly praised, and most of the others were commended. Only a few were extremely wicked, and they introduced idolatry into the temple, which led to the captivity of Judah. Though the nation was warned and judgments were threatened, the time came when they had to be shown that God would no longer tolerate their voluntary disobedience. Consequences of their decisions came in the form of captivity in which they became slaves to kings who didn't know their king. So it could be with any nation that voluntarily rejects God.

We've witnessed through the prophets over four hundred years of God's work. Now it will be left to each individual whether or not he or she initiates repentance. Although there will be a long period of silence for the Israelites to deal with, God will not forsake them. I feel it is not too dissimilar from our situation today. We have His word in plentiful supply if we care to consult it. The Israelites had Malachi's words ringing in their ears along with the words of many other prophets who had pleaded with them to be prepared for the coming day of the Lord. In the absence of books the prophets filled a vital role in God's foundation.

Where does this lead us? Prophets have been replaced with preachers. People still teach by their influence or their lack of influence. The world we live in is dramatically different yet the same, while accessibility to God is still available. We rush about in our busy lives, lives too busy and too uncaring to seek Him, to praise and worship Him. What will the day of the Lord bring to us? We are heedless that He speaks to us in the thunder and the lightning, in the tsunamis, the floods, the earthquakes, in life and in death, yet His message remains the same: "Repent, seek me, and you will find me." His purpose remains the same, the gift of life. He will not force it on you. It is up to you to reach out for it, to say to Him, "Yes, I believe. Please help my unbelief," and He will hear you and answer your prayer.

Study Guide—Chapter 8

Q. To what could we compare the role of the prophet today?

A. We have preachers who come nearest, being like the prophets, except they aren't directly inspired by God, and I would have to say many are not inspired at all. However, some are, and without enough of those who are to feed us adequately, we are on our own. We must learn to feed ourselves in this regard. After all, it is our individual responsibility.

Q. Does this help you to understand the apostasy of the Israelites, or does it make it more difficult to understand your own?

A. I'm afraid it makes it harder to understand theirs because the prophets had what you might call *inside information* since they were inspired by God. Knowledge should make apostasy (sin) more deplorable, but on the other hand, we have tons of information just waiting to be used and even our Bibles must be dusted off occasionally in order to use them.

Q. Which prophet shows most clearly the love and sorrow God felt for the necessity of chastening His children?

A. Jeremiah, known as the weeping prophet, wept over the chastisement of the people by allowing them to go into captivity, and while they were gone, Jerusalem was destroyed. And he wept over the city. Many years later during Jesus' ministry and shortly before His crucifixion, Jesus did the same. "Oh Jerusalem, Jerusalem, who kills the prophets and stones those who are sent to her! How often I wanted to gather your children together, the way a hen gathers her chicks under her wings, and you were not willing" (Matthew 23:37).

Q. What was the purpose of their chastening, and how does it show God's continuity?

A. God allowed the chastening because of idolatry. Remember the two nonnegotiable principles? "You shall have no other gods before me, and shall not make for yourself any idol…neither to worship or to serve" (Exodus 20:1–2). His principles have not changed. Remember that God chastens those that He loves.

Q. In Habakkuk 2:4 we learned that pride leads to death because it cannot accept faith but that the righteous live by faith, which leads to life. Correlate this to God's plan of reconciliation as we know it today.

A. There is no difference. This recalls the old saying that says a gift is not yours until you have accepted it. It is true also with spiritual gifts. God reserves the right not to recognize anyone in judgment who hasn't repented.

Chapter 9: Books of Poetry

I don't know how many times I've heard people say, "Poetry! Who cares?" If I could only convince them of what they are missing, they would be so blessed. Poetry is a way of seeing God. It is a way of understanding His love. It is a human response to the Father, a method that overcomes those things that do not lend themselves to understanding.

Poetry responds to God and His creation on a basic level—whether it is in reaction to a single perfect flower or a range of awesome mountains, an attempt to understand the world in which we live or an effort to understand one's self. It can be a prayer of thanksgiving or a cry of despair. Biblical poetry is usually presented majestically and often elicits wonder, awe, or fear. It's through poetry that we are able to draw closer to His comfort and security, where we find a loving God. Our responses can be quite different, depending upon the circumstances for which we seek help. After I read David's prayers in the Psalms, I knew I could take all of my wounds to Him for healing. He is the same yesterday, today, and tomorrow.

Poetic Form

Poetry as a type of writing touches on all aspects of the human experience. It is difficult at times for us to define biblical writings as poetry because their forms are so different from what we think of as poetry. However, there is much to be gained from these books of poetry because they portray the rich and varied experiences of God's people in such a way that we may find inspiration, comfort, strength, and guidance.

Hebrew poetry followed not so much rhyme and meter as parallel thoughts. These thoughts could be synonymous, contrasting, or simply developed and enriched.[29] (Nelson 1995). The poetry usually falls into one

---

29 Nelson's New Illustrated Bible Dictionary, copyright 1995 by Thomas Nelson Publishers, (published by Thomas Nelson Publishers, Nashville), Poetry, (Authorship and Date),

of three categories: lyric (musical and songlike), didactic (instructive), or dramatic (striking, forceful, and emotional).The books of poetry include the Psalms, Proverbs, Ecclesiastes, Song of Solomon, and Job, and I have also included Lamentations. Even though it is characterized as prophecy, the entire book is poetry. Many poetic passages are found outside these five books, especially in the prophetic writings. However, those books are classified by their primary content with the exception of Lamentations and Nahum, which is lyric verse.

Job

Job is a theological debate on why those who are righteous suffer. Many consider it the oldest book of the Bible[30] (Nelson 1995), even dating it as far back as patriarchal times. This would indicate an incredible amount of revelation prior to written Scripture, but the content of Job seems to do just that. It has several messianic passages, a beautiful discussion of wisdom (chapter 28), and several chapters of outstanding poetry (chapters 38–41). The foundational concept is trust. A secondary concept is that God uses suffering in His divine plan as a means of perfecting character. The challenge of reading Job as well as other poetry at times is to understand the author's intent. Often you'll find that a poem speaks in a different way to different readers, which extends the beauty of the message; however, it is beneficial to go back again and again for the wisdom a poem offers, especially in the book of Job.

While it is generally considered that Job was written during the time of Solomon, internal evidence involving the living conditions and historical events not mentioned here points to a much more archaic setting (Nelson 1995)[31] (MacArthur 2005)[32].

1. Job's wealth was measured in cattle, flocks, and herds, which were an indication that Job lived in patriarchal times.

---

30 Nelson's New Illustrated Bible Dictionary, copyright 1995 by Thomas Nelson, (published by Thomas Nelson Publishers, Nashville), Poetry, Job, (Authorship and Date)

31 Ibid

32 MacArthur, John, MacArthur Bible Commentary, copyright 2005 by Thomas Nelson, (published by Thomas Nelson Publishers, Nashville), Job, (Author and Date).

2. His children remained a part of his household, subject to his rule.

3. Job's priestly functions within His family (Job 1:5) and his life span of about two hundred years fit with the patriarchal period, comparing in length with Abraham who lived 175 years and his father, Terah who lived 205 years. This is contrary to earlier times when people lived for multiple centuries, such as Noah who lived 950 years and his father Methuselah (his father) who lived for 969 years.

4. Similarity to the book of Ecclesiastes suggests Solomon might have written it.

5. The Chaldeans who murdered Job's servants were still nomads instead of city dwellers at the time of the murder.

6. There is no mention in the book of God's Covenant with Abraham, Israel and the exodus from Egypt, or the Law of Moses. Neither is there mention of the tabernacle or the temple, which would suggest an earlier writing.

Job also reveals that Satan had access to God despite his many acts of rebellion and evil. I feel that the timing of this revelation is also important in tracking his decline because it reveals God's sameness and His continuity. Perhaps you wonder why the timing is important. I think it is important primarily because it reveals a great deal of revelation prior to Scripture. God's communication with the patriarchs was much more extensive than one would know without knowledge gained from the book of Job. It is important because of the relationship it reveals between God and man. It demonstrates the *how* with which one deals with suffering by trust. Because of the conversation between God and Job, we recognize that God truly has not changed but deals with man in the exact same way He has done from the beginning. "Believe and obey God," He tells Job. It isn't essential that you understand.

Trust, I think, is the key word to remember in regard to Job.

Psalms

Psalms is a book of praise, which is its core concept. The Greek word from which it was taken meant "a poem sung to the accompaniment of musical instruments." It deals with every question of religion and human experience, past, present, and future. Both God's sovereignty and goodness are recognized. There are 150 spiritual songs, poems, and prayers. They are quoted more frequently in the New Testament than any book except Isaiah. This book sets the example for appropriate praise and prayer. The different types of Psalms serve different types of worship, even as we select certain songs today to complement the theme of a service like praise, prayer, or instruction. The Psalms are rich in concepts for godly living. In fact the primary theme of Psalms is the idea of living in the real world, where two dimensions work simultaneously. The horizontal relationships are those with family, friends, employers, businesses—all of the people we know or come into contact with in our daily lives. The other dimension is our relationship with God, our worship and praise, our spiritual sacrifice, our contact with people. Oops, did you catch that? They blend into one. Don't worry. They are supposed to. That's sort of what *symbiotic* means. We need each other. We help each other, and we are good for each other. Live your spirituality 24-7, and while you're doing it you are helping others to live theirs. Our relationship with each other and with God joins us together in spiritual cohesiveness, which will keep Satan at a distance. He doesn't want any of that two-dimensional symbiotic spirituality. In light of these teachings it is obvious that we should spend extra time in the Psalms.

Proverbs

Proverbs pleads the case of wisdom. Proverbs are simple comparisons or contrasts held up against life's most profound truths. Proverbs is a collection of pithy sayings that are practical and not theoretical. They were common to all nations of the ancient world and were probably designed for the purpose of making God's truth accessible, as they point to God with instructions on holiness. This collection, although not written in its entirety by Solomon, is attributed to him. He is said to have uttered three thousand such proverbs in his lifetime. His wise counsel was in conflict with his example, especially in the latter part of his life. Here is an example: "The fear of the Lord is the beginning of wisdom, and the knowledge of the Holy One is understanding" (Proverbs 9:10).

Ecclesiastes

Ecclesiastes means *preacher* in Hebrew. It is probably autobiographical by Solomon and questions the vanity of life apart from God. It is the reflections and experiences of a philosopher whose mind is in conflict over the problems of life. His conclusion is that there is a holy God who will bring everything to judgment. Apart from God, all is vanity. Neither amassing wealth nor accomplishments bring happiness; true satisfaction is testimony to the dreariness of life without God.

Song of Solomon

This book is a love song that is possibly allegorical, comparing the love of God for Israel and the love of Christ for the church. It also characterizes beauty, joy, and love, which are much deeper than attraction. The book was designed to last a lifetime, and it does not reflect cultural changes. Conceptually you may see the following: "Marital love is pure as ordained by God."

Lamentations

Lamentations means *elegies of Jerusalem* or *plaintive poems*. Written by Jeremiah, who had so eloquently prophesied the capture and destruction of Jerusalem, he now laments the fall and expresses hope for Judah's future restoration. He recognizes that God's harsh punishment is for the purpose of saving man from eternal doom, a lesson we are constantly in need of. Though much shorter Jesus lament over the city was similar (Luke 13:34).

Note: The book of Lamentations is always listed with prophecy, and I have not altered the numbering for either division. Because Lamentations is a poem, I wanted to share its structure with you as a poem. The poetic content is similar to what we would call a dirge, although the form is quite different. It is doubtful that there is either rhyme or meter in Lamentations, but Jeremiah made use of the method called parallelism in which a thing is said twice. For example consider Lamentations 2:7: "The Lord has rejected his altar and abandoned his sanctuary." There are other methods used in Lamentations, but repetition seems to be a constant for whichever form is used.

Life as a dirge, it is a sad poem, but I suspect there are many things we can learn from it because the subject is such an important one. Let me know what you think.

Summary

The books of poetry have diverse foundations:

1. Trust God.

2. Offer songs of prayer and praise.

3. Love is a gift.

4. Marital contentment is a result of love.

5. Apart from God (who brings judgment), all is vanity.

6. Jeremiah weeps for the destroyed city of Jerusalem.

Conclusion

These thirty-nine individual parts make up the book we call the old covenant between God and man. They were written over a period of a thousand years in the Hebrew language. There are five books of law, twelve books of history, seventeen books of prophecy, and five books of poetry. They tell of a war in heaven and the fall of Satan and his angels. They tell of God's creation of man and man's fall through the sin of unbelief. They tell of a law that prepared man for the Messiah who would reconcile him to God and the mystery of how that reconciliation would be achieved. They reveal that God's plan to achieve His purpose existed before the foundation of the world, and then they tell us how God executed His plan by first laying a foundation from which man could learn of His unchanging principles. Each part of the plan contributes in its unique way to the central theme of God's eternal plan. The parts are also necessary for one to understand how Satan attempted to undermine God's work, which resulted in the war we are engaged in when he was thrown out of heaven. Prior to that event, man was secondary in Satan's ambition as he wanted what God had. Actually he wanted to be God and he wanted to get rid of the Son. Satan was successful in deceiving Eve, and he was a part of the curse God placed on man, which resulted in his hatred of woman (who he blamed for the way it turned out). He focused his attention on harming the Father until the Son was sent to earth. Then he had to focus on the Son; however, those plans weren't successful, and when Michael defeated his challenge and won that battle, mankind was all that was left for him with the result that enmity between woman's seed and Satan accelerated his determination to make himself equal with God. Many battles ensued. He won far too many of them as he used man against God. For instance, the conflict between Cain and Abel was lost. There was also the loss of an entire generation in the flood and the evil that replaced it. And then God had to destroy the cities of Sodom and that first evil generation that was destroying too much of what had been accomplished. The evil that popped back up in Sodom and Gomorrah had to be cleansed to protect the people.

Giving man the choice, God was still victorious over Satan because of such strong men and women of faith as Abraham, Job, Noah, Ruth, Deborah, the prophets, David, the king, and those who quietly lived their lives by faith, trusting in the Father, such as the seven thousands of Israel "whose knees have not bowed to Baal nor kissed him" (1 Kings 19:18). Such would be seed for the remnant from which the final pieces of God's plan would burst forth when the time would be complete. It would be then that Satan and his helpers would receive their punishment and the world would be free, and the Israelite remnant and the Gentile followers of Christ will be one and will unite with those of the heavenly kingdom above.

The remnant stands as the final completion for the hope of the future when the church is finally one, Jew and Gentile together.

Study Guides—Chapter 9

Q. How many books of poetry are there?
A. There are only five books of poetry, which makes it the smallest division of books in the Bible; however, Psalms is the largest book. Psalms is also quoted more than any other Old Testament book. Theology in this division is based on day-to-day reality and the soverigtny of God (but not at the expense of human responsibility), and it also rests on the light of divine providence[33] (MacArthur 2005).

---

33 MacArthur, John, MacArthur Bible Commentary, copyright 2005 by Thomas Nelson, (published by Thomas NelsonPublishers 2005, Nashville), Poetry, (Introduction).

Q. Poetry deals with all aspects of the human experience. What then might we expect to gain from these books?

A. Poetry is a great source of knowledge and understanding because it allows you to see in a different light and in different ways. All poetry does this, even some you wouldn't care to read because of its somewhat immoral tone. The book of Psalms is no different except that these include more about God and His sovereignty.[34]

Q. This division begins with Job, a man who had everything and lost it but was blessed again, and it ends with an allegory of married love. How do these diverse situations help to lay God's foundation?

A. The book of Job teaches the sovereignty of God through faith, trust, and loyalty[35] (NKJV 1982). I believe you would agree these are all characteristic necessary for getting along well with people and in businesses. Let me remind you that practicing spirituality involves getting along with and understanding people. Proverbs is a book of wisdom. It teaches "the ability to live life skillfully and Godly in an ungodly world." It does this by teaching practicality as well as establishing a relationship with God, children, neighbors, and government.[36] Ecclesiastes teaches that all is vanity apart from God.[37]

Q. Psalm 8:2 (NIV) indicates that it is praise for God that will silence the Avenger. In light of this, how important do you feel the role of praise has been in your life? (This is a thought question.) Even though it is a thought question for you, I want to point out that this is something I never would have learned without being a reader of the Psalms. I am working really hard on this one. Won't you join me?

A.

---

34 The Holy Bible, giant print ed., red letter ed., copyright 1982 by Thomas Nelson, end of ref., ed., 2006, (publisher Thomas Nelson Publisher, Nashville), Psalms, (Introduction).

35 Ibid, Job, (Introduction)

36 Ibid, Proverbs, (Introduction).

37 Ibid, Ecclesiastes, (Introduction).

Q. God knows all things. Why then does He want us to acknowledge all that He has done, ask for what we need, tell Him when and how we hurt and why we are glad, and praise Him for all that He is?

A. Let's begin by assuming that you talk to those you love. That is the normal pattern of our behavior. We are family with God. Prayer is the way we have conversation with Him. He wants to hear from us because He loves us. In our human families we dislike hearing from them only when they need something. It is the same with the Father. Plus He appreciates hearing you thank Him for what He does for you.

Q. Given that prayer is our conversation with God, Scripture is His conversation with us, and knowledge is how we are able to understand, how do you feel you need to alter your relationship with Him? By the way wisdom comes from asking.

A.

Chapter 10: An Interlude

An interlude is an intervening episode or period of time. We are looking at a period of time, I think though perhaps not. I have no experience with four-hundred-year events or episodes so the discussion at hand may be both an episode and a period of time. We are interested in this interlude because we need to learn if anything happened during this period that affects God's purpose and His plan. First we will look at the last book of the old covenant. Written about a hundred years after the return of the captives, Israel is again disillusioned as they begin to doubt God's love. Their enthusiasm for rebuilding has disappeared, and they have begun to offer animals that are defective as sacrifices, while at the same time they fail to make other offerings and tithes (contributions). In the midst of this situation God gave them a promise regarding the great and terrible day of the Lord that would come.

Look at Malachi 4:5 with me, "Behold, I am going to send you Elijah the prophet before the coming of the great and terrible day of the Lord." Although there is controversy over the interpretation of this day, I don't believe it can refer to anything except the day of judgment, which would apply in both a near and a far manifestation. Malachi is saying to them (and to us) before that day comes I'm going to send you a teacher, so "don't wait to repent, repent now, and be ready for that great and terrible day." The importance of preparation *now* is that we do not know when that day will come for us on an individual basis. There will eventually be a universal day of reckoning; however, then all time will cease, and it will be too late for a teacher to reap a harvest of souls. So what is this about the prophet Elijah?

John the Baptist announced himself as a type of Elijah (John 1:19–24), meaning *one like*. Therefore, we need to know in what ways they were alike to understand what John was saying. When the word *like* or *as* (and similar words) are used, it doesn't mean that this person who will come will be Elijah. The person who comes will be *similar*, a comparison.

The most important comparisons include the following:

- They each taught repentance and reconciliation.

- They each would be filled with the Holy Spirit and power.

- They each had taught regarding inward as well as outward obedience.

- They each emphasized faith.

- They each taught against arrogance and false piety.

- They each would be independent and nonconformists compared to what might have been expected.

From the final words of Malachi 4:5 to the coming of John the Baptist (Matthew 3:1–5) there is no recorded message from God[38] (MacArthur 2005), at least none that fits the canon by which authenticity was evaluated. This is the period of silence of which we speak. Malachi uttered his last prophecy (424–425 BC), and John the Baptist began his ministry (AD 28–29), so four hundred years is close, even without allowing for error in the dates for Malachi's end and John's beginning.

They were not easy years for God's people, but a remnant remained to keep the faith of Abraham alive. The most glaring piece of information perhaps was God's silence. He did not speak to them regarding the law, their lack of trust, or their faithlessness. He was silent regarding repentance and judgment. He did not communicate with them through priests, but when the time was complete for the coming of His Son, He broke His silence and sent John the Baptist to prepare the way for the one who would be their Messiah. Like Elijah, John preached repentance to turn their hearts back to God just as Malachi had prophesied (Malachi 4:6). It was almost as if God had rescued them so many times and had granted forgiveness over and over again that it was up to them now to decide what they intended to do. Have any remained faithful? Do they still want to retain their covenant relationship with God?

---

38 MacArthur, John, MacArthur Bible Commentary, copyright 2005, Intertestmental ,(Malachi to Matthew).

In spite of political upheaval and idolatry in the world at the time, the Jews, encouraged by Alexander the Great, colonized the city of Alexandria in Egypt. There the translation of the Old Testament began around 285 BC. This translation would have a tremendous bearing on the Gentiles[39] (Scofield 1988).

In 198 BC Judea was divided into five provinces, three of which were Galilee, Samaria, and Judea where Jesus would minister. Judea revolted under the leadership of a family called the Maccabees, and war was the result. Civil authority was established with war ending in 63 BC by Roman conquest of Judea and Jerusalem. Herod was appointed governor of Galilee and later king of the Jews. After he married he appointed his wife's brother as high priest in complete disregard of God's instructions regarding the priesthood.

What have we learned of importance? We learned how Israel's nation came under Roman rule, how Herod came to be the governor of Galilee, and about his arrogance before God, but what do those things mean to the war that was brewing between God and Satan in which we are engaged as Satan's primary targets?

To begin we have learned that "though the voice of God was silent, the hand of God was actively directing the course of events during these centuries"[40] (MacArthur 2005), demonstrating His faithfulness. We still see the Israelites lack of trust in God by the fact that they still cling to idolatrous ways. Under the Romans the Israelites would be persecuted and killed, and those who remained would become enslaved to the Romans; however, others became a part of the diaspora (dispersion) settling in all parts of the known world. God would use this dispersion of His people after Pentecost when people began to preach the gospel.

Other than the political environment, there were changes that affected the religious life of Israel. In the absence of a temple in which to worship, people began to build synagogues wherever the dispersion took the Jews. Synagogues were used as meeting places, and on the Sabbath, they were used to offer prayers and read Scripture as a way to worship. Rabbis took

---

39 The New Scofield Study Bible, copyright 1967 by Oxford University Press, (ed. C. I. Scofield, rev. 1967, NAS,1988 (publisher Oxford University Press, New York, World Bible Publishers, Iowa Park), Intertestmental: (Malachi to Matthew).

40 MacArthur, John, MacArthur Bible Commentary, copyright by John MacArthur 2005, (publisher, Thomas Nelson Publications, Nashville), Introduction to Intertestmental Period.

the place of priests as teachers, but they were a source of burden to the worshipping Jews because opinions and differing interpretations as well as tradition took the place of God's Word. Opinions were superimposed upon the law, and obedience was transferred from the law to the interpretation[41] (Scofield, 1309). Sects began to dominate worship as those of differing opinions pushed their ideas on the people. These problems were chiefly observed between the Pharisees and the Sadducees, who differed over the resurrection and approached the law with differing attitudes. The Essenes were an overly aesthetic group that lived more secluded lives.

It is important to note that although there was no word of judgment or exhortation from God during this period of time, the prophecies were quite busily being fulfilled. As mentioned they were not easy years, but there was always a remnant to keep Abraham's covenant with God alive. The question seems to hang in the air now as we speculate, "Will there be enough who have remained faithful?" It will not be easy, for their world is full of political upheavals. As the period ends not only are their lives difficult from a political standpoint, but their spiritual lives have been traumatized by their own leaders. Rabbis compete with rabbis, sects with sects, resulting in a chaotic atmosphere. It was into this mix of "divide and conquer" as every person attempted to prove that he was *right* and the other person *wrong* in which our Lord would come. Of course, disagreements are one thing, but the animosity and bitterness between those who disagree did not bode well for the atmosphere for the coming Messiah. It was normal for those who differ to want to come out on top in a discussion, but whether they knew it or not, division was created by their determination to prove themselves right.

I think you'll agree that there are many events listed here that had a bearing on the coming of the Messiah. Rome's rule was perhaps one of the most important in the sense that they provided roads and access for travel, which would facilitate the spread of the gospel. The synagogues provided a place in which Jesus would be able to address the Jews, and the impurity of the priests left a vacuum for which there was a strong need for leadership. The quarreling between sects brought questions and indecisions regarding their spirituality, and the Jews were in fact looking for the arrival of the Messiah. Covenants did not seem to be of paramount

---

41   Scofield Study Bible, NAS ed., copyright 1988 by Lockman Foundation, published by Oxford University Press, Oxford University Press, New York, World Bible Publishers Iowa Falls), Intertestmental Period.

importance, as complaining and arrogance toward God showed many to be openly rebellious.

With Abraham God promised blessings in return for faithfulness and a channel through which His blessings could flow. Without the priesthood there was no longer a channel until the new channel would be provided. This possibly could explain God's silence because priests were no longer qualified to serve. Let us now look at the new covenant.

Note: There are no questions for the chapter dealing with the interlude.

Chapter 11: The New Covenant

~~~~~~~~

We've mentioned that God has been building a foundation for a symbolic building. Work on it has been going on for centuries and is near completion. In the meantime the Jews were taught by the law regarding holiness, sin, sacrifice, and the coming Messiah. At the time the covenant was made with Abraham it was made with the understanding that it was conditional on obedience. In spite of continual sin, God chose to continue teaching the Israelites what was expected in the way of obedience. Please understand that both the old covenant and the new covenant are contracts between God and man and was valid until it would be fulfilled, replaced, or broken. Because the covenant made with Abraham was broken by the people and would be fulfilled by the Messiah when He came, one would assume that a new covenant was forthcoming. Biblical history provides a solid background on which to build faith, but we also need to learn about the history of God's relationship with man, His principles, and how they relate to salvation. The old covenant is God's Word, and we should continue to study it for no reason beyond that, knowing that the law is no longer binding but the principles that preceded the law are things that we need desperately.

There are multiple parts by which to understand the new covenant, but we will address the time line first. We have mentioned several times that the law was not perfect because a single mistake would make one guilty of the whole law. This was because the law didn't provide forgiveness. There were reasons for that which basically boiled down to the fact that the Israelites needed a "cause and effect" type of teaching with discipline as a part of the learning process. It would have been no different for us. Mankind was still in its juvenile stage; they were in many ways still children. The time line is important to prevent confusing it with the law. God's purpose preceded His foreknowledge about who would be saved. His purpose was that reconciliation would be for all men. His foreknowledge indicated that only those who chose to believe would be sanctified by the indwelling Holy Spirit to receive forgiveness. This is important because it leaves the choice with man. Choice is what Satan's war is about because his premise was that man would always choose him over God if given a choice.

The Priesthood

The priesthood was a vital part of the law. In fact without the priesthood the law could not have existed as the priests were the vehicle through which God spoke to the people regarding the law. Hebrews 7:12 tells us that "of necessity" the priesthood had to change. Priests weren't just appointed. They had to be born to the right family in order to be priests. Priests were appointed by the right of being descendants of Aaron. The high priests were direct descendants of Aaron, who entered God's presence in the Holy of Holies to make the sin offering once a year. The rest of the priests couldn't enter through the veil at all.

What was the veil? I believe the first time I heard about the veil it was for the tabernacle when God was bringing the Israelites out of Egypt. There it was—a heavy, ornate curtain of many layers that separated the Holy of Holies, where God dwelled, from the holy place, which was a separate room or enclosure. When Solomon's temple was built, the veil still served as a curtain that separated man from the glory of God. The temple that's spoken of in the first century when Jesus walked the earth would be the temple built by Herod or at his order, and the purpose was not quite the same. In Herod's temple the curtain was just a separation like a door that separated the inner court from the outer court. This was the curtain that split from top to bottom, and the split indicated that there was a new way that would be open to God (Matthew 27:51). This occurrence has been taken to indicate that as children of God we will no longer be separated from Him but will have communion with Him as Adam did in the garden. The fact that Jesus entered through the veil in heaven as a forerunner for us is an indication of the new way in which Jesus our high priest will "confess our names before Him" and as he intercedes on our behalf, He will also explain our weaknesses to the Father and plead for mercy for us in the presence of the Father. Another ironic aspect of this new priesthood is that we (you and I) are the priests, not the high priests but the other priests. We have continual access to God through our High Priest, who is the resurrected Jesus.

Aaron and his descendants were priests because of their heritage. Jesus, on the other hand, became a priest by on oath of God. "The Lord has sworn and will not change His mind, 'you are a priest forever,' so much the more also Jesus has become the guarantee of a better covenant" (Hebrews 7:21–2). These are the basics of the new priesthood.

Sealed with the Spirit

The old covenant was sometimes called the covenant of circumcision (Acts7:8a) because circumcision was the "seal used by God to authenticate His chosen people."

A seal was used in biblical times to demonstrate the following:

1. Proof of authenticity (1 Kings 21:8, Esther 8:8, Jeremiah 32:10, Daniel 6:17, and Matthew 27:66)

2. Proof of ownership (Ezekiel 9:4, Ephesians 4:30, 2 Timothy 2:19, and Revelation 7:3, 9:4, and 14:1)

3. A down payment for something yet to come 2 Corinthians 1:22 and Ephesians 1:13–14)

In Abraham's situation circumcision was all three. It was a promise of salvation to come, and it was proof of Abraham's authenticity to the Jews who would be under the law. God's new covenant required a different seal because we are told, "In Christ Jesus neither circumcision nor uncircumcision means anything, but faith working through love" (Galatians 5:6). The new seal would be a seal made without hands, an indwelling seal, and one that would be received not on the eighth day of infancy but through the symbolic act of baptism. God, the Holy Spirit, would secure the seal. It is His indwelling presence that marks us as authentic to both Satan and the world, and it is both proof of God's ownership and a down payment on redemption.

Colossians 2:11–13 says the following:

In Him you were also circumcised with a circumcision made without hands, in the removal of the body of the flesh by the circumcision of Christ; having been buried with Him in baptism, in which you were also raised up with Him through faith in the working of God, who raised Him from the dead. And when you were dead in your transgressions and the uncircumcision of your flesh, He made you alive together with Him, having forgiven us all our transgressions.

Made without hands means it was not physical circumcision but an inner mark of the Holy Spirit. The body of flesh refers to fleshly desires that have been replaced by the indwelling spirit and the yearnings of the soul. It correlates with the circumcision of the old covenant in which an actual piece of flesh was removed. Baptism is the physical manifestation of the new covenant, which marks you as belonging to God, much as circumcision of the flesh marked the Jew as belonging to God. This mutual transaction between you and God marks you as a Christian who has come from death of the flesh to life of the Holy Spirit.

Acts 2:38 says, "Peter said to them, 'Repent, and each of you be baptized in the name of Jesus Christ for the forgiveness of your sins; and you shall receive the gift of the Holy Spirit.'" This gift is the indwelling of the Holy Spirit, and the gifts He brings are tied to your spiritual growth. It is the promise of Jesus as He prepared to ascend into heaven (Ephesians 1:13–14). The Holy Spirit is with us as a pledge, a promise. It is a promise in the same way that a buyer gives money to an owner or a lawyer. That money is a guarantee, a surety of your intent. This is an example of what is known as earnest money. It was at Jesus' request that the Father left this Helper with us, "I will ask the Father, and He will give you another Helper, that He may be with you forever; that is the Spirit of truth" (John 14:16–17). The Holy Spirit is God's promise to you.

Timothy 2:19 says, "Nevertheless, the firm foundation of God stands, having this seal, The Lord knows those who are His." What a blessing and a comfort to realize we are not out here alone at the mercy of evil. He knows us! He is with us to help us refrain from wickedness. The decision to belong to God requires action on our part. It is said that the Devil believes but trembles. They cannot bring themselves to obey. Will you choose God's side, or will you choose Satan's side? God wants everyone to receive the reconciliation that will guarantee protection from His wrath in the day of judgment.

Summary

God's purpose, known before the foundation of the world, was that man would be reconciled to Him through Christ Jesus and the shedding of His blood. To this end, He foreknew that those who responded by the sanctification of the Holy Spirit would obey the commandments required for reconciliation and would thus be cleansed of sin. It is this act of obedient faith in the cleansing blood that grants us the indwelling Spirit as children of God, fellow heirs with Christ and Abraham's seed by faith. Without faith separation from the Creator is the result, and like Satan we would then be condemned to darkness, for without God there is no light.

Because of the change in the Aaronic priesthood, the law of necessity had to change. Without the priests, there was no line of communication with God, and no sacrifices could be made according to God's instruction. Through Christ's eternal nature, He became the new High Priest, and believers became the new priesthood.

Study Guide—Chapter 11

Q. Why was a new covenant necessary?
A. The new covenant was needed because the old one was imperfect in that it didn't grant forgiveness. Under the law God's system was for the purpose of teaching people in which they demonstrated their faith by their belief that they would have forgiveness with the advent of the Messiah.

Q. God's purpose and His plan were in place before the foundation of the world. Why is it important that His purpose preceded His foreknowledge of those who would be conformed to His Son (another way of saying they would be sanctified).
A. God's purpose demonstrated that He desired salvation for all people, but His plan recognized that only those who would obey would receive it. This can be compared to a person who has left money in a will but has to prove first that he is who he says he is. A gift is not owned until such a requirement is met. God's requirement is that we be *conformed* to His Son. The way we become conformed is by listening to the indwelling Spirit who comes to us through baptism. This leaves the choice to the individual.

Q. To be sanctified is to be set apart. How does one become sanctified? Is this the same as reconciliation?
A. To be sanctified is another description of conforming in that we are set apart for righteousness. The process is again by the Spirit. Reconciliation is a gift of God when He recognizes an individual's desire to be conformed and set apart. The best way to let your desire be known is by baptism,

which demonstrates both to the world and to Satan that you belong to God.

Q. There are those who believe that God decides arbitrarily without consideration of man's choice who will be saved and who will be eternally lost. In light of the fact that reconciliation has always been God's purpose, is this a logical assumption?

A. This is definitely not a logical conclusion. The deciding factor has always been choice. The choice a person makes shows in the life he leads. By the same token the act of baptism doesn't save, but it puts you in contact with God and tells Him you want salvation. A changed life is what saves by the grace of God.

Q. God's plan resulted in the death of His beloved Son in order to make salvation available to all mankind. Explain how man's salvation hinges on a basic principle present throughout all the ages.

A. That principle on which all others is connected is belief, and it is belief that leads to faith. And faith leads to obedience. The sacrifice of His beloved Son shows us how much God loves us and how far He was willing to go to redeem us from eternal death.

Q. Circumcision, which had been the seal for the first covenant, is no longer of value. What did God use to seal the new covenant?

A. The new seal is an inward seal (not made with hands). It is the indwelling of the Holy Spirit as our helper to guide us, teach us, and comfort us. The Spirit is granted at the time of baptism.

Chapter 12: The World of His Birth

God's covenant relationship with Israel had served its purpose. God had both revealed His divine nature and prepared the world through prophecy for a Savior. Since the law was given, He relates to man as a nation, a chosen people. Now some two thousand years later, that relationship would evolve. Fulfillment of the final part of the prophecy to Abraham was about to unfold. "And in you all the families of the earth shall be blessed" (Genesis 12:3). The blessing, which was previously nationalistic, was about to become universal. God's plan had not changed. Salvation (reconciliation) is still for people of faith. Again, as before, there is a shift of emphasis, this time from one nation to people of all nations. The preparation for this event has been lengthy and often painful, but there have also been almost limitless blessings that should speak to us of God's great love. Not all the Israelites were ready for this shift of emphasis; however, some were, and it would be those who would respond immediately. The message would be directed to all.

A New Leader

To accomplish this shift of emphasis, there had to be a new leader but not an Abraham, a Moses, or a Joshua, not a Saul or a David, not even an Isaiah or a Jeremiah. No, this time God sent Himself in the form of man. "And the Word became flesh, and dwelt among us, and we beheld His glory, glory as of the only begotten from the Father, full of grace and truth" (John 1:14 NKJV).

The term *Word* refers to Jesus (John 1:1). John explains that not only is God eternal without beginning or end, but His Son is also eternal. "He was in the beginning with God" (John 1:1–5), and "He created all things by the command of the Father" (Hebrews 1:3). I agree it is not something easily grasped that the Father, the Son, and the Holy Spirit are separate yet one, but for a moment look at it as you might view a rope that secures a ship to a wharf. It is easy to see that one rope is attached to the wharf, but on closer examination we find three ropes are blended into one. It isn't a completely accurate illustration because there is much more to the one than to the other, but consider this: If the ropes are separated, they will not achieve their purpose. God the Father, whose stamp is on all things as the Architect and whose Son created all things as the Builder, accompanied by the Holy Spirit, who established the plan at Pentecost and within the hearts of every believer, are one. Their dream is one. Their cooperation is one, and their faithfulness is one. God the Son became mortal man in order to fulfill the promise, and the Holy Spirit breathed His blessings on the day of Pentecost and remained with man as an indwelling guide. This unity represents the church, where each person is vital to the dream.

A New Covenant

Jesus said in Matthew 5:17 "Do not think that I came to abolish the Law of the Prophets, I did not come to abolish, but to fulfill." What does Jesus mean when He says "I did not come to abolish"? There is a tremendous difference between *to abolish* and *to fulfill*. To abolish indicates to do away with; however, if something is lacking on a document, it must be completed, or if it is a matter of fulfilling an obligation, it must be taken care of before it can be considered finished legally. After fulfillment it can be put away for future reference.

It is the same with the Mosaic law. Until it was fulfilled, it was a valid document subject to obedience but not yet complete. It would be complete with the crucifixion of Jesus but only on condition of His resurrection. It was the resurrection that would enable forgiveness and the putting away of the old covenant. It was the resurrection that fulfilled the covenant. It has not been thrown away or buried as if it were now useless. It will never be useless because it is God's Word, which identified sin and brought people to Christ. It also teaches God's principles. As a book of law, however, it is no longer a law that people must follow because it is now obsolete.

God has prepared for the new covenant by creating a foundation, first through the prophets and then through the apostles. Through Moses He gave a law that would teach humility, grace, and obedience but from which its students would also learn discipline. Then His Son came in the form of humanity so that His blood would provide forgiveness, paving the way for Him to be our mediator with the Father.

It is His resurrection that gives authenticity to all that has been prepared. Still an active law until after the resurrection and its fulfillment, it required obedience to its mandates. When the blood price was paid and the resurrection occurred, it became like a wise old grandpa who remembers the whole thing and can tell you how it was. And that is so good because God said the law would be a tutor to bring us to Christ, and there are a whole lot of people out there who haven't found Him yet. So what we need are more grandpas and grandmas who can tell about the law and the foundation and the prophets so that people are ready to follow God when they learn of Him. That is the difference between *to abolish* and *to fulfill*.

The law, which leads to Christ, also allows us to be "justified by faith" (Galatians 3:24). What does it mean to be justified by anything? In a spiritual sense, justice is moral rightness. To the rest of the world, it could be said that justice is fairness. In a courtroom justification has to do with defense. Otherwise there would be no trial. In life there is no defense for sin, and many things are unfair and perhaps will never be sorted out until God enters the picture as a judge. He will not be like an ordinary judge who may or may not be interested in what he is doing and who doesn't care one way or the other about the decision that comes down. God is not only interested in the procedure, He wants you to be justified; therefore, He probes as He extends His mercy, seeking circumstances to determine guilt or innocence regarding any act of sin. He might ask Jesus, our mediator, "Of what significance was the heart in this sin?" Was it planned, or was it committed for lack of training? Was the sinner sorry or glad? What else played a part in this sin? If God is satisfied with the answers and decides the heart is pure, the sin will have been justified, and no punishment will follow. This is why it is called forgiveness.

Without the law there would have been no justification for Jew or Gentile. Without the teaching of the law man would have failed again to walk uprightly with the result that there would not have been a righteous people through which the promised blessing would come. This explains Israel's role as God's people. You could say they enabled God's plan for forgiveness. Although God promised Noah that He would never again destroy all flesh by water, an avenue was needed through which people could be taught. Man needed a way to have a chance to overcome the sinful nature within him. It is almost as if God leveled the playing field for us. In the absence of teaching, desire will always rule the heart, so it was necessary to provide a way for justification to occur.

Jesus' birth, His life, His death, and His resurrection were all in fulfillment of prophecy. Because it is fulfilled, why are we interested in the prophecy? There are probably many reasons, but the most important one is that it proves that His death satisfied the requirement of the law because His pure, sinless blood provided cleansing. "Now that faith has come, we are no longer under a tutor," but are "sons of God through faith in Christ Jesus" (Galatians 3:24–9). Understand that in the same way that mortal man must die in order for a last will to become effective, Jesus had to die for His will to become effective.

> The new covenant would be mediated by His blood (Hebrews 9:15–17). Mediation means that any settlement between two parties must be equitable for both sides. It does not mean that both will be happy with the decision made. For justice to be served in the case of sinful man God gives mercy to the repentant by the grace of His forgiveness; however, He issues condemnation for the unrepentant, and justice has been served according to God's plan. In this situation the blood of Jesus reaches to those of the past (those under the law and before the law) who lived by faith, those of the present who live by faith, and those of the future who will live by faith. His blood makes all men equal under God's love, mercy, and forgiveness. Jesus said,

- "By this all men will know that you are my disciples, if you have love for one another" (John 13:35).

It is almost inconceivable to realize that love is that evident in our lifestyle. The love we have for each other is an imperfect duplication of the love given to us by God the Father and God the Son. Together they enable the new covenant to be written not on tablets of stone but on the heart.

- "You are our letter, written in our hearts, known and read by all men; being manifested that you are a letter of Christ, cared for by us, written not with ink but with the Spirit of the living God, not on tablets of stone but on tablets of human hearts" (2 Corinthians 3:2–3).

This verse always brings to mind the neighbors of my young years as I observed their loving service to neighbors and to the community at large by way of food, yard help, garden help, laundry, sitting with the sick, or whatever was needed. It is surely evidence that God is in your heart. These people are unsung heros and heroines, but their relationship with God is visible.

As a final point on the inadequacies of the law, let me remind you that when one single aspect of the law was broken, the perpetrator was guilty of breaking the entire law. God knew it was not a perfect law, but it was a teaching law and one that was necessary for their growth. It was much more complicated than the single law God presented to Adam and Eve, but then while they were not babies physically, they were children with no concept of circumstances.

Background

It has been said that the time was right for the coming of Jesus, and of course it was because God chose the time. Looking back, however, at least five reasons can be given for this rightness.

1. Under the yoke of Roman oppression, the Jews were actively look-ing and hoping for a Savior. They were also under the yoke of their own leaders who had become extremely legalistic in their interpretation of the law.

2. The Jews were scattered throughout the known world, and wher-ever they went, they built synagogues, which were used for meet-ing and teaching places. Therefore there was an available network of facilities from which the Jewish community could be reached.

3. The oneness of government, the Roman Empire, assured a uni-versal language, Greek. The Jews had even translated the Old Testament into Greek (the Septuagint).

4. A huge network of roads had been built by the Romans to con-nect their empire, making it possible for people to quickly take the gospel to the world.

5. Roman influence and power made travel possible to countries out-side the empire, making it feasible for people to move from country to country.

A Melting Pot of Ideas

The Jews were a long way from Mount Sinai, where God gave Moses the law. After the destruction of Jerusalem and the Babylonian captivity, worship as they had known it was pretty much a thing of the past. Even with the rebuilding of the temple post-exile temple worship was available only to a few because of the dispersion. For many, however, the synagogue replaced the temple, and the rabbi (teacher) replaced the priest. This gave rise to sectarianism (or sects), where interpretations of the law became as important as the law, and leaders demanded obedience to the interpretation. Many special interest schools of thought were the result of this process.

For example the Pharisees were the most powerful of the religious sects. They were characterized by self-righteousness and rigid, legalistic thinking. Because they believed in the resurrection, they had many followers among the Jewish middle class[42] (Nelson 1995).

The Sadducees were a religious sect of the upper class. They considered themselves freethinkers and did not believe in angels or the resurrection[43] (Nelson 1995).

The Essenes were a radically pious religious sect characterized by an affected or exaggerated reverence and austere self-discipline. It is possible they were the occupants of the Masada stronghold against the Romans[44] (Nelson 1995).

Other influences on Jewish life and culture included the Samaritans, a hybrid of the Jewish religion whose principle crime occurred when one married outside the Jewish faith. Persian mysticism, so called "because they kept their rituals secret" and Greek humanism were prevalent dogmas of the time. In addition there were numerous political groups within the Jewish community. Some of those were traditionally patriotic, but others were more vocal. The openly rebellious groups were zealots, and the politically active were Herodians.

---

42 Nelson's New Illustrated Bible Dictionary, copyright 1995 by Thomas Nelson Publishers, Pharisees.

43 Nelson's New Illustrated Bible Dictionary, copyright 1995 by Thomas Nelson Publishers, Sadducees.

44 Nelson's New Illustrated Bible Dictionary, copyright 1995 by Thomas Nelson Publishers, Essenes.

Summary

Governed by Rome, peopled by the openly corrupt, even within the Jewish community, the devout and the less-than-devout, both of whom anticipated His coming but were torn by religious controversies, our Lord would come into this setting. The event, which was known before the foundation of the world, promised to Abraham, and in fulfillment of prophecy, was about to happen. It would be the beginning of a new relationship between God and man and the start of a new era.

Study Guide—Chapter 12

Q. Why did the destruction of Jerusalem and the captivities end worship as the law had prescribed?

A. The dispersion was not a single act. It took place over many years, and then when the captivities occurred, thousands of Jews remained in their city of captivity. After the last Babylonian captivity Babylon fell to the Persians, and those who went back to Jerusalem had no temple in which to worship because of the destruction of that city by Rome. The temple was rebuilt; however, by then thousands of Jews had become accustomed to synagogue worship in the cities where they were, and the priesthood was becoming very small with very few who could make the sacrifices. Many Jews had replaced temple worship with synagogues, and the priesthood was largely lost.

Q. What two things were most instrumental in the advent of sectarianism?

A. Sectarianism arose because of differences of opinion about various interpretations of Scripture. Rabbis had virtually replaced the priesthood, and *sects* came into existence, with the people following the one they considered right. One of the major problems of the sects was that opinion took the place of law with equal enforcement as the law. This is one of the reasons the Jews were so burdened by their religious leaders at the time of Jesus' ministry.

Q. Name the primary philosophy that divided the Pharisees and the Sadducees.

A. The sects were divided by the idea of the resurrection from the dead. The Pharisees believed in the resurrection, and the Sadducees did not.

Q. Tradition and interpretation of Scripture were taught not only orally but by means of rabbinical writings collected in what was known as the Talmud. Explain how this Jewish writing helped set the stage for the coming Messiah.

A. The Talmud, a collection of writings penned by various rabbis was read in the synagogue, which provided a setting for discussion in which Jesus participated, however, even more to the point they showed themselves as divided.

Q. Explain the new shift of emphasis that is about to occur in God's relationship to man.

A. The shift has not yet occurred, but when it does (after Pentecost and the establishment of the church), God will no longer speak to His people through the priests but will speak through His Son who would speak to each person individually through His Word.

Chapter 13: Jesus, the Christ

The Promised Seed

The second part of the promise made to Abraham so long ago will be fulfilled through Jesus. The seed, Isaiah tells us, prophesied to be a descendent of Abraham, Isaac, and Jacob and also to be of the tribe of Judah would be called Immanuel ... or by definition, *God with us*. Matthew 1:1 identifies Him as the child Jesus, and Matthew 1:18–23 tells of His birth.

The law would be in effect until after the blood was shed, and the resurrection gave proof He was the Son of God. "Behold, a virgin will be with child and bear a son, and she will call His name Immanuel" (Isaiah 7:14 and Matthew 1:22–3).

"But as for you, Bethlehem Ephrathah, too little to be among the clans of Judah, from you one will go forth for me to be ruler in Israel" (Micah 5:2).

This refers to the little town of Bethlehem, of which we sing at Christmastime. "Now after Jesus was born in Bethlehem of Judea in the days of Herod the king, magi from the east arrived in Jerusalem, saying, 'Where is He who has been born King of the Jews we have come to worship Him'" (Matthew 2:1–2).

Now the magi had no idea that Herod's interest in this new birth meant trouble for a lot of people. Herod is a perfect illustration of greed and jealousy. By means of his father's help he took his own throne from the Hasmonian king, who had been appointed by Rome, and when Herod heard the magi's news, he was afraid he would be replaced as king and that he would lose his position, power, and prestige. So he issued an edict commanding that all the male children two years old and under in Bethlehem and its vicinity be killed; but Joseph had received a dream telling him to take the child and flee to Egypt because of Herod's plot. This was the nature of the man named Herod—evil, callous, self-centered.

His Identity

Jesus, the seed, came with unimpeachable credentials because His identity was crucial to all He would say and do. It was also crucial to the administration of God's hidden wisdom, which would soon be revealed. The Jews, who had been told of His coming for generations, were aware of the prophecies concerning Him. Among those who rejected Him the chief priests and rulers had agendas of which their own personal power was a major factor. One might ask in light of the prophecies, "How could they have been so unseeing?" Nevertheless as with Adam and Eve and all men of all times, they were at liberty to make a choice. Even the apostles who were with Him every day and who made the right choice in following Him had difficulty from time to time in recognizing Him as the Son of God. It seems they, too, were often confused by this king who came to serve rather than to be served, and they would, on occasion, ask in awe, "Who is this man?" While they were beginning to comprehend that He was the Messiah, they had not as yet come to terms with His identity as God in the flesh or the crucified God. That was unthinkable.

Jesus would ask His apostles, "Who do people say that the Son of man is? Who do you say that I am?" (Matthew 16:13). "Unless you believe that I am He, you shall die in your sins" (John 8:24). While acceptance of Him as the Christ, the Son of God, is inherent in their burgeoning belief, it is most likely that their starting point was acceptance of Him as the promised seed, the Messiah. Why? Because they were not yet sure about the role He would play as their Messiah. They, too, hoped for an earthly king. After all one from heaven was too way out there. Surely, God would send a man, one they could relate to and who would relate to them. That's really all that their expectations included.

He Grew as a Man

The human side of Jesus is perhaps the most difficult aspect of His life to comprehend. We understand that He is God, so how is it conceivable that He could also be less? If we grasp the truth of His birth (the incarnation), we soon begin to waver and attribute His lack of sin to His divine nature. This is in error. Hebrews 4:15 points out that He was tempted in all things as we are tempted, yet he did not sin. To the human mind it is almost inconceivable that He did not use His divinity for Himself while He was on earth. After all He had the power. Why could He not benefit by it? First we need to understand the purity by which all parts of the godly person functioned. We are not talking about humans here. Our natures without God are base, even evil. Without God there is nothing to pull us up out of the mire of ugliness within us.

I'll give you what might seem like an improbable example by using a sweet, precious infant. From the moment of birth a baby is obsessed with his (or her) own needs. With food, diaper, and sleep plus a proper amount of devoted attention he is an angel of perfection, but wait. Such self-absorption may be narcissistic, but it's normal for a baby. Of course it is, but watch him when he's two. Unless you apply some discipline as training, he will become a screaming temper tantrum with full benefits. We would probably call it something else by then, maybe spoiled, but in a few years one glance at him and his self-absorption would cause people to run in the opposite direction.

This is only one example. I'd say it is pretty normal. But what about the pretty little girl who likes to torment little dogs or cats? Where does that evil originate? It's sad, but it's true that evil originates from within. We need God's help to be able to develop righteousness or right-doing. The human side of Jesus accomplished a life without sin. If He had not, He could not have empathized with our weaknesses. It is also His human side that allows Him to mediate issues between God and man with fairness to both sides.

- "And Jesus kept increasing in wisdom and stature, and in favor with God and men" (Luke 2:52).

- "This is my beloved Son in whom I am well pleased. Hear Him" (Matthew 3:17).

- "And being found in appearance as a man, He humbled Himself by becoming obedient to the point of death, even death on a cross" (Philippians 2:8).

Deuteronomy 21:23 calls such a one who hangs on a tree accursed by God. Was He really accursed? I don't know, but we know that the sin He carried was accursed. Men cursed Him, and that is difficult to figure out. I know also of His infinite love. You can ask yourself this question, "If God hadn't turned His back on Jesus, would there be any salvation for anyone?" The answer of course is no, but at what terrible cost to the Father and to the Son.

We can understand from Scripture that God turned away from the Son because of the sin of the world that He carried to the cross. Crucifixion on a cross involved torture as well as execution, and it was the Roman's most severe form of punishment reserved for slaves and criminals. To the Israelites it was a disgusting mode of execution, yet they obtained authorization to have Jesus crucified. It says in 1 Corinthians 1:23–4, "We preach Christ crucified, to the Jews a stumbling block, to the Greeks, foolishness; but to those who are called, both Jews and Greeks, Christ, the power of God and the wisdom of God." This is the human Jesus.

There is yet another aspect of His humanity often overlooked and that is the role His obedience played in shaping Him as a man. In Exodus 20:12, we have the commandment to "honor your father and mother," the first commandment with promise. We may not completely know exactly what the promise involves, but if one considers it in light of Jesus' purity, one begins to see the far-reaching aspects as they relate to the soul. His obedience to His parents helped to prepare Him for the roles He would subsequently assume. His obedience to God the Father not only fulfilled prophecies but also set the example for us and provided for the forgiveness of sin (Acts 5:30–1).

It was the man Jesus who grew in wisdom, stature, and favor with God and man. It was the man Jesus who was tempted in all ways as are we. It was the man Jesus who walked the earth and ministered to those who suffered and were in need. It was the man Jesus who was rejected, suffered, and died on the cross. This was the human Jesus, the man, the Son who would be obedient to the point of death. It is vital to understand, however, that He was God at the same time (Colossians 2:9). All the fullness of deity dwells in Him in bodily form. How is this explained? To have power and not use it is far superior than not, and it is yet another way of showing His subjection or submission to the Father. By withholding His power He maintained His subjection as He hung on the cross and accomplished His mission of salvation for man. This is parallel to the examples of the beatitudes. Restrained power of the individual is an art of Godliness and one to which we should aspire.

His Authority

Biblical authority usually refers to a person's right to do certain things because of the position or office he or she holds. It also can refer to the legality and right of that person to exercise those authorities.

It is further defined as intrinsic or derived. "Because all authority is intrinsic to God" (Romans 13:1), man's authority is derived and therefore secondary, and in time it will be returned to God. An example of derived authority is the Bible because it is God breathed or inspired (2 Timothy 3:16 and 2 Peter 1:20–1). Jesus Christ has the same intrinsic power as God the Father (John 10:25–30), which was given to Him by the Father, just as the authority of the Holy Spirit is given to Him from the Father and the Son (John 14:26, 15:26, and 16:13–15). Jesus' authority is multifaceted.

- His authority is eternal (Isaiah 9:6–7).

- His authority is universal (Zechariah 9:9–10).

- His authority is over all of nature (Matthew 8:27).

- His authority is over the church (Ephesians 1:22).

- His authority is heavenly (John 5:26–7, 10:17–18, and17:2).

Reflect on these passages as you consider His authority: "And after being baptized, Jesus went up immediately from the water; and behold, the heavens were opened, and He saw the Spirit of God descending as a dove, and coming upon Him, and behold, a voice out of the heavens, saying, 'This is My beloved Son, in whom I am well-pleased'" (Matthew 3:16–17). "The multitudes were amazed at His teaching; for He was teaching them as one having authority, and not as their scribes" (Matthew 7:28–9).

Methods of Teaching

It is surprising how little information Jesus gave to His apostles regarding instructions on *how* to do things. I wonder if it is because a lot of information is beneficial but not absolute and lots of people are locked into methods and don't see a need to change. I do believe God knows our capabilities and expects us to use the intelligence He has given us to do whatever needs doing. If we learn His principles sufficiently, we will be knowledgeable of those things that violate them. I do know that just as God changed His method of communication as the world grew, changes are often a good thing.

By Example

John 15:10 says, "If you keep my commandments, you will abide in my love; just as I have kept My Father's commandments, and abide in His love." And 1 Peter 2:21 states, "Christ also suffered for you, leaving you an example for you to follow in His steps."

God asks of us only those things for which He has left an example.

Hebrews 12:1–2 says, "Let us run with endurance the race that is set before us, fixing our eyes on Jesus, the author and perfecter of faith."

Focus is vitally important. It is perhaps the only thing that can help as we struggle in the immediacy of Satan's temptations.

By Parables

"All these things Jesus spoke to the multitudes in parables, and without a parable He did not speak to them" (Matthew 13:34 NKJV).

This goes back to the heart and the desire to understand. For those who only wanted to argue, knowledge would not have been beneficial.

By Miracles

Matthew 4:23 says, "Jesus was going about in all Galilee, teaching in their synagogues, and proclaiming the gospel of the kingdom, and healing every kind of disease and every kind of sickness among the people."

Outside of these three types of teaching, methods are not mentioned. I don't know why these instructions were not given, but I can speculate that God wanted man to use his common sense while he also utilized all the means that were available to him. We do have the example of the Pharisees who quibbled over the crossing of a "T" and the dotting of an "I," which our Lord compared to staring at a gnat while swallowing a camel. Perhaps the absence of instruction allows the heart's attitudes to dictate method, thereby illustrating whether one's position is an arbitrary one or motivated by an attitude of love. It is possible that when we become so addicted to a how, we lose the why.

His Roles

I think you will agree that role models teach a stronger message by example than by means of the spoken word. There is an old adage that expresses the thought: "I'd rather see a message any day than hear one." As you look at these roles perfected by our Savior, look for the method He uses to demonstrate His principles.

Creator

"In the beginning was the Word, and the Word was with God, and the Word was God. He was in the beginning with God. All things came into being through Him, and apart from Him nothing came into being that has come into being" (John 1:1–3).

Prophet

"Behold, I have made Him a witness to the peoples" (Isaiah 55:4).

"God, after He spoke long ago to the fathers in the prophets in many portions and in many ways, in these last days has spoken to us in His Son, whom He appointed heir of all things, through whom also He made the world" (Hebrews 1:1–2).

Priest

Responsibility was twofold:

1. First there is the offered sacrifice. "For if the blood of goats and bulls and the ashes of a heifer sprinkling those who have been defiled sanctify for the cleansing of the flesh how much more will the blood of Christ, who through the eternal Spirit offered Himself without blemish to God, cleanse your conscience from dead works to serve the living God?" (Hebrews 9:13–14).

    A comparison is made here between the animal sacrifice and the sacrifice of His Son. Please note that Jesus was offered one time to cleanse all repentant sin for all ages, whereas animal sacrifices were made daily.

    Animal blood was sufficient to sanctify, but the blood of Christ cleanses.

    "As it is appointed for men to die once and after this comes judgment, so Christ also, having been offered once to bear the sins of many shall appear a second time for salvation without reference to sin, to those who eagerly await Him" (Hebrews 9:27–8).

    This verse refers to the second coming, which will not have anything to do with sin because that was taken care of at the cross.

Those who await Him are cleansed and anxious to join Him in heaven.

2. Second this makes intercession a possibility: "And the former priests, on the one hand, existed in greater numbers, because they were prevented by death from continuing, but Jesus, on the other hand, because He continues forever, holds His priesthood permanently. Therefore, also, He is able to save forever those who draw near to God through Him, since He always lives to make intercession for them" (Hebrews 7:23–5).

This verse points out the difference between the human and the divine.

The former priests refer to those who were priests under the old law. In referring to Christ He states that He is eternal and is therefore our High Priest in correlation to the priests of the old covenant. In the old covenant, the High Priest was only allowed in God's presence one time a year as He went into the holy of holies. Jesus, on the other hand, as the Son of God, is forever in His presence to advocate in our stead.

King

"Say to the daughter of Zion, Behold your King is coming to you, gentle, and mounted on a donkey, even on a colt, the foal of a beast of burden" (Matthew 21:5).

Zion is a figurative name for Israel as the people of God (Isaiah 60:14). This verse refers to the triumphant entry of Jesus into Jerusalem before the arrest and crucifixion.

"The King will say to those on His right, 'Come, you who are blessed of My Father, inherit the kingdom prepared for you from the foundation of the world'" (Matthew 25:34).

This verse tells us again that God's plan was made before the world was made, but here it has reference to the end of time when the righteous are referred to as sheep and the wicked as goats. "He who overcomes, I will grant to him to sit down with Me on My throne, as I also overcame and sat down with My Father on His throne" (Revelation 3:21).

Overcomers is a phrase from Revelation that indicates that one has been faithful to death. It speaks of the trials of life, the temptations of Satan, and perseverance.

Savior

It was always God the Father's intention that His plan for salvation would be accomplished through the Son. This resulted in the incarnation of Jesus, which was preceded by the miraculous birth of John the Baptist, who prepared the way for the Lord. "For today in the city of David there has been born for you a Savior, who is Christ the Lord" (Luke 2:11).

The city of David is the tiny town of Bethlehem. "The God of our fathers raised up Jesus, whom you had put to death by hanging Him on a cross. He is the one whom God exalted to His right hand as a Prince and a Savior, to grant repentance to Israel, and forgiveness of sins" (Acts 5:30–1).

Here we see the usage of Israel, which appears many times in the New Testament in reference to the New Israel, the church, which is composed of Jews and Gentiles. (See Romans 9:6–8, John 1:49, and Luke 2:30–2.)"It was now about the sixth hour, and darkness came over the whole land until the ninth hours, for the sun stopped shining. And the curtain of the temple was torn in two. Jesus called out with a loud voice, 'Father, into your hands I commit my spirit.' When He had said this, He breathed His last" (Luke 23:44–6).

This speaks of the final moments of the crucifixion when Jesus died as he called out to the Father. The curtain of the temple, sometimes called a veil, was split in two, which signifies the end of God's separation from man.

Jesus appeared to the remaining eleven apostles and other disciples on the resurrection day. They were startled, thinking they had seen a ghost. He said to them, "Why are you troubled, and why do doubts rise in your minds? Look at my hands and my feet. It is I myself! Touch me and see; a ghost does not have flesh and bones, as you see I have" (Luke 24: 37–9 NIV).

Judge

Before Jesus ascended back to the Father in heaven, the eleven apostles met Him on a mountain in Galilee, and Jesus said to them, "All authority in heaven and on earth has been given to me. Therefore go and make disciples of all nations, baptizing them in the name of the Father, and of the Son, and of the Holy Spirit, and teaching them to obey everything I have commanded you. And surely I am with you always to the very end of the age" (Matthew 28:16– 20).

This verse preceded Jesus' return to heaven, where He was exalted and seated at the right hand of God in preparation for the final time when all men will be judged through Him. His command to the apostles is often called the great commission, through which all who come to Him become ambassadors of His Word. "And He ordered us to preach to the people and solemnly to testify that this is the One who has been appointed by God as Judge of the living and the dead" (Acts 10:42).

"God will judge the secrets of men through Christ Jesus" (Romans 2:16).

There will be no secrets on the day of judgment. He can see into the heart and will judge accordingly. There is an old gospel song I think of in this regard that says, "Is your heart right with God? Washed in the crimson flood, cleansed and made holy, humble and lowly, right in the sight of God?" It is the most important question you will ever answer.

We understand from each of these texts that this judgment will be a serious situation. When it occurs, there will be no time to change our destiny because time as we know it will no longer exist.

Under the new order believers are allowed to come to our heavenly Father as priests who approach Him through Jesus Christ, our High Priest, our interpreter, and our mediator. The marvelous thing is that we can come as often as we wish. Think about it. Are we making use of that privilege? There is a word in Scripture that is translated as *Abba*, and it has somewhat the same meaning as *Daddy* has to us. *Daddy* is a special word to children. It indicates a close relationship, perhaps even one of a loving confidant. This is the relationship God wants with us—a loving confidant who is always there for us. He can be our Abba Father if we let Him be.

The dialogue that follows is an imaginary conversation between God the Father and God the Son. Because it is a principle that is being illustrated, the concept is true. In this imaginary scene Jesus explains to the Father on behalf of the accused the charges brought by the Accuser, Satan. He fills the Father in on the particular incident, explaining as He goes.

And the Father will speak, "And how did the Accused feel before and after this thing was done? And what was in his heart at the time when it was only a thought?"

And our Lord would reply as He considered His experience as a human, and the Father would murmur, "Hmmm."

And again He would ask, "Had teaching been available to him or opportunities to understand how temptation works? How knowledgeable was he that such a thing as this could happen ... and if he had such knowledge, did he take steps to avoid it?"

After Jesus' had explained the background and the opportunities of the one before the throne, the Father asked His final questions.

"After the event" He said and paused, "was the accused sorrowful for himself or for the victim? Was he concerned that he might be caught, or did his conscience hope that he could confess and take responsibility?" Then he added, "Does he allow the Spirit's guidance, or does he shut Him out of his heart?"

Mediation complete, the verdict would be rendered with no hope of appeal to a higher court, but the verdict would be tempered with mercy based on the offender's belief or on justice in the absence of belief.

We seldom think of the judgment that is waiting for us in a literal way. We have no need to dwell on it because we can be assured of salvation. However, we do need to practice self-evaluation and pray for forgiveness as we offer praise and thanksgiving. Today as always is the day of salvation.

Summary

Jesus, Son of God, Creator of all things, lived among us as His name Immanuel implies. He "emptied Himself, taking the form of a bond-servant" (Philippians 2:7). A bond servant had no rights except what the master gave him. He completely belonged to the master. Jesus was here to do the Master's bidding, and the Master was God the Father. A bond servant yet, within Him was all the fullness (capabilities) of God. "Though He was rich, yet for your sake He became poor, that you through His poverty might become rich" (2 Corinthians 8:9). Our Jesus was the bond-servant of His Father, but the Father gave to the Son all of His own fullness. Jesus emptied Himself even of His life-blood, and it was from that poverty that we will become rich.

Can you imagine the glory He left in heaven to dwell among us? I seriously doubt this verse speaks of money in saying He was rich. Yet He was rich in a way that defies the concept of wealth we hold. Not only can we be rich in joy, fellowship, righteousness, and beauty, but we are rich in all it entails to be sons. It is an interesting concept that speaks to the inner qualities of the heart. I can't wait to learn the answer. As a prophet, He spoke to man for God; however, in becoming a man, He would speak to God for man, and in so doing He would become a high priest forever, making intercession before God on man's behalf. From the knowledge He gathered as a man He would make judgment as a Savior and would gather to Himself the children of obedience to reign with Him forever in the eternal kingdom. There are numerous examples of behavior established for us by Jesus that enable us to grow spiritually. However, to emulate an example, a certain amount of understanding is required. Perhaps a good place to begin would be an examination of the controlled power Jesus exhibited throughout His ministry.

Study Guide—Chapter 13

Q. What is the meaning of the name Immanuel? Why is it such an appropriate name for Jesus?
A. Immanuel means God with us. I think it is appropriate because it both explains who He is and what He has come to do.

Q. Why do you think Scripture repeatedly refers to Jesus as the man?
A. I know that the Old Testament frequently referred to Jesus as the "Son of man" or as "the man," so my first thought is that it was to help identify Him to the Jews. It was likely also to identify His humanity.

Q. At what point did Jesus the man become God the Son? Explain.
A. I don't know that I can give you the answer to this question either, but I did want you to think about it. Jesus died as a man (even though He was still God). We know this because Scripture tells us that He possessed "all the fullness" of God, yet He did not call on his powers as God while He suffered on the cross *or* during His time on earth. When He suffered, He suffered as a man. I would classify this in somewhat the same light as our

choice to live for God. We still have the ability to do evil, but we choose to live for God instead. I realize it is not a true comparison, but on a grander scale the Son of God had the ability to use His power to end the suffering He endured on the cross. However, He chose to suffer. By that choice He completed the responsibility He assumed by offering to be the sacrificial Lamb. He gave all humanity the right of redemption from eternal death. He earned the right to be our High Priest and to advocate for us before the Father. He enabled the Father's plan to be completed. And not to be forgotten, He defeated Satan. I hope we can learn from His example to reach for the impossible.

Q. Can you understand why both the human and divine aspects of Jesus' nature are crucial to His role as priest and judge? Explain.
A. Because He lived as a man, He is able to intercede with the Father on our behalf, explaining the different aspects of temptation, man's struggle to overcome (or His lack of struggle), and how His heart helped or hindered Him in the ordeal. As a priest He is able to intercede.

Q. What characteristic enabled this man, the Son of God, to carry out His mission on earth?
A. This ability is the characteristic of love.

Q. Name three methods by which He taught and give the purpose of miracles.
A. Jesus taught by parables, miracles, and example. Miracles enabled belief.

Q. Name two responsibilities of a priest.
A. The two responsibilities of priests were to offer sacrifice and to make intercession.

Chapter 14: The Power of the Spirit

The Final Preparation

In rejecting Jesus His enemies were successful in taking His life, not realizing that in doing so the law they fought to protect was fulfilled. In an ironic twist of circumstance their act of hateful violence made it possible for them to receive forgiveness. And Jesus said, "Father, forgive them, for they do not know what they are doing" (Luke 23:24).

Please consider the enormity of Jesus' faith. Not only was it submissive to the point of death, but at the peak of His suffering He begged the Father to forgive them for their cruelties. He maintained His dignity and His love for sinful man while He refused drink that would have eased some of His pain. Then He saw His mother by the apostle John, and He gave her unto His care and John unto His mother's care. It is this love that has enabled and provided our reconciliation

His Death

"And so they crucified Him in a place called the Skull, and innocence was charged with the sin of mankind. The charge they put above His head read, "Jesus, the King of the Jews" (Matthew 27:37), but they had no understanding that they proclaimed the truth.

In spite of the attitudes of the Roman Guard, which was indifferent or scornful, Scripture tells us that the creation He brought into existence responded to His agony. Luke 23:44 NKJV tells us darkness prevailed from the sixth to the ninth hour (noon to 3:00 p.m. Hebrew time), while Matthew 27:51 tells us the earth shook, rocks split, and tombs gave up their dead. Symbolically the veil of the temple, which separated the holy place from the holy of holies, was torn in two from top to bottom. The destruction of this curtain, through which the high priest had been allowed entrance once a year (Hebrews 9:30), signified a new order in which all believers could approach God through Christ, the eternal one.

His Resurrection

Our Lord was alone without benefit of God the Father or God the Holy Spirit. When He raised Lazarus from death's hold, He was on the outside of the tomb and cried out, "Lazarus, come forth" (John 11:43). No one was on the outside to call the Son forth. The Father was also alone in heaven in grief that His Son carried the weight of the world's sin as He hung on a cross. God had turned His back. In my conscious memory I've always had some understanding that this situation was necessary, but I didn't know then how reprehensible sin is. I only knew that God as light could not at that moment bear the sight of His Son, who was not light. I realize now that there is more to it than that. The crucifixion and the burial served more than one purpose. Firstly there had to be a blood sacrifice for sin; however, there were those who didn't believe Jesus was the Son of God, and that, too, had to be proven. Jesus cried out, "My God, My God, why have you forsaken me?"(Mark 15:34). I know that Jesus knew why, but the agony of separation was death itself. I would love to have seen Him come forth triumphant from the grave, in all the glory and power that was His. He had accomplished what the Father knew He would, and in the process He proved to the world that He was (and is) the Son of God.

His Exaltation

The dictionary defines exaltation as the act of being lifted up, glorified, praised, and honored. That he was exalted solidifies the authority that was already His. Scripture indicates that no one will escape his own moment of truth when realization finally penetrates the heart that Jesus is the Son of God. Even those in the darkness of their tombs will experience that truth. "God highly exalted Him, and bestowed on Him the name which is above every name, that at the name of Jesus every knee should bow, of those who are in heaven and on earth, and under the earth, and that every tongue will confess that Jesus Christ is Lord, to the glory of God the Father" (Philippians 2:9–11). "He is at the right hand of God, having gone into heaven, after angels and authorities and powers had been subjected to Him" (1 Peter 3:22).

The Ministry of the Spirit

You probably recognize that we are talking of the Holy Spirit when we say "the Spirit," but it may be hard to understand that He has a ministry just as the Father and the Son have their own particular work to accomplish. The Spirit has not been front and center up to now, but He accomplished what He does somewhat behind the scenes. Not so in this chapter. That's okay because our challenge as believers is to continually learn and utilize that which has been learned. I would suspect that for most of us our first knowledge of the third member of the Trinity comes when we are baptized and someone says, "In the name of the Father, the Son, and the Holy Spirit." Others may have known He was also there but with little comprehension of what He did, and that's okay too; however, now it is time to understand the Helper, as Jesus called Him. Perhaps you will even want to thank Him soon. It is impossible to learn about every detail all at once. In fact I can say with great confidence that no one will ever learn it all, much less all at one time.

While the term Holy Spirit appears in the Old Testament only three times (Psalm 51:11 as well as Isaiah 63:10 and 11), His work is evident throughout that message, and it's often repeated in the New Testament regarding the ministry of Jesus. There are three ways in which the word *spirit* is used in Scripture. The meaning of each is as follows[45] (Nelson 1995):

- There is the immaterial part of a man's body, meaning that it will not decay (Hebrews 4:12 and Galatians 6:18). Jesus used it in reference to His own body in John 11:33 as Paul did of himself in Acts 17:16.

- It is used in reference to good and evil spirits, such as angels or demons who are beings other than God or human (Psalm 104:4 and 148:8 for angels and Mark 9:25 for demons).

- The term *the Spirit* refers to the Spirit of God, who is the Holy Spirit and is found in both the Old and New Testament. Examples in the Old Testament enabled service to God in a special way (Exodus 31:3–5) and enabled the judges to lead armies to victory (Judges 3:10). In the New Testament the Spirit enabled the fulfill-ment of prophecy (Judges 2:16–21, 3:18, and 28:25–7; Acts 2:4; Acts10:44–8; 2 Corinthians 3:18; 2 Thessalonians 2:13; Acts 10:20 and 16:6–7). And when applied to Jesus, it allows others to relate to Him. In this capacity He is called the Helper (2 Corinthians 3:17, Romans 8:9, Galatians 4:6, and John 14:16–17).

---

45 Nelson's New International Bible Dictionary, copyright 1995 by Thomas Nelson Publishers, Spirit, p. 1197-8

Methods of Receipt

- The direct administration of the Spirit was an example at Pentecost. It was also received in this manner with Cornelius and with Saul.

- With the benefit of prayer the apostles would lay their hands on individuals to transfer abilities to others to perform miracles, prophesy, or speak in tongues. This was used at least three times in Scripture with the seven deacons (Acts 6:1–8), the Samaritans (Acts 8:14–16), and the Ephesians (Ephesians 19:1–6).

- In addition the Spirit is received by baptism, which is identified as an indwelling measure of the Holy Spirit (Romans 8:11).

Manifestations of the Spirit occurred in order that hearers might believe and become "witnesses of God's grace through the Spirit" (Acts 2:38). There are many such examples in the book of Acts and the gospels. I'm quite certain the following is a partial list.

- The Spirit is the power by which believers come to Christ (1 Corinthians 12:3).

- The Spirit is the power by which we see with faith (Romans 8:11).

- The Spirit speaks to us of the Father and Son, not of Himself. It is the Spirit who gives new life (John 6:63) as we walk and live (Romans 8:3–6) in building Christian character and bearing fruits of righteousness (Galatians 5:22–3).

- It is the Spirit as the Helper that Jesus promised would come to His disciples after the ascension, and it is through the Helper that Father and Son abide with disciples (believers) (John 15:26).

- The Spirit is proof of Sonship (Romans 8:16–17).

- The Spirit serves as an intercessor on behalf of our prayers "with groanings that can't be uttered" (Romans 8:26–7).

- It is by the Spirit that Scripture was inspired (2 Peter 1:20–1). It is through the Spirit that we are sealed or authenticated as belonging to God (2 Corinthians 1:21–2).

- Christian liberty stems from the Spirit (2 Corinthians 3:17–18).

Regarding liberty, I would say that all of life demonstrates the liberty of choice, but as we keep our gaze on Him it begins to show in the reflection of the one we see in the mirror (self). This can only be a result of "beholding as in a mirror the glory of the Lord." This is the process of transformation. Choice plus focus on Him bathes the believer in His glory by the Spirit of the Lord (3:18).

My conclusion from these texts is that while the Son is the way to the Father, the Spirit is the way to the Son (Romans 8:11) and consequently the Father as well (Romans 8:14–15). It is He who bears witness to us that we are children of God (Romans 8:16–17). It is through Him that the "deeper things of God" are revealed to us (1 Corinthians 2:10-12), and it is through Him that we realize the mystery of Christ (Ephesians 3:3–5).

The Unity of the Trinity

It is through unity within the Trinity that the message of sin, righteousness, and judgment awaits our acceptance of the gospel. The apostle Paul ends his second letter to the Corinthians with a prayer for their well-being, and in a different way his prayer demonstrates the unity of the Trinity because Paul's message was by inspiration. Second Corinthians 13:14 says, "The grace of the Lord Jesus Christ, and the love of God, and the fellowship of the Holy Spirit, be with you all." Notice also that Paul prayed for them that they, too, would have grace, love, and fellowship.

At the beginning of Jesus' ministry unity is shown by the presence of the Trinity. The Father's voice, the Spirit in the form of a dove, and the Son were all present at His baptism by John. This example is recorded in all of the gospels (Matthew 3:16, Mark 1:9–11, Luke 3:21–2, and John 1:33), and it was an appropriate beginning to demonstrate unity. It bears some resemblance to the outpouring of the Spirit at Pentecost—except in that instance Father and Son were the supportive team for the beginning of the church in which the Spirit assumed the more active role.

Romans 15:13 tells us that it is through *the expressed power of the Trinity*, whose evangelistic power was poured out at Pentecost for the early church, and through His indwelling presence that we have the hope of our belief. Somehow this connects to the admonition not to "grieve the Spirit" because it is through Him that we find and understand the commandments of the Father through the Son. It is He who guides us into all truth and teaches us to walk and live for God (Ephesians 4:30). We must listen to His guidance, or else the hope that is within will surely die.

The New Era

The new era has been accomplished. The latter days are here. We are living in the final age. While the principle of salvation for people of faith remains the same, we see that God's grace is for all mankind not just the Jews. Through the newly converted Paul, God directs the inclusion of the Gentiles in the new mission.

> "Therefore remember, that formerly you, the Gentiles in the flesh, who are called uncircumcision by the so-called circumcision, which is performed in the flesh by human hands … remember that you were at that time separate from Christ, excluded from the commonwealth of Israel and strangers to the covenants of promise having no hope and without God in the world. But now in Christ Jesus you who formerly were far off have been brought near the blood of Christ." (Ephesians 2:11–13)

The wall that separated Jew from Gentile has been removed. We are now one in Him, heirs of Abraham and salvation.

Summary

We found that because of Jesus' death, resurrection, and ascension, we are now connected in an unusual manner to the Holy Spirit, the third member of the Trinity. The Spirit dwells within each believing person as a guide, a helper, and a personal tutor to keep us on the right track. We can ignore His teaching as it is still a choice, but the results of that choice will leave us alone in our inability to understand God's will, the path we should choose, the way to make decisions, and the way to live in the faith we have professed.

It is somewhat strange to learn that the Spirit has a ministry just as Jesus' did—strange but intriguing. There are so many things that the Spirit does for man that it may come as a shock when we begin to realize we are recognizing

His work in us. Some of the Spirit's work involves fulfillment of Old Testament prophecies, but beyond that most of the rest seems to be for man individually not collectively. We have a huge responsibility to witness about Jesus. Anything less shows an incredible amount of ingratitude for all that's been done for us. You may notice that the Spirit doesn't talk much about Himself. His emphasis is on Jesus and the ministry of sin, redemption, and judgment. We must learn to follow that example.

One thing that is hard to understand is that the Trinity is one. I think that must mean they are of the same mind because they surely do have different jobs, though I do see that they seem to focus their goals on sin and judgment as well as redemption, and I have to tell you I like that a lot.

Another thing that seemed strange at first was that in this particular situation, the Spirit is the one who is termed *the expressed power* of the projects. It is my belief that this simply refers to the assignment of responsibilities. God was the architect of this building called the church, and Jesus was the builder; however, there also had to be someone around who could put all the pieces together and see that it got done, and it looks like that's the Spirit. I do not believe that one has more power than the other. Remember that the Spirit was also with Jesus in the creation, and I love the text that refers to Him as "moving over the face of the waters" (Genesis 1:1). The NKJV says He hovered over the water, which to my mind is very descriptive. I often carry that picture in my mind as I behold the glory of the universe.

Study Guide—Chapter 14

Q. What did the manifestation of the Holy Spirit confirm in the first century?
A. The manifestation of the Holy Spirit confirmed the authenticity of the church.

Q. What three methods did the Holy Spirit use?
A. The Spirit manifested itself to believers directly by the laying on of hands and by baptism.

Q. For what purpose does the Holy Spirit become manifest regardless of the method used?

A. The purpose of the manifestation of the Spirit was for belief in the Son of God.

Q. In what way was the manifestation received by Jesus different from all others?

A. The manifestation of the Spirit received by Jesus was *without measure*.

Q. Our measure of the Spirit, which we know as the indwelling Spirit, is a gift that comes through baptism. How does it manifest itself?

A. Our measure of the Spirit is manifest in a changed life.

Q. We saw God's emphasis move from the individual to heads of families, to a nation, and now to people of all nations individually. What connecting principle binds them together and shows God's continuity?

A. God demonstrates His sameness by continuing to speak to man but also by changing His methods as population as need arises. This is also a demonstration of His love.

Q. How did the resurrection grant forgiveness to those who lived and died in prior ages?

A. Forgiveness is granted to all who have ever lived by faith. God tells us that there is no excuse for living without faith because there is an avenue by which all man has had opportunity to learn. Those avenues are nature (which speaks of God), the law (which taught of God), and Scripture (which tells us about God). God does not change. These speak of God's sameness and His continuity.

Q. How did persecution help to spread the early church, and what were its sources?

A. Troubles between the chief priests (assumed to be the high priests) and the priests broke out while Felix was procurator under Nero. They "formed bands of revolutionaries who stoned and abused each other as if it were a city without government." That was written by Josephus (2007), an early church historian, about 54 AD. "Such shameless audacity possessed the chief priests that they sent slaves to the threshing floors to snatch the tithes owed to the priests, so impoverished priests could be seen perishing of want. The violence of the factions thus completely vanquished justice."[46] These were the types of persecution that went on within the priesthood. In addition, there were arguments between sects, dividing the people over what they were to believe, and harassments of all kinds especially of those who were then martyred. And then there were the persecutions that stemmed from the government—banishment, imprisonment, and martyrdom. You can easily see the motivation for leaving for other places to live. The interesting thing is that everywhere the Jews went they took their faith and taught it to others.

---

46   Eusebius: Maier, *Church History,* copyright 2007 by Paul L. Maier, 2.20.

Chapter 15: The Book of Acts

Have you had any experiences in your life where you put your whole self into something, feeling you might never cross the river, climb the peak, or make it until morning? It is an awe-inspiring moment, one that both drains and exhilarates. Today I'm having one of those moments, and what is really strange about it is that I'm synchronizing my internal time clock with the year AD 30 or a little earlier or possibly a little later. No one knows for sure the exact year that our Lord was crucified because even calendars were altered by His presence. Whatever the date was, it was the beginning of a new age, a different era, and a time that our Lord referred to as these latter days. It is stunning after I have spent hours upon hours in study to prepare myself for this moment that I didn't have any idea what it would be like, and here I am considering their moment instead of mine. What must it have felt like for Jesus, for He was not quite yet the Messiah, the Christ. He was still Jesus, son of Mary. Oh, yes, He was still the Son of God too, but we're talking here about how it would have *felt*. He was not quite over the mountain peak. There were a still a few things that had to be finished before He ascended back to the Father. He needed to see James, His brother, and He wanted to break bread with the apostles. And He still needed to appear before a number of people who would have their own eyewitness account of His resurrection. The word *complete* was more and more often in His mind, and he found Himself longing for what it implied, the completion of this particular episode and the beginning of the next.

The Book

And when the day of Pentecost had come, they were all together in one place. And suddenly there came from heaven a noise like a violent rushing wind, and it filled the whole house where they were sitting. And there appeared to them tongues as of fire distributing themselves, and they rested on each one of them. And they were all filled with the Holy Spirit and began to speak with other tongues, as the Spirit was giving them utterance. (Acts 2:1–4)

This was the day for which the world had unknowingly waited. We can just barely recognize now that we need what God gave to man on that wonderful day. How could they have known? It seems to me that until we begin to know ourselves there is no hope of knowing what we need especially in the way of spiritual nourishment.

Acts was sometimes called the Acts of the Apostles and at other times the Acts of the Holy Spirit or even just Acts, but whatever you call it, the writing is by the physician Luke, who is a Gentile by the way. Did you know that? No matter. He was evidently a fine man. He wrote the book of Luke by the way. The Lord gathered everyone together by means of the Holy Spirit and gave instructions that they were to stay in Jerusalem and wait until "that which the Father had promised came." "John," He said to them, "baptized with water, but in a few days you will be baptized with the Holy Spirit." Obviously their minds were in another channel because they asked if "this was the time when He would restore the kingdom to Israel."

And Jesus replied "It is not for you to know times or epochs which the Father has fixed by His own authority. But you shall receive power when the Holy Spirit comes upon you; and you shall be my witnesses both in Jerusalem, and in all Judea and Samaria, and even to the remotest part of the earth."

"And after He had said these things, He was lifted up while they were looking on, and a cloud received Him out of their sight." And two angels asked, "Why do you stand looking in the sky? This Jesus, who has been taken up from you into heaven, will come in just the same way as you have watched Him go into heaven."

And that is the way the new era began.

The Ministry of the Apostles

Can you imagine how chaotic it must have all felt? They recognized the responsibility the Lord laid on them, but how they would achieve it wasn't quite clicking within them. I think they had determination and more than a little stress. The point in time when they could just *do* hadn't yet come.

The first thing the apostles did was to select someone to replace Judas, someone who had been with them from the baptism of John until the day the Messiah was taken up into heaven. They drew lots and prayed. The lot fell on one Matthias, and he was added to the eleven.

It was clear as the apostles began to plan how they would begin the work Jesus had so specifically left for them that it would be different. How different they were not yet sure, but the feeling among them was that it could never be the same without Jesus in their presence. Perhaps they would know more when they received that which the Father was sending.

Pentecost

It is said that the gift from the Father arrived ten days later when they were gathered together to celebrate the feast day of Pentecost, which was celebrated fifty days after the first day of Passover. This feast was also known as the Feast of Weeks and the Harvest Feast, and the offering to God was to be of the firstfruits of the harvest. The firstfruits that came on that day from God (the outpouring of the Holy Spirit) were the firstfruits of the believer's inheritance. Symbolically those who were gathered together were also firstfruits of all the believers who would come after them. So there are in this beginning three types of firstfruits, which I believe establishes a pattern.

- Firstfruits from the believer were to honor God.

- Firstfruits from God blessed the believer.

- The gift of self then is the only appropriate thanks to God for the blessing He bestowed.

One might ask if the power of the Holy Spirit would have been recognized had there not been this visual picture of sound and movement. It correlates in my mind with the reason Revelation was written to *show* (Revelation 1:1), and John was summoned to be the recipient of the *showing*. Some things must be seen and heard in order to gain comprehension.

The importance of Acts is in the fact that it tells us of the establishment of the church, not just a church but God's church. Although we can't see the building, I'm sure it is a beautiful building, one not made with brick or stone but rather a spiritual building that will hold God's people, who are a representation of Christ's resurrected body.

161

The book of Acts is church history as established in the first century. As mentioned, Luke, the author, was a physician, an educated man, one whose writing has been referred to as art. In addition to the ascension and the happening on Pentecost, Luke records the spread of the church as the apostles carried out the commission given them by Jesus prior to His ascension, and we must remember that this beginning was in fulfillment of the prophecy by Joel (and others) as far back as the years 835- 796.

"This is what was spoken of through the prophet Joel: 'I will pour forth my Spirit on all mankind; and your sons and your daughters shall prophesy, and your young men shall see visions, and your old men shall dream dreams; even on my bond slaves, both men and women I will in those days pour forth of my Spirit and they shall prophesy'" (Acts 2:16–18).

Peter and Paul were the two most prominent characters of Acts, although all of the apostles and others as well were ambassadors of the gospel news. You may not know that *gospel news* refers to the death, burial, and resurrection of Jesus Christ and is the information that the apostles were told to take to the world. Beginning on the day of Pentecost, the Holy Spirit was revealed as the strength and power that guided the apostles' activity. Indeed, we also learn that essentially all Christians became teachers, at least by example. Are we to conclude then that they all "went about preaching the Word" (Acts 8:4) as the apostles did? Probably not, but they were so changed by their faith in Christ and the indwelling Spirit that their transformed lives were a gospel message to all. Driven from Jerusalem by persecution, the gospel spread very quickly to Judea and Samaria and "even to the remotest parts of the earth" (Acts 1:8).

Thought at first by the Jews to be a gospel for the Jews alone, after Cornelius's conversion it was proven to be the enactment of the promise to Abraham, whereby all people of the world would be blessed. You might ask, "What exactly is all the excitement about? There have been many others who were crucified by the Romans without all the excitement this Jesus of Nazareth has caused. What is it that is happening? Has everyone gone crazy?"

In chapter 3 we presented faith as a spiritual growth that stems from belief in that knowledge creates the desire to know God while it also motivates obedience. Faith comes principally from hearing God's Word (Romans 10:17), but it is good to know that faith generates more faith and is inspired by example. Hebrews 11:1 tells us that faith is the "substance of things hoped for and the evidence of things not seen." That means that we see by faith and we obey by faith. As I've said many times, faith is what was found by the early Christians, but contrary to craziness, it is the substance of life as it opens the door to salvation. In the book of Acts we are privileged to witness this transformation. So in answer to the hypothetical question, I would have to say that people are not crazy. They have just waked to reality.

The church marks the end of an age and the beginning of the last age. With the advent of Pentecost it marks the beginning of a new covenant, which allows salvation to rest on the choice of each individual. Our God desires obedience, but the emphasis under this covenant is the heart. He knows we will make mistakes. He is willing to forgive in the presence of repentance. Repentance is an important principle to remember. It connects with faith and the longings of the heart, and it keeps you within God's grace. We have to understand that there are neither little sins nor big sins. All sin misses the mark of the perfection He desires for us. Continuing to try, continuing to seek, and continuing to worship and praise Him means that at the end of our journey on this earth, He will reward us with perfection just as if we had earned it. As far as I can see He has the playing field stacked in our favor. There is nothing we can lose except the lust of the flesh and the pride of life.

Acts gives us the baptisms of believers and the opposition of unbelievers. It records differences of opinions between Jewish and Gentile believers and shows how the differences were resolved. And as we've mentioned it tells us of God's oneness. It is a narrative full of activity, color, and excitement as Luke records our Savior's accomplishments and the accomplishments of those who were told to "go preach."

We saw the beginning of God's church in all its simplicity and magnificence, in its joy and sorrow, and I realized in a moment of pure insight how blessed we are that we are the recipients of that legacy, which was forged by men and women much like you and me, people who had the courage of their convictions and followed the Lord.

Summary

I'm not at all sure how to summarize a book like Acts, especially when we viewed it as more of an outline or overview. I hope I've been able to show you the vastness of God's project and how the Spirit has taken over His part with joy and enthusiasm. We don't know as much about the Holy Spirit as we do about God and Jesus, and I can tell you why. Think about this: Jesus tells us (and also did when He was on earth) about the Father. And who is it that the Father speaks of? He speaks of the Son "in whom He is well pleased" always. He speaks to us of the Son. And what is the Holy Spirit doing all of our waking minutes? He is telling us of the joys of heaven, the marvels of the Father and Son as He convinces us that is where we want to be and what is necessary to achieve that dream. Believe me. He never takes a vacation. He is always there within us, teaching, guiding, comforting. So I know we don't listen like we should, or we would be getting to know Him better. He looks after us and continues to be with us as our helper today. I hope you will keep in mind that it is through the Helper that we find relationship with the Father and the Son, that it is through Him that we learn, and that through Him we can realize the strength necessary to withstand Satan, and though we didn't cover all of the aspects of His nature, I want you to know that it is through Him that we find comfort in times of sorrow.

Acts is orderly and chronological in regard to both the history of the day and the accounting of Jesus' accomplishments in his three-year ministry. Luke also mentions the growing opposition of the Jewish leaders to the gospel message and speaks of the Holy Spirit more than fifty times. He emphasizes that Jesus of Nazareth is Israel's long-awaited Messiah and that the gospel is for all men, connecting prophecies from the Old Testament to the events of the day regarding the spread of New Testament Christianity.

We have reemphasized faith as the key to salvation with obedience as the partner that authenticates our faith. To see these principles come alive in the study of Acts is to see the church alive with enthusiasm. The Spirit, dominant on the pages of Acts, reveals Himself in all aspects of our faith. We know from previous studies how the Son is our advocate before the Father. I have learned in this lesson that the Spirit is the advocate for both the Son and the Father and that they are advocates for the Spirit. It is interesting how the three blend as they always speak of each other, rarely of self.

Study Guide—Chapter 15

Q. How is the book of Acts classified?

A. The book of Acts is a book of history, specifically church history.

Q. What is the historical significance of Pentecost?

A. Pentecost was first celebrated in the Old Testament as a Harvest Feast that came fifty days after the first barley sheaf. The feast itself was on the first day of Pentecost and was called the Feast of Weeks. It was in celebration of God's outpouring of blessings, which had enabled the harvest. The eschatological significance is that for Christians it is the beginning of His church, but it is connected to the first Pentecost in that they are both outpourings of blessings from God. Passover historically celebrates the deliverance of the Jewish people from the bondage of slavery, but it is connected to Pentecost by the fact that the memorial feast in memory of our Lord was instituted on the last Passover celebrated before the crucifixion.

Q. What is the theme of Acts?

A. This is not an easy question. I would say that it *is* an historical record of the establishment of the Lord's church. Luke, the writer, says it *is* an orderly account of the Lord's life and activities on earth. As we've mentioned before it is often called the *Acts* of the apostles or the *Acts* of the Holy Spirit. After consideration I believe I would say the theme is evangelical, meaning the spread of the Gospel.

Q. Name the event that came before the resurrection that upon its completion made forgiveness possible.

A. I hope you know (without this reminder) that without the foundation none of the rest of God's plan would have been possible. (Two big reasons: the creation of the nation of Israel which taught the law to the Israelites as well as information regarding the coming Messiah). Of course, these are only two pieces of the foundation.

Q. Tell me where I can find Jesus' last will and testament. I also need to know when a will is read. And while you're at it, please tell me what I have to do to be included in His will. Thanks.

A. You probably have a copy of it, maybe with you. The New Testament is His last will and testament, and a will is never read until there is the death of the testator (the one who made it). Okay, here is what you have to do. Firstly you must believe that Jesus is the Son of God and that He came to this world in the flesh and lived and died as a sacrifice for the forgiveness of our sins. Secondly that belief has to develop into faith because just by itself it sort of shrivels up and dies and there is no growth in the life you are offering to God. On the other hand, if it develops into faith, you have in your heart the substance of that for which we hope (eternal life) and the evidence of our faith, which is unseen (God). The third thing you must do is obey His commandments. Now it isn't as if He piles a whole bunch of things on you and says, "Now I want all of these things done by tonight at 9:30 or by tomorrow at noon." No, it doesn't work that way.

Okay, so what are these commands? Well, it's really hard to say because that is an individual matter of when and how you and God work this out. But I will tell you this: When you learn of a command, then is the time you become responsible for it. From that time forward you can no longer say to God, "But I didn't know." So the way I see it, if you knew nothing else at this moment other than what I just told you, then you would have a responsibility to open your heart to belief and learn whatever else He wants you to do. We've mentioned lots of things in the pages of this book, but they won't all come at you at once. If you begin to study for yourself, it will begin to come to you what you are ready to do. I don't like to call obedience *steps* because it makes it sound as if there are a few things you must do and then outside of that you're okay. The truth is that the life lived for Christ is just that, a life, a growing process, and as you learn God will expect more of you.

If you click with what I have shared and the way it has been shared, then this book would be a good one to begin with along with your Bible. I'm told there isn't another on the market like it right now that can take you from beginning to end while it show how it connects. However, don't ever just take someone else's word for what God wants you to do. Check it out for yourself.

Chapter 16: God's Mystery: The Church

~~~

The promise to Abraham has been fulfilled, at least in the sense of spiritual blessings that are ours in this age. The heavenly kingdom of God is yet to come, and when that completion comes, there will be blessings beyond our imagination. Spiritual blessings for the current kingdom that belong to the here and now are bountiful, with the indwelling of the Spirit, our mediator, Jesus Christ, in heaven with God the Father, the interpretation of our prayers to Him by the Spirit, who comforts, guides, and teaches. Yes, these blessings are ours in Christ in this age, but there will be unimaginable blessings in the heavenly kingdom as we dwell in His presence. Just think of all that has happened and remember that God is faithful. It doesn't matter that 430 years passed from the promise to the law. Nor do the intervening centuries that prepared the way for the incarnation matter. All was completed that was necessary prior to the establishment of the church. God's timing is always perfect, and only He will know when this age in which you and I live will be complete. In the meantime there is much to do. We'll look first at the establishment of His church and then at the method He chose by which to spread the news. Only when He recognizes that His work is complete will He move us on into judgment and eternity.

Upon the resurrection the foundation was complete. A means of reconciliation had been established, and its purchase price had been paid. The requirement of the law for a blood sacrifice had been fulfilled. With that blood He purchased a church that would be the instrument of instruction for the new covenant just as the law had been the instrument of instruction for the old covenant. This time there would be a connection between the two, specifically in the resurrected and exalted Christ. The following verses illustrate the coming together of the church as the forgiven and sanctified body of Christ growing into the glory of the Savior. Do you understand the implication that each forgiven, sanctified person in Christ must continue to grow? We just are not born spiritually full-grown. It takes a lot of growing to achieve the glory that God wants for us.

- "All things are cleansed with blood, and without shedding of blood there is no forgiveness" (Hebrews 9:22). Why there must be the shedding of blood isn't clear. Perhaps it is needed to signify the value of that which was sacrificed, the Son of God.

- "As Christ also loved the church and gave Himself up for her; so that He might sanctify her … so He might present to Himself the church in all her glory, having no spot or wrinkle or any such thing; but that she would be holy and blameless" (Ephesians 5:25–7). We are set apart from the world just as a good apple might be taken from a bushel that contains many bad apples. The setting-apart saves it from contamination. We can assume, therefore, that sanctification is a form of protection. "Having no spot or wrinkle" means that she has been cleansed. Keep in mind that the cleansing was from the blood of Jesus. When He was resurrected, he was raised to immortality. His death therefore is symbolic for Christians of putting off the old man of sin (mortality) and putting on the new man of Christ, who gives us immortality. We are allowed to make contact with that symbolism through the act of baptism when the old man of sin is cast off and the new man of Christ emerges from the watery depths of baptism.

- Of baptism, we might add that just as circumcision was the mark of the Jew, baptism is the mark of the Christian (Romans 6:4), signifying to walk in newness of life as the visible mark.

A Miraculous Beginning

Before specifics of the new law could be revealed, there was a miraculous beginning, which fulfilled prophecy (Joel 2:28–32) and preached the Lordship of Christ. This next verse refers to Pentecost, a day of Jewish celebration in which the Israelites celebrated their miraculous deliverance from Egyptian bondage. The visitation of the Spirit associated with Pentecost (Acts 2), marked the beginning of God's church.

- This event on the day of Pentecost illustrates the direct method of receiving the Spirit. "And when the day of Pentecost had come, they were all together in one place. And suddenly there came from heaven a noise like a violent, rushing wind, and it filled the whole house where they were sitting. And there appeared to them tongues as of fire distributing themselves, and they rested on each one of them. And they were all filled with the Holy Spirit and began to speak with other tongues, as the Spirit was giving them utterance" (Acts 2:1–4). This outpouring was the event our Lord instructed the apostles to wait for in Jerusalem. Not only did the worshippers speak in tongues they did not know, but those who were listening each heard words in their own languages.

- The indwelling Spirit is received by the act of baptism. "Those who had received his word were baptized; and there were added that day about three thousand souls" (Acts 2:41).

- Those who believed accepted the message, proclaiming their belief by the symbolic act of baptism. "And they were continually devoting themselves to the apostles' teaching and to fellowship, to the breaking of bread and to prayer" (Acts 2:42).

In this new age of the church the Passover still represents salvation from the bondage of slavery, but for Jew and Gentile alike it now represents for all men a miraculous salvation from the bondage of sin.

His Church Roles

In our language we would say of Jesus that because He bought the church with His blood it is undoubtedly His. Speaking from the spiritual aspect it is a little more complicated. It is His, but according to Scripture the church is referred to as His bride (Revelation 21:9 and 22:17). He also has many roles within the church, which describe who and what He does or has done for her.

The Foundation

Without Jesus the foundation would never have been completed. It is easy to grasp this concept if you realize all teaching before, during, and after the law points to the coming of Jesus. He became part of the foundation with the incarnation, His life and ministry, the crucifixion, the resurrection, and the ascension. With the resurrection He became the primary and indispensable part that we refer to as the cornerstone. "No man can lay a foundation other than the one which is laid, which is Christ Jesus" (1 Corinthians 3:11).

The Cornerstone

Both foundation and cornerstone refer to the spiritual building. I see the cornerstone as a connecting unit of the two covenants, but I also see it as a connection of the mind and spirit of those within. As Jewish heirs of Abraham as a whole begin to understand that Jesus is their Messiah, there will be a bonding of Spirit that has yet to occur in His church. The oneness of salvation for Jew and Gentile will be the crowning glory for all within and the fulfillment of the plan for the Trinity.

"You are fellow citizens with the saints, and are of God's household, having been built upon the foundation of the apostles and prophets, Christ Jesus Himself being the corner stone" (Ephesians 2:19–20).

What exactly is a cornerstone? I admit I consulted a dictionary to find out how a cornerstone fits into our foundation. This is what I found. A cornerstone is the indispensable (the part you can't do without it) and fundamental (most important piece) of something. Our *something* is God's church, and the cornerstone connects two walls or two stones without which neither could function.

Psalm 118:22 and Acts 4:11 identify the cornerstone of this foundation as the rejected, crucified, and resurrected Christ and the foundation to which He belongs as the one built on the apostles and prophets (Ephesians 2:20). The two covenants are the intersecting walls. The old covenant could not forgive sin, but it promised forgiveness. The new covenant forgives sin but only after the blood price has been paid by the one who made the covenant. That condition was met with Jesus' death. His resurrection fulfilled the old covenant and allowed the forgiveness of sin to apply equally to obedient believers under both the old covenant and the new covenant.

You may understand why the followers of the law need to be connected to our wall. (They want to obtain forgiveness for the faith they exhibited in following the truths they had been shown.). But why do we need to be connected to their wall? It is a good question, but the answer is so simple you will be astonished to hear it. The answer is love—love of the Father who gave His Son, love of the Son who gave His life, and love of the Spirit who dwells within each believer. The love of those who believe today provides forgiveness and completion for those who lived under the law by faith. The love of the martyrs of the first century and those of today, who loved God more than they loved their lives, helped to defeat Satan. This is why the new covenant is sometimes called the covenant of love.

The Head

We recognize that there must always be a leader, a head who knows all about what he is doing and why. In the church, Jesus is the head, and the body is the church.

"He is also head of the body, the church; and He is the beginning, the firstborn from the dead" (Colossians 1:18).

"We are to grow up in all aspects into Him who is the head, even Christ, from whom the whole body, being fitted and held together by what every joint supplies, according to the proper working of each individual part, causes the growth of the body for the building up of itself in love" (Ephesians 4:15–16). This is saying that while we are not like Him now, our goal is to grow until we are like Him. To do it properly we must work together in love with the talents and the abilities of each person, and it is love that will bring growth.

The High Priest

How did we become priests? The priesthood ended when the law ended. Jesus became our High Priest with continual access to the Father in place of the old system, where the high priest could enter God's presence only once a year.

"You also, as living stones, are being built up as a spiritual house for a holy priesthood, to offer up spiritual sacrifices acceptable to God through Jesus Christ" (1 Peter 2:5).

Individually, Christians are the dwelling place of the Holy Spirit, living stones, and a part of the spiritual house of God. The symbolism is that Christians are the stones of which the building is constructed; the difference is that we are *living stones* who offer our lives as sacrifices to Him by worship, praise, and living for Him.

What kind of sacrifices does this refer to? In addition to worship and praise it includes prayer (which is our conversation with Him), study (which is His conversation with us), doing for others in love and kindness, practicing self-control, developing godly attitudes, and practicing patience. In short it is an effort to be like Jesus. It is obviously something that doesn't happen overnight, but it is the desire and the striving-for that God is pleased with.

As we've mentioned before the priesthood is gone, and Christians have been given the responsibility and the privilege of approaching the throne of God through Jesus, our mediator. The law had been fulfilled. The priesthood was no longer valid. Therefore there was of necessity a change of law (Hebrews 7:12).

"As I have planned, so it will be, and as I have purposed, so it will stand" (Isaiah 14:24). This speaks of the plan itself because God emphasizes that each covenant must serve the purpose for which God created it.

Salvation

Because we have been bought, can we also be rejected? Does God have to keep what He has purchased, or is He at liberty to reject the less than perfect? Such a rejection would include all of us, as Romans 3:23 tells us, "All have sinned and fall short" of His glory. Are His promises true? Will He forgive our imperfections? While it is true that He cannot condone sin, He allowed His Son to take our sin upon Himself and die in our place. Jesus's words on the cross were these: "My God, my God, why hast thou forsaken me?" My understanding is that sin is so reprehensible to God that

He turned His back on His Son as He carried the sin of the world. It was by this act of profound love that both Satan's power over death was destroyed and sinful man's debt was paid. Because there was also a resurrection, God's plan was implemented. Now when God sees us, He doesn't see our sin but our justification.

Isaiah 1:18 says, "Though your sins are as scarlet, they shall be as white as snow." We are "justified as a gift by His grace" through the redemptive blood of Jesus (Romans 3:24). This gift of grace achieves a miraculous transformation in that we are no longer lost because of sin but justified by faith. I would point out that in order for a faith to justify it must be an obedient faith, or it takes on the essence of Eve's approach. James, the brother of our Lord, points out that faith without works is dead being alone (James 2:17). Verse 22 adds that "faith working with works perfects faith." His example cites demons who also "believe and shudder" (James 2:19).

Second Corinthians 6:1 indicates that this marvelous gift can be received in vain. Sanctification is done by the Spirit (Galatians 5:16). If we do not allow ourselves to be led by the Spirit but instead indulge in the things of the flesh, we are warned that we will not inherit the kingdom of God (Galatian5:16–21).

God's continuity is again demonstrated in that the choice is ours, which includes both a decision and an action as usual. As with any gift, it must be accepted before it is possessed.

In Hebrews 10:14, the writer states He has "perfected for all time those who are sanctified" (Romans 5:1). Sanctification produces faith. Faith completed (meaning until death) produces perfection, not by our own abilities but by His strength, a gift at the end of our physical journey.

"Conduct yourself with fear while you are here on earth, knowing that you were not redeemed with perishable things like silver or gold from your futile way of life inherited from your forefathers, but with the precious blood, as of a lamb unblemished and spotless, the blood of Christ" (1 Peter 1:17–19).

Again I must point out that liberty in Christ does not mean you can do as you like. Freedom is not synonymous with license. Our freedom is to choose. License, on the other hand, is anarchy, indicating a lack of control, confusion with every person doing as he likes. Our biblical example in the historical account of the period of the Judges demonstrated that confusion.

Hidden Wisdom

With the advent of Pentecost and the establishment of the church, it is time to reveal God's hidden wisdom. Until such a revelation could be made, however, the church has been identified as the mystery through which His wisdom would be demonstrated. His hidden wisdom was revealed with the elimination of all distinguishing characteristics between the Jew and the Gentile, thus making them joint heirs of the promise (Ephesians 3:3–11).

Paul tells us that God gave to him the privilege of administering the mystery (Ephesians 3:3), which is another way of saying that he was chosen to take the gospel to the Gentiles. Now, he says, according to God's purpose of reconciliation, the wisdom of His action would be made known "to the rulers and the authorities in the heavenly places."

Who were these rulers and authorities? They are undoubtedly all those who have received their authority from Satan, his coworkers, his converts. Ephesians 6:12 identifies at least some of them as world forces of darkness and spiritual forces of wickedness in heavenly places. Judging from the secrecy of the message that Jews and Gentiles would be united as one in His church, I can only surmise that these forces of darkness under the leadership of Satan would have found many ways to hinder the completion of the plan and that they are no doubt utilizing those methods to delay the inevitable result.

Now that the sacrifice has been made, the resurrection accomplished, and Satan defeated, both the mystery of the church and the wisdom of oneness in Christ are revealed.

What a devastating blow this must have been to Satan! The mystery had been foretold but never explained. It is my opinion that Satan had the mistaken concept that Abraham's descendants had already received their blessing by becoming a great nation. I don't believe he ever dreamed that God would become man, that He would purchase man's salvation by His own death, or that through a church, the representation of His resurrected body, He would eliminate all distinguishing characteristics that separated Jew and Gentile, thus uniting every believer in His body. We learn now that this had been the plan from the beginning. If Satan had realized the scope of God's plan, he would have made even more problems for the Israelites.

His Eternal Purpose

The following verses say again that God's purpose from the beginning was that salvation would be for all people and not just the Jews; however, it does not bring to mind for the reader all the work that's gone into the construction of the foundation to prepare for this revelation. Because of what went before as well as the creation of the church, it is now time to reveal the next steps in His eternal plan, which now openly includes the Gentiles.

"This was in accordance with the eternal purpose, which He carried out in Christ Jesus, our Lord, in whom we have boldness and confident access through faith in Him" (Ephesians 3:11).

Paul comments on this next scripture, saying that when his Ephesian brethren read it they will understand the insight he has had concerning the mystery, which in prior generations had not been made known but has now been revealed to the apostles and prophets who belong to Jesus.

"To be specific, that the Gentiles are fellow heirs and fellow members of the body, and fellow partakers of the promise in Christ Jesus through the gospel" (Ephesians 3:6). This is the unity that God wishes for us, the unity of Spirit, which makes us one.

"And if you belong to Christ, then you are Abraham's offspring, heirs according to promise" (Galatians 3:29). This, too, is an act of unification. How can Gentiles be heirs of Abraham, who was a Jew? Let's find out. God says we are all shut up into disobedience so that He may show mercy to all. To be *shut up* means that everyone is guilty. This is a call to obedience for all (Romans 11:32) people regardless of race.

Jesus became human to give aid to the descendants of Abraham, who were descendants by faith (Hebrews 2:16).

He reasoned that He was needed as a High Priest for the heirs of Abraham, who would like Him be tempted by Satan. The incarnation enables Him to be our High Priest (Hebrews 2:17–18).

Because the outpouring at Pentecost was the first happening in the Lord's church, we know the new covenant is in effect now. Therefore Abraham has two lines of descendants, they are (a) believers, children of faith who are blood descendants, and (b) believers, children of faith who are not blood descendants (Romans 9:6–8 4).

"That being justified by His grace we might be made heirs according to the hope of eternal life" (Titus 3:7). Look closely at the means of justification " ...grace comes from God ... so it is a gift; Therefore, the work we do is a matter of the desire to obey and not in order to receive grace.

Fulfillment of the Promise

God's promise to Abraham can be understood now in its wisdom and simplicity. God is not a respecter of persons as some have thought because

He had a chosen people (Romans 2:11). Salvation is for everyone! His purpose was revealed when the time was right for the Gentiles just as it was revealed when the time was right for the Jews. Only the right combination of events would reveal it, and that was accomplished after Pentecost.

Unity

Paul offers this information in regard to unity. He is in prison in Rome, writing his letters, encouraging believers in faith, keeping spirits alive for the work that needs to be done. This is what he has to say, "I implore you to walk in a manner worthy of the calling with which you have been called, with all humility and gentleness, with patience, showing tolerance for one another in love, being diligent to preserve the unity of the Spirit in the bond of peace" (Ephesians 4:1).

These are his instructions for dealing with controversial matters. I find it extremely interesting that he calls for tolerance first. This is an attitude with which I agree. I don't really understand why Christians feel it necessary at times to pull out the punching bag in order to make a point that is already lost because of attitude.

"There is one body and one Spirit, just as also you were called in one hope of your calling; one Lord, one faith, one baptism, one God and Father of all who is over all and through all and in all" (Ephesians 4:4). The body referred to here is God's church, and the Spirit is the Holy Spirit. And we hope for eternal life.

"There is salvation in no one else; for there is no other name under heaven that has been given among men, by which we must be saved" (Acts 4:12).

Summary

Both God's mystery and His wisdom have been revealed. In His church, a representation of His resurrected body, Jew and Gentile are united by Jesus blood.

The church that has been purchased with the blood of Christ is now the instrument of instruction as the law was in the old covenant, and the two are connected by the resurrected and exalted Christ. Reconciliation for the Jews has moved from the role of children who no longer require a tutor to a new position as heirs directly responsible now only to the Father. Paul spoke to young Jewish Christians and said, "Therefore, my brethren, you also were made to die to the Law through the body of Christ, that you might be joined to another, to Him who was raised from the dead, that we might bear fruit for God" (Romans 7:4). That fruit would be the fruit of obedience … and the sacrifice of spiritual gifts.

The Spirit authenticated the miraculous beginning and continued to do so with the apostles as they went about preaching the word. One must remember that the church in this context is not a denomination created by man, but is God's church, purchased with the blood of Christ. It remains therefore that only He is the guide. Like the Bereans, we must search the Scriptures daily to determine the truthfulness of what is taught (Acts 17:11). Scripture testifies of Jesus (John 5:31–2) in the same manner that Jesus was testimony of God. We are told that if we seek Him with the heart we will find Him (Jeremiah 29:13).

Faith continues to be the key to salvation, one that opens the doors to motivation and obedience as it increases both love and faith. James, the brother of the Lord, makes the challenge regarding faith versus works and states that faith is perfected in works.

We took a look at the many roles that were made perfect by our Lord as He assumed the responsibilities of His church and found that He is the foundation, the chief cornerstone, the head, and our high priest and advocate with the Father.

In addition we learned how the word Spirit is used in the Bible and how the Spirit works in us today. The Father, the Son, and the Holy Spirit are in harmony about all things, unified in the message regarding sin, redemption, and judgment. It was suggested that we know more about the Father and Son than we do about the Spirit (Holy Spirit) because it is He who speaks to us of them. The Spirit is our Helper and dwells within us. He came to us on the day of Pentecost and stayed in order that we may have a bountiful harvest for the Lord.

Study Guide—Chapter 16

Q. What did the blood of Jesus purchase?
A. Jesus' blood purchased a church which is the representation of His resurrected body.

Q. Beyond the fact of forgiveness and salvation, what primary principle was achieved by the establishment of the church?

A. Probably the most important principle is unity. God says that the church has broken down the wall of enmity between Jew and Gentile, and we are now one faith, one hope, one body, one Spirit with one Lord and Father of all.

Q. What did Paul have reference to when he said that it was his privilege to bring to light the administration of the mystery?

A. Paul was speaking of having been commissioned by our Lord on the road to Damascus to take the gospel to the Gentiles.

Q. Besides being the foundation, the cornerstone, and the head of the church, Jesus is said in Colossians to be the beginning. What does that mean?

A. Jesus was the beginning as the firstborn from the dead, the first to escape the bonds of death and resurrected to life eternal.

Q. Together all Christians are a holy temple, a dwelling of God and a spiritual house. What is a Christian individually?

A. Christians are individually the temple of God.

Q. Through what principle does faith work?

A. Faith works through obedience and the grace of God.

Q. How does one obtain faith?

A. Scripture says that faith comes by hearing the Word of God, and I believe we can add from wherever we find truth. It can be from "hearing the word" as you read Scripture. It can be from the example of friends or acquaintances. It can be from observing all that God has done to make our world beautiful. He says, "Seek and you will find, knock and it will be opened to you,"

Chapter 17: Books of the Beginning

The books of the Gospel, Matthew, Mark, Luke, and John, give us most of the available biographical information concerning Jesus. A biography of His early life is incomplete because very little of Him is known from that time. However, Luke 2:40–51 lets us know that He grew physically and mentally in the same way that all children grow, but in addition we are told that He was regarded favorably by both God and man, which tells us of His reputation. We also know that as a twelve-year-old He was capable of learning from and teaching the rabbis in the temple at Jerusalem, where His family went each year to celebrate Passover. At that young age He already felt the need to be engaged in His Father's work.

Though I have not called this chapter the Gospels, each book was assigned that title along with the author's name sometime after it was written. They are synoptic, which means that they tell a story from a similar point of view. In this case that is the story of Jesus life and ministry. Though all deal with the same subject, each is written uniquely from his own perspective, which reveals elements of the writer's personality. They are amazingly in harmony regarding Jesus' ministry. "Together they weave a more complete picture of the God-man, Jesus of Nazareth who was perfect in humanity and deity the only sacrifice that could have been acceptable for the sins of the world"[47] (MacArthur 2005).

The etymology of the word *gospel* goes back to the Anglo-Saxons and the derivation is *godspell*, which can mean either a *good story* or a *story about God*. When harmonized with the Greek word for gospel, *evangellion*, it means *good news*, which is a good report on an important event. How perfectly this fits the life, sacrificial death, and resurrection of Jesus of Nazareth[48] (MacArthur 2005).

---

47 MacArthur, John, MacArthur Bible Commentary, copyright 2005 by Thomas Nelson, Mark, (The Synoptic Problem), p. 1191, #8.

48 Ibid, Mark, (Introduction), p.1095.

Our focus will be on the books as we analyze the content, and we will provide some information about the author and the approximate date of writing, purpose, theme, emphasis, and characteristics chosen by the author to get his message across to the audience he specifically addressed.

The synoptic purpose of the Gospels is both theological and apologetic as expressed by John (John 20:31). They provide authoritative answers to questions regarding His life and ministry while they also provide strength to the believer and assurance regarding the reality of his faith (Luke 1:4).

I feel that it is important to know a little about each book both individually and as a group because they complement each other and in some instances give additional information not available in the first. It is a method of study in that you begin to have a tool that will help you find specifics for which we all search from time to time

The Books

The Gospels are unique because they write about a common subject, yet as I said earlier they are amazingly in harmony while they maintain four different viewpoints. That in itself makes them fascinating. Luke was most likely the first of the four written with John the last coming at least thirty years later after his release from Patmos, where he was a prisoner. Jesus is the theme of each book, although each has a different focus. Matthew writes to a Jewish audience, and his purpose is to convince the Jews that Jesus is the promised Messiah, the Son of God. He focuses on what Jesus said. Mark addressed his information to a Roman audience who were generally impatient with anything abstract and just wanted the *facts*. His focus was on what Jesus did, so his gospel was an active, fast-paced one. Luke's gospel is the most complete and the most orderly. He wrote the gospel before he wrote Acts. John almost didn't write a gospel. He was three or four years away from his one hundredth birthday, but he was still active and was urged by friends to write about what Jesus was *really* like, so his theme is the nature of Jesus' person. Don't make the mistake I made in thinking there was not much to his gospel. At first you may think it is simplistic, but think again. Before John gets through with you, you will know his words are profound.

Matthew

Matthew was originally called Levi. He was one of the original twelve apostles, a Jewish tax collector, honest but wealthy from a profession that was despised by his fellow countrymen because tax collectors worked for the Roman government and because they were dishonest for the most part. Because there is no prophetic mention of the destruction of Jerusalem within the book, it was assumed to be written before that event transpired in 70 AD. Written to a Jewish audience, Matthew traces Jesus back to Abraham, the father of the Jewish nation, and gives His legal lineage through the father, which was considered the legal lineage. He cites Jewish customs without explanation, refers to Jesus as the Son of David, uses the term *kingdom of heaven* instead of the *kingdom of God*, to which the Jewish audience would have objected, and quotes from the Old Testament sixty times, emphasizing fulfillment of prophecy.

Tradition says that he remained in Jerusalem for thirteen years following the death of Jesus, after which he preached in ancient Babylon to the Persians, Parthians, and Medes, and died a martyr's death in Egypt.

Two main characteristics of his writing besides being Jewish are that it was *didactic* (a teaching gospel) and *kingly emphasizing the royalty of Jesus*.

Mark

Mark was known as John Mark, who was the nephew of Barnabas (Colossians 4:10) and the son of Mary (Acts 12:12). His father was well-to-do as they owned a house and slaves in Jerusalem, where the disciples met (Acts 12:12). Barnabas was also a man of property, for he sold a field and laid the money at the apostles' feet (Acts 4:36–7).

Mark was not an apostle but was closely associated with the apostles from the beginning. Through the influence of Barnabas he was taken on the first missionary journey but turned back, causing a rift in his relationship with Paul, a rift that was later resolved (2 Timothy 4:11).

Of Jewish background he is nevertheless familiar with the Roman mind as he had lived and traveled under the Roman influence. Written to a Roman audience, he appeals to the Roman mind in his style of writing, which is terse and to the point, stressing facts rather than topics. He also stresses the power and authority of Jesus and what he did. He uses no references to Jewish law or genealogy, explains all Jewish terms, and computes or reduces Jewish forms of money into Roman terms. Finally he also explains Jewish customs.

Mark elicits wonder in the telling of even facts by the use of vivid detail and by recording the response of Jesus' audience.

Tradition says that Mark was a companion of Peter, that he founded the church in Alexandria (Egypt), and that he died a martyr.

Luke

Luke was a physician (Colossians 4:14), a Greek-speaking Gentile, and a man of culture and learning. He was often a companion of Paul in his travels. (See *we* and *us* sections of Acts 16:10, His is the most complete gospel with much material that is not found in the other gospels. Written to a Greek audience he traces Jesus back to Adam, father of the human race, rather than to Abraham. He explains Jewish customs and sometimes substitutes Greek names for Hebrew names. There is no knowledge concerning Luke's age at death or how he died, but tradition says that he was an artist. It is said that Luke's diction in the Greek is a marvel of combined simplicity and meaningfulness. He presents Jesus as the ideal man, and while his purpose was to give an orderly account of Jesus life, it is predominately historical. It is also a gospel of culture and refinement as well as being doctrinal as he connects historical reality to the basis for preaching repentance and forgiveness of sins.

Luke also stresses the human sufferings and sympathies of Jesus and devotes His narrative to Jesus' relentless path to the cross beginning at 9:51 for about ten chapters as he emphasizes the purpose for which Jesus came to earth, "For the Son of Man has come to seek and to save that which was lost" (Luke 19:10).

John

John was the son of Zebedee (Matthew 4:21) and one of the twelve. Both he and his brother, James, were susceptible to hot tempers. Consequently they were known as "sons of thunder" (Mark 3:17). John later became known as the apostle Jesus loved. It was to him that the care of Jesus' mother was entrusted at the crucifixion.

John was imprisoned on the Isle of Patmos, where he wrote the book of Revelation. After the death of the Emperor Domitian in AD 96, he was released by the Emperor Nerva (AD 96–98), who was the next to ascend the Roman throne. According to Eusebius (Maier 2007), John wrote the gospel of John in Ephesus at an advanced age because upon examination he found that the other three gospels began after John the Baptist's imprisonment, and he was moved by the Holy Spirit, to compose a spiritual gospel[49] These statements seem to offer proof that the book of John was written after his release from Patmos.

---

49 Eusebius: Maier, *Church History*, copyright 2007 by Paul L. Maier, published by Kregel Publications, (John's Writings), 3.24.

In his introduction to the Gospel his use of Logos or the Word in reference to Jesus is interesting in that it doesn't denote any particular religious background. For example the term *Christ* would have been relevant only to people of Jewish background. Lord was strictly a Gentile term, and Jesus was a common human name. This philosophical terminology points up John's emphasis on the universal nature of Jesus' ministry.

The spiritual (theological) emphasis of John's gospel is meant to inspire belief in Jesus Christ as the Son of God. Among other things it shows the nature of His deity. It shows His personal nature in relationship with man. It shows His humanity. It gives us the meaning of faith, and it gives us a unique vocabulary that uses both figurative language with a technical meaning (examples include life, light, darkness). And it gives us an abstract language with a philosophical meaning (examples: truth, true, hate, know, and it is a teaching gospel which demonstrates a deeper understanding of the abstract qualities that relate to both the Father and the Son but are generally foreign to our human nature. This allows for a richness of the texture in which we are enabled to see them.

Tradition says that John was the last of the apostles to die and the only one to die a natural death.

Summary

The word *gospel* has reference to Jesus' death, burial, and resurrection, and therefore it is the good news for mankind. A brief look at word derivation lets us know that the term originated with the Anglo-Saxons and then made its way to the Hebrews, the Greeks, and the English. That the Gospels are also rich in information regarding His life makes them invaluable as a source from which we can know Him. It is from the Gospels that we become familiar with His attitudes and His love. It is from the Gospels that we learn to pattern our own lives to His, and it is from these four books that we learn what it means to follow Him. From the Gospels, we can also learn to internalize His sacrifice for us and finally recognize our own roles in life, namely to live for Him.

I think if this manuscript were a three-act play, we would recognize the Gospels as the third act with all the drama, the suspense, the people, the countries visited, the Romans and their cruelty, the crucifixion of an innocent, the unbearable that must be borne, pathos, rejoicing.

Each time I study the Gospels it strikes me anew how different the four writers were—Matthew (the outcast tax collector), Mark (a young man from a rich family), Luke (the professional, a physician who was cultured and artistic), and John (the beloved fisherman). It is truly amazing that Jesus' life was chronicled by these four, isn't it? I feel it is an illustration of how love can bring us together regardless of background.

The comparison becomes even more interesting. Matthew wrote to a Jewish audience, Mark to the Romans, Luke to the Greeks, and John to the world. In their writings, they chose what would interest their particular audience the most. We see Mark, our young man, presenting the Romans with a picture of power, authority, and facts. Anything else would have been a waste of time with that audience. John, on the other hand, sees no boundaries. He writes to the universality of the world, evangelistic to the end of his life, teaching of a saving faith. Matthew proves his points with the Jews by what Jesus had to say, but Mark tells the Romans, "Let me tell you what He did!" Luke and John see Jesus' compassion and His humanity and want to pass it on—John because he witnessed it at the hands of Jesus, Luke because he was convinced by what he heard and saw in the lives of others.

In some ways Matthew and Luke are the same. Matthew as a Jew keeps his message within Jewish boundaries, except that he warns in humility against the Pharisees and the Samaritans. "They are leaven that must be avoided," he says (Matthew 16:11–12). In spite of Jewish sensibilities, he also portrays Jesus as victorious returning in glory (Matthew 24:30). Luke, on the other hand, is the same in a different way. He methodically follows the path of Jesus on His way to the cross, never deviating. For ten chapters his focus doesn't change, his devotion to detail and accuracy making it possible to identify the historical context of the events he describes. It is perhaps more unusual that Luke, who was not an eyewitness but a convert, would have this kind of persistency.

It is evident that each man wrote from his own perspective, and I feel it is also evident that by setting them side by side, we are able to see something of their lives and of their personalities that was perhaps not evident before the comparison. I am also able to feel their conviction, the reality of their love, and their devotion to the Lord they served. Each gospel is distinctive, yet together they are a complete testimony of Jesus.

Study Guide—Chapter 17

Q. John says about the Son that the Word became flesh and dwelt among us. It has been said that John's use of Logos or Word denotes the universal nature of His ministry. Can you think of another implication of the use of that particular word?

A. What I think of is the Word of God, which is the Scripture. This application of an abstract word as Jesus' name becomes literal after you meditate on it for a time. Jesus is the Word. He is God.

Q. Name three things that were made subject to the Son before His reign began at the right hand of God.

A. One might say all things were made subject to Him—the power of forgiveness and the power over death (remember He just came out of the tomb and ascended to heaven after He conquered death), the power over authorities, the power of judgment, and the power over nature.

Q. Matthew gave the legal genealogy of Jesus because he wrote to an audience of what people?

A. Matthew as a Jew wrote to his countrymen, the Jews, hoping to convince them that Jesus is the long-awaited Messiah.

Q. What was the theme of the book of Matthew?

A. Matthew wrote in regard to the things Jesus *said,* quoting from the prophets and their prophecies from the Old Testament.

Q. To what audience did Mark write, and what was his theme?

A. Mark as a young man wrote about what Jesus *did.* His is a gospel of action to appeal to the Roman mind. It is pointed, terse, and clear for the Roman audience which was impatient with abstractions.

Q. Why did Luke trace Jesus back to Adam instead of Abraham?
A. Luke wrote to the Greeks, who were not interested in Jewish genealogy, so he caught their attention by connecting them to the Father of mankind. In an orderly fashion he described our Lord as the ideal man stressing Jesus' perfect humanity.

Q. John's theme of belief makes use of both figurative and abstract vocabulary. Give an example of each.
A. Words such as *life*, *light*, and *darkness* are figurative words with a technical meaning, while such words as *truth*, *hate*, and *know* are examples of abstract words with a philosophical meaning.

Chapter 18: Spiritual Guidance

The end of national life in Judea occurred centuries before the destruction of Jerusalem in AD 70. The beginning of this process occurred with the first invasion of the Babylonians, and by the time of the last invasion in 581 BC Jeremiah tells us it was in effect the end (Jeremiah 52:28–30). According to Jeremiah's report, many Jews had left Israel before the captivities began and were living in various cities of Egypt. Even so these settlements were small in comparison to the ones left behind in Assyria, Babylon, and Persia. These were composed of those who chose to remain in the country of their captivity. They comprised the largest part of the dispersion, referred to in the New Testament[50] (Nelson 1995). Just as Jeremiah mentions having ministered to those in Egypt (Jeremiah 43:8, 44:1), Christians took responsibility to minister to converts wherever they were.

Looking at that period of time from this end, it is just all very sad. I know without it being said that there was blackness in those years for the Israelites. Thankfully there were cycles so that those who were trying to live for God had periods of rest before a new cycle would begin.

Although Paul made his missionary journeys to encourage and teach, he also continued to preach the gospel wherever he went. The recorded history of that time comes to us by these letters to various congregations.

It is unfortunate that persecution continued not only in the Roman colonies but even around the world to a degree. Around AD 49 Emperor Claudius (AD 41–54) expelled all the Jews from Rome because of a famine in the country. This resulted in an even greater dispersion, and everywhere these expelled Christian Jews went, the gospel was taken. Following the destruction of Jerusalem in AD 70, there were very few, if any Jews left in the city.

---

50   Nelson's New Illustrated Bible Dictionary, copyright 1995 by Thomas Nelson, (published by Thomas Nelson Publishers, Nashville), Dispersion, p. 361.

There are a total of twenty-one letters in this category, thirteen of them written by the apostle Paul. Of the other eight, two were written by the apostle Peter, three by the apostle John, and two by brothers of our Lord, James and Jude. These letters were all written to Christians to advise them how to best live the Christian life. The subject matter addressed ranges from persecution to problems of daily living to spirituality. Various types of persecution may change. Individual problems change, but the call to spirituality and the principles by which problems and persecution are resolved remain the same. It is for this reason that these letters remain so vital.

The first thirty years of the church are explored in the book of Acts. These letters plus the book of Revelation will cover the next period of time up to the death of John and the end of the apostolic age. To enhance the significance of the time in which each letter was probably written, we will examine them somewhat chronologically. Of course this is a subjective decision, and in no way alters the message of each letter.

For the most part the letters do not follow one theme; however, there is usually one that stands out. This does not mean that it will be the one that will speak with the greater emphasis for you. We will highlight both the author and the book, give approximate dates for the writing, and provide a theme, a purpose, and the emphasis within the text. This will be followed by two scriptures taken from the highlighted book, which I hope will illustrate the type of spiritual guidance you will find within that book.

The Letters: From the Dispersion to the Imprisonment

These books are in the form of letters, a few of which are for individuals; however, the majority of them are addressed to congregations, and it is believed that most would have been passed around to other congregations. When we consider the abundance of books in our world, that thought is archaic. As a final thought I have selected two verses from each book to demonstrate the basic type of message you will find in that book. The verse will not necessarily be the most well-known verse of the book but one representative of the book.

James

This book was written around AD 48–49 and historically was probably the first one to be circulated. It was written by James, the brother of our Lord. He was probably converted after the resurrection. We know that the risen Lord appeared to him (1 Corinthians 15:7), that he was a leader in the church at Jerusalem (Galatians 1:19 and Acts 15:13), and that he wrote to the twelve tribes who are dispersed abroad. James was probably written shortly after Paul's first missionary journey but before the Jerusalem Conference of AD 49–50. It is Jewish in content, and it reads like Proverbs with short, pithy, direct statements for encouraging uncompromising obedience. It has been said that James was not a Jewish Christian but a Christian Jew.

The James we know seems a perfect choice to write to the dispersed tribes that are now composed of many Christians. Think about it. Had he been a Christian who was no longer Jewish in outlook, he could have done very little to assist them in their transition as he would have had very little influence with their spiritual problems. However, as a Jew who was a Christian, he was both knowledgeable and beneficial in resolving the problems of combining the traditions of the law with the requirements of their faith. In short the new Jewish Christians had respect for James because he had retained his Jewishness. This doesn't mean He followed the law. He followed Christ, but he didn't abandon his background as a Jew. Nor should he.

James wrote on such subjects as faith, partiality, controlling the tongue, wisdom, patience attitudes, and the misuse of riches. His theme seems to be practical Christianity with the purpose of aiding Christians to live in such a way that they will bear spiritual fruit.

1. "Spiritual fruitfulness is the bearing of fruit for the Spirit" (Galatians 5:22–5), and these fruits are the result: love, joy, peace, patience, kindness, goodness, faithfulness, gentleness, and self-control." (This verse is not from James, but it gives an excellent definition of fruitfulness.)

2. "Therefore, putting aside all filthiness and all that remains of wickedness, in humility receive the word implanted, which is able to save your souls. But prove yourselves doers of the word, and not merely hearers who delude themselves" (James 1:21–2).

3. "Pure and undefiled religion in the sight of our God and Father is this; to visit orphans and widows in their distress, and to keep oneself unstained by the world" (James 1:27).

Galatians

This book was written around AD 50.

Galatians was probably the first of the letters written by Paul to the churches in Galatia around AD 50 after the first missionary journey and after the Jerusalem Conference. Paul visited the churches in Galatia on both his first and third journeys, but there is no record that he was the founder of those congregations. He was warned by the Holy Spirit not to visit them on his second journey (Acts 16:6). The subject matter of this letter parallels the discussion of the Jerusalem Conference where the problem of Judaizing teachers was resolved.

Paul wrote on perversion of the gospel, liberty, faith, the law, sonship, and the spirit of love.

His theme centers on justification by faith for the immediate purpose of countering Judaizing teachers who would insist that Gentiles must be circumcised after the law. His emphasis was on salvation by grace.

1. "Christ redeemed us from the curse of the law, having become a curse for us, for it is written, 'cursed is everyone who hangs on a tree' ... in order that in Christ Jesus the blessing of Abraham might come to the Gentiles so that we would receive the promise of the Spirit through faith" (Galatians 3:13–14).

2. "I have been crucified with Christ; and it is no longer I who live but Christ lives in me; and the life which I now live in the flesh I live by faith in the Son of God, who loved me and gave Himself up for me. I do not nullify the grace of God, for if righteousness comes through the law, then Christ died needlessly" (Galatians 2:20–1).

First Thessalonians

First Thessalonians was written around AD 51.

This Thessalonian letter was written by Paul while he was on his second missionary journey soon after the congregation was established (Acts 16:1–18:22). When violent opposition to the message arose, he was forced to leave the city quickly in the night, but later he sent Timothy back (3:2) to strengthen the young congregation. Inspired by Timothy's report of their love and concern for him, he wrote this letter, which for that reason is more personal than most of his letters. As he anxiously inquires after their welfare we see a softer side of Paul than we usually see. Thessalonians was a city in Macedonia. The letter was written from Corinth.

Paul wrote to the Thessalonians on the subjects of thanksgiving, the second coming as correlated to the message of Acts, spiritual growth, attitudes, sanctification, love, and Christian conduct.

His theme for this letter was the second coming of Christ for the purpose of comforting those who were concerned for their loved ones already deceased.

1. "May the Lord cause you to increase and abound in love for one another, and for all people, just as we also do for you; so that He may establish your hearts without blame in holiness before our God and Father at the coming of our Lord Jesus with all His saints" (1 Thessalonians 3:12–13).

2. "But we do not want you to be uninformed, brethren, about those who are asleep, so that you will not grieve as do the rest who have no hope. For if we believe that Jesus died and rose again, even so God will bring with Him those who have fallen asleep in Jesus. For this we say to you by the word of the Lord, that we who are alive and remain until the coming of the Lord, will not precede those who have fallen asleep. For the Lord Himself will descend from heaven with a shout, with the voice of the archangel and with the trumpet of God, and the dead in Christ will rise first. Then we who are alive and remain will be caught up together with them in the clouds to meet the Lord in the air, and so we shall always be with the Lord. Therefore comfort one another with these words" (1 Thessalonians 4:13–18).

Second Thessalonians

Second Thessalonians was written around AD 51.

This Thessalonian letter was probably written only a matter of weeks after the first letter, which would have been late AD 51. He wrote to clarify misunderstandings that were a result of the first letter. Some thought that the second coming was eminent and felt that their persecution was a sign that the end was near. Paul reminds them that there will be apostasy and lawlessness before the end comes, and he warns against idleness, which creates unrest. Those who think the end is near need to be occupied. Paul visited this congregation twice on his third journey.

In this second letter, Paul wrote about thanksgiving and perseverance, discipline, choice, the man of lawlessness, and encouragement. His emphasis is on maintaining a healthy church

Again, Paul's theme is the second coming, but in addition to offering comfort, he also corrects and confronts those who are idle and who are agitators.

Emphasis: How to maintain a healthy church.

1. "With regard to the coming of our Lord Jesus Christ and our gathering together to Him, that you not be quickly shaken from your composure or be disturbed either by a spirit or a message or a letter as if from us, to the effect that the day of the Lord has come. Let no one in any way deceive you, for it will not come unless the apostasy comes first, and the man of lawlessness is revealed, the son of destruction, who opposes and exalts himself above every so-called god or object of worship, so that he takes his seat in the temple of God, displaying himself as being God" (2 Thessalonians 2:1–4).

2. "Stand firm and hold to the traditions which you were taught, whether by word of mouth or by letter from me" (2 Thessalonians 2:15).

First Corinthians

First Corinthians was written around AD 55.

The church in Corinth was founded on Paul's second missionary journey (Acts 18:1), and this letter was written by him from Ephesus during his three-year stay there (around AD 55) on his third missionary journey. Priscilla and Aquila along with Paul worked together in this very corrupt city of some four hundred thousand people. He had established the church in Corinth on his second journey (Acts 18:1–18), and it had become infected with evil more from the standpoint of the Corinthians' carnal nature than from heresies. The Corinthians were proud of their intellect and their abilities, but their so-called wisdom was leading them astray. Paul writes in response to information he received from members of Chloe's family that there were divisions among them. He defends his apostleship and admonishes in grief and indignation over the unspiritual, immoral condition of the church in this pagan city. In spite of their corruption, Paul calls them brethren and saints (MacArthur, 1561–3).

In this letter Paul wrote of unity, wisdom, dependence on the Spirit, spiritual growth, stewards, immorality, arrogance, lawsuits, marriage, and liberty, comparison to Israel, overconfidence, orderliness, the Lord's Supper, spiritual gifts, and the importance of love and the resurrection.

Paul's theme for 1 Corinthians centers on purification of the church, emphasizing correction of behavior by instilling foundational truths that will promote spiritually.

Purpose: Paul's purpose was to promote foundational truths in order to have godly behavior.

1. "Flee immorality. Every other sin that a man commits is outside the body, but the immoral man sins against his own body. Or do you not know that your body is a temple of the Holy Spirit who is in you, whom you have from God, and that you are not your own? For you have been bought with a price therefore glorify God in your body" (1 Corinthians 6:18–19).

2. "Therefore, consider the members of your earthly body as dead to immorality, impurity, passion, evil desire, and greed, which amounts to idolatry. For it is because of these things that the wrath of God will come upon the sons of disobedience and in them you also once walked, when you were living in them. But now you also, put them all aside: anger, wrath, malice, slander, and abusive speech from your mouth. Do not lie to one another, since you laid aside the old self with its evil practices, and have put on the new self who is being renewed to a true knowledge according to the image of the one who created him" (Colossians 3:5–10).

Second Corinthians

Second Corinthians was written about AD 56.

This Corinthian letter was written from Macedonia within a year of the last letter. Paul had left Ephesus after a confrontation with Demetrius and the silversmiths (Acts 19:23–41), and probably because he was also anxious to hear from Titus about how the Corinthians had received his letter. Not finding Titus at Troas, he went on to Macedonia, where Titus joined him. This letter is a very personal one in which the apostle opens his heart in regard to his ministry, his motives, his spiritual passion, and his love for the church. Troubled by those who would discredit him, he again defends his apostleship against those who would undermine his work on the grounds that he was not one of the twelve.

In this second letter to the Corinthians Paul wrote in regard to the new covenant, his ministry and integrity, the temporal versus the eternal, fellowship of brothers in Christ, generosity, the inner man, his vision, and self-examination.

Paul's theme for this letter is defense of his apostleship. He also expresses his fulfillment in them and in the ministry.

1. "We are ambassadors for Christ, as though God were making an appeal through us; we beg you on behalf of Christ, be reconciled to God. He made Him who knew no sin to be sin on our behalf, so that we might become the righteousness of God in Him" (2 Corinthians 5:20–1).

2. "For the ministry of this service is not only fully supplying the needs of the saints, but is also overflowing through many thanksgivings to God. Because of the proof given by this ministry, they will glorify God for your obedience your confession of the gospel of Christ and for the liberality of your contribution to them and to all, while they also, by prayer on your behalf, yearn for you because of the surpassing grace of God in you. Thanks be to God for His indescribable gift" (2 Corinthians 9:12–15).

Romans

Romans was written around AD 56.

Romans was written by Paul from Corinth during his three-month stay there after he left Macedonia (2 Corinthians 13:1 and Acts 20:2–3). He expressed his desire to visit the brethren in Rome, but he felt he had to go first to Jerusalem partly to deliver the relief funds for the poor that were being sent from Macedonia and Achaia (15:23–28).

Perhaps in an effort to establish his credentials before he came to them, he explained his understanding of the gospel in comparison to the Law of Moses and gave practical applications from it for transforming one's life. It was about AD 58, and he was planning to sail soon for Syria, which would end this third missionary journey. Instead he learned of a plot against his life and returned by land to Macedonia, where he sailed for Troas from Philippi (Acts 20:3–6). Then he made his way down the coast of Asia and across the Mediterranean Sea to Tyre and eventually found his way to Jerusalem.

To the Romans Paul writes of unbelief and its consequences, the impartiality of God, the universal guilt of sin, justification by faith, the evidence of justification by faith in the Old Testament, the results of justification, the conflict of two natures (carnal and spiritual), grace, deliverance from the bondage of sin and victory in Christ, Israel as children are physical descendants, and Israel as heirs of the promise are spiritual descendants, knowledge, government, conscience, self-denial, love, and unity.

Paul stayed for seven days in Troas, where he preached on the first day the week until daybreak. From there he walked to Assos, where he met Luke, and together, they sailed to Miletus, which was some miles south of Ephesus. He had bypassed Ephesus, not wanting to spend time in Asia because he had taken a vow to be in Jerusalem for Passover. However, he sent for the elders of the churches in Ephesus and asked them to come to him so that he could bid them farewell, knowing that he would not see them again (Acts 20:16–38). Finally they sailed for Tyre, where Paul was warned he would be arrested in Jerusalem. After seven days at Tyre he left for Caesarea, where he was again warned about what awaited him.

In Jerusalem he gave his report to the brethren, took a vow of purification, and went to the temple, from where he was dragged and beaten by local Jews who had been stirred up by men from Asia. The Asians, angry over his work in Ephesus, had followed him with the intent of creating trouble. He was arrested, taken before the Sanhedrin, informed by God that he would witness in Rome, made his defense before Felix in Caesarea, and was imprisoned for two years. During that time Felix was replaced by Festus, who sought to try him in Jerusalem in order to please the Jews. On the basis of his Roman citizenship Paul appealed to Caesar, made his defense to the visiting King Agrippa, and was sent to Rome.

Paul's theme is God's righteousness. He approaches it by emphasizing justification by grace through faith. His purpose is to teach the truths of the gospel of grace to those who had never before received apostolic instruction.

1. With respect to the promise of God, he (Abraham) did not waver in unbelief, but grew strong in faith, giving glory to God, and

being fully assured that what God had promised, He was able also to perform. Therefore it was also credited to him as righteousness" (Romans 4:20–1).

2. "But now apart from the law the righteousness of God has been manifested, being witnessed by the law and the prophets, even the righteousness of God through faith in Jesus Christ for all those who believe; for there is no distinction; for all have sinned and fall short of the glory of God, being justified as a gift by His grace through the redemption which is in Christ Jesus" (Romans 3:21–4).

Colossians

Colossians was written about AD 60–62.

Colossians was written from a prison in Rome (Acts 28:16–31), where Paul was awaiting his hearing before Caesar. After two years in jail in Caesarea Paul as a Roman citizen exercised his right to make an appeal to Caesar, and he was put aboard a ship for Rome (Acts 24–6). The church in Colosse was started during Paul's three-year ministry at Ephesus (Acts 19), but it was not started by Paul. Epaphras, a member of the Colossian church, went to Rome to consult with Paul regarding the heresy that was overtaking the congregation. It is one of Paul's four prison letters.

Paul warns the Colossian church against trusting in worldly wisdom, angel worship, and asceticism and instructs concerning purity, the family, relationships, and knowledge according to divine wisdom. Paul's theme is the deity of Christ for the purpose of correcting doctrinal errors. His emphasis is on Christ, the head of the church.

1. "And He is the head of the body, the church" (Colossians 1:18), "holding fast to the head, from whom the entire body, being supplied and held together by the joints and ligaments, grows with a growth which is from God" (Colossians 2:19).

2. "Instead, speaking in truth, we are to grow up in all aspects into Him who is the head, even Christ from whom the whole body, being fitted and held together by what every joint supplies, according to the proper working of each individual part, causes the growth of the body for the building up of itself in love" (Ephesians 4:15–16).

Philemon

Philemon was written around AD 60–62.

Philemon is a personal letter from Paul to a well-to-do Christian in the congregation at Colosse, and it could have been sent by the same messenger. The letter is written on behalf of Onesimus, Philemon's slave who had fled to Rome, where he came in contact with Paul and became a Christian. Paul calls him a faithful and beloved brother (Colossians 4:9) and would have preferred to keep him but felt it his duty to return him to Philemon, his master (Philemon 12–14). He asks Philemon to forgive and restore Onesimus as a brother (Philemon 15–18).

Paul's advice reflects God's example toward all men regardless of race or status. It is interesting to note that the early Christians were not commanded to release their slaves but to treat them as brothers. That covers a lot of territory. Would you force a brother to stay if he wished to leave? On the other hand, would he want to leave if he were treated as a brother? Of course circumstances create their own necessities, and two brothers would be aware of those necessities and work them out between them. There is no shame in being a worker; the shame comes from the ignorance of those who mistreat others. As Christians we are to be in subjection to each other, which simply means we are under obligation to think of others before we think of ourselves.

Paul returns the slave Onesimus and pleads for forgiveness for him for running away from his master. He reminds the owner that they are both Christians and that he must treat him as a brother Emphasis is focused on the spiritual qualities of master and slave.

1. "I appeal to you for my child Onesimus, whom I have begotten in my imprisonment … perhaps he was for this reason separated from you for awhile that you would have him back forever, no longer as a slave, but more than a slave, a beloved brother" (Philemon 1:10–16).

2. "If he has wronged you in any way or owes you anything, charge that to my account" (Philemon 1:18).

Ephesians

Ephesians was written in. AD 60–62.

Ephesians is a third prison letter written at the same time as Colossians and Philemon, and it was carried by Tychicus to their destinations. There is some indication that this letter was meant as a general letter not to be addressed to any specific congregation, as the words *at Ephesus* in the salutation are missing from the best manuscripts. Colossians 4:16 indicates that Paul had previously written to the Laodiceans, and it's possible that this letter is the one referred to. If so, the salutation would read appropriately without the words *at Ephesus*. Certainly the truths that are presented are universally applicable, yet the letter doesn't address problems of a specific congregation as Paul's other letters do.

Paul gets right into it with the Ephesians, reminding them of how blessed they are from the message of redemption. They were dead, he says, with no knowledge of God, but now they are alive. He talks with them about the mystery hidden for years that has now been administered through him ... and of his thankfulness to God that they are now rooted in faith and love. He speaks of unity, one body, one Spirit, one hope, one Lord, one faith, one baptism, one God and Father of all. He speaks of the grace given to each and the ability that grace provides that each in his own way has a way to encourage and build up God's church, thus enriching and encouraging all in the daily walk with God. And then he teaches people about marriage and its similarity to the church and family relationships.

The theme of Ephesians is the church, Christ's body and the Holy Spirit its lifeblood. It was written for the purpose of encouragement and admonition with emphasis on the blessings in Christ.

1. "Blessed be the God and Father of our Lord Jesus Christ, who has blessed us with every spiritual blessing in the heavenly places in Christ" (Ephesians 1:3).

2. "In Him we have redemption through His blood, the forgiveness of our trespasses, according to the riches of his grace which He lavished on us" (Ephesians 1:7–8).

Philippians

Philippians was probably written about AD 61.

Philippians is the final letter of the so-called prison letters. During the time of these four letters Paul had been under house arrest, but he was more or less free to come and go. His letter to the Philippians is a spiritual love letter to acknowledge their gift of money brought to him by Epaphroditus, who became ill after he joined Paul and was sent back to Philippi with this letter of love. The church at Philippi had a very small beginning with Lydia and the Philippian jailer and his family as the first converts, (Acts 16:12–34). Founded by Paul on his second missionary journey, it was now well established, having both elders and deacons. However, it appears to be having internal problems regarding Judaizing teachers and strife between members. Nevertheless it was a congregation very close to Paul's heart. On his third journey he was in Philippi twice, bringing his total visits there to three.

In Philippi Paul gives thanks for their fellowship and prays for their development and ability to discern real knowledge in order to recognize the things of God. The NAS uses the term *sincere*, (Philippians 1:10) which was a term used by actors and artists in the first century. If a performance, a portrait, or a sculpture was so perfect that it seemed like an exact replica, it was said to be sincere. Paul is admonishing the Philippian brethren to be filled with the fruits of righteousness, thus attaining the glory of Jesus Christ to His glory and praise, and in so doing achieve that quality of being sincere. He tells them to beware of false teachers, to think on excellence, to rejoice in the Lord, to be anxious for nothing, and to be prayerful. Further, he says people should dwell on things that are true, honorable, right, pure, lovely, of good report, excellent, things worthy of praise, and the peace of God would then guard their hearts and minds.

There is no evidence that upon arrival in Rome Paul's case was heard in any court. We know that he had his own living quarters with a very light guard and that he was free to have guests, a situation that allowed him to continue preaching and teaching. We also know that within three days of his arrival, he invited the Jewish leaders to visit and that he had some converts as he proclaimed to them the good news regarding Jesus Christ (Acts 28:17–31). For two years he continued in this fashion until he apparently was released for at least a year, probably longer, during which time he traveled and continued to preach and teach.

The theme of Philippians is encouragement through spiritual goals. His purpose in writing is to thank them for their gift of money, and his emphasis is Jesus Christ.

1. "Have this attitude in yourselves which was also in Christ Jesus, who, although He existed in the form of God, did not regard equality with God a thing to be grasped, but emptied Himself,

taking the form of a bond-servant, being made in the likeness of men. Being found in appearance as a man, He humbled Himself by becoming obedient to the point of death, even death on a cross" (Philippians 2:5–8).

2. "But one thing I do: forgetting what lies behind and reaching forward to what lies ahead, I press on toward the goal for the prize of the upward call of God in Christ Jesus" (Philippians 3:13–14).

The Letters: From Paul's Release to Revelation

There has been a lot of speculation about where Paul may have traveled during this period of release before he was rearrested and returned to Rome. The only scriptural evidence is in two of his later letters in which he makes reference to incidents that could not have occurred on his previous journeys. By piecing those passages together, it would seem that Paul traveled from Rome to Crete, where he left Titus to set things in order in the congregations there and to "appoint elders in every city" (Titus 1:5). On his way to Macedonia he stopped at Miletus to leave Trophimus, who was sick, (2 Timothy 4:19–22), left Timothy in Ephesus to instruct regarding false teachers, (1 Timothy 1:3–11), and stopped at Troas, where he left a cloak with Carpus (2 Timothy 4:9–13).

First Timothy

First Timothy was written around AD 62–64.

This book was written by Paul to Timothy, his "true child in the faith" (1 Timothy 1:2). Timothy was the son of a Greek father and a devout Jewish mother. He joined Paul on his second missionary journey, and he was with him in Corinth, Macedonia, Ephesus, and Jerusalem. The letter was probably written from Macedonia (1 Timothy 1:3) after Paul's release from prison in Rome about AD 64.

In this letter Paul deals with public worship and private instruction on proper conduct, using the tone of a father instructing a son. He covers personal conduct as it applies to godly living for older men, older women as examples and guides to young women, young men as maturing and sensible adults, and people steadfast in purity. Let all be obedient to those who have the rule over you. He encourages the pursuit of righteousness, godliness, faith, love, perseverance, and gentleness, and he also gives the qualifications for those who will serve as elders.

The theme of this book is organization and conduct, and the purpose is to give authoritative guidance in regard to church order with emphasis on sound doctrine,

1. "I urged you … to remain on at Ephesus so that you may instruct certain men not to teach strange doctrines, nor to pay attention to myths and endless genealogies, which give rise to mere speculation rather than furthering the administration of God which is by faith" (1 Timothy 1:3–4).

2. "O Timothy, guard what has been entrusted to you, avoiding worldly and empty chatter and the opposing arguments of what is falsely called knowledge" (1 Timothy 6:20).

Titus

Titus was written about AD 65.

Titus was written by Paul, who had left him on the Island of Crete to strengthen the church work there. He was evidently a reliable, responsible helper who had been Paul's messenger to Corinth (2 Corinthians 8:16–24), a companion to Paul and Barnabas to Jerusalem (Galatians 2:1), with Paul in Rome during the imprisonment (2 Timothy 4:10), a Gentile (Galatians 2:3), and a beloved friend and partner (2 Corinthians 2:13 and 8:23). In the letter he states that he plans to leave shortly for Nicopolis (on the western coast of Greece), and hopes that Titus will meet him there (Titus 3:12).

Both Titus and 1 Timothy give the fullest teaching available on the qualifications of elders and deacons. In addition Paul teaches regarding duties of both older and younger men and women as well as slaves. All are to be subject to rulers, and all are to subject themselves to godly living, for the kindness of God did not save us because of our righteous deeds but according to mercy.

The theme is church organization and discipline for the purpose of serving as a guide for Titus in his work at Crete as the congregation is set in order. Emphasis is on good works.

1. "Remind them to be subject to rulers, to authorities, to be obedient, to be ready for every good deed, to malign on one, to be peaceable, gentle, showing every consideration for all men" (Titus 3:1–2).

2. "Avoid foolish controversies and genealogies and strife and disputes about the law, for they are unprofitable and worthless" (Titus 3:9).

First Peter

First Peter was written around AD 64–65.

Peter to the exiles of the dispersion throughout Asia Minor. After the Jerusalem Conference, Peter wasn't mentioned, but there is evidence in his writings that he was familiar with Paul's letters. They had worked with some of the same people, such as Silas and John Mark, and their paths had probably crossed. He sends this message of encouragement and admonition to the churches largely founded by Paul. Dated about AD 62–64, it was written from *Babylon* (1 Peter 5:13), which is thought to be a pseudonym for Rome.

The early Peter, the one who was impulsive and full of weaknesses, did not write this letter, but rather it was the man who had been strengthened by years of sufferings and trials, the Peter who wept in shame after he denied His Lord and later witnessed the crucifixion—that's who wrote this letter. This seasoned Peter could write to the dispersion about suffering and victory with knowledge and empathy. He talks about the foreknowledge of God and refers to Christ as our living hope and sure salvation, and he urges that the mind be fixed on Him in obedience, which purifies the soul for a sincere love of the brethren. Such love is *born again* and is not perishable because it is of and through the enduring love of God. As newborn babes we put away malice, deceit, hypocrisy, envy, and slander and long instead for the pure milk of the Word. He describes us as *living stones*, a royal priesthood, submissive in all things, an example of Godliness, fervent in love, willing servants, sharing in the suffering of Christ. This is the Peter who asked to be crucified upside down because he wasn't worthy to die as our Lord had died.

Peter's theme is submission and suffering for the purpose of living victoriously in the face of persecution. His emphasis is sound doctrine and good works.

1. "It is better, if God should will it so that you suffer for doing what is right rather than for doing what is wrong. For Christ also died for sins once for all, the just for the unjust, so that He brings us to God" (1 Peter 3:17).

2. "Therefore humble yourselves under the mighty hand of God, that he may exalt you at the proper time, casting all your anxiety on Him, because He cares for you" (1 Peter 5:6–7).

Second Peter

Second Peter was written around AD 67.

Second Peter is not written to a specific person or congregation but to all Christians. It is traditionally believed that the letter was written from Rome shortly before his death. He knew his life was almost over, and he predicted his coming death (2 Peter 1:14). In Rome he was martyred by crucifixion, head downward. Tradition says that he was put to death on the same day as Paul.

Similar to Paul's letters to the Thessalonians in regard to the second coming, Peter also warns against corruption and false teachers, exhorts to spiritual diligence, and refers to the validity of Old Testament prophecy.

Peter's theme here is a denunciation of heresy whether in doctrine or in life, and he is probably saying this must be done by exposing false teachers. His emphasis is on true spiritual knowledge.

1. "He has granted to us His precious and magnificent promises, so that by them you may become partakers of the divine nature, having escaped the corruption that is in the world by lust. Now for this very reason, also, applying all diligence, in your faith supply moral excellence, knowledge, and in your knowledge, self-control, and in your self-control, perseverance, and in your perseverance, godliness, and in your godliness, brotherly kindness, and in your brotherly kindness, love, For if these qualities are yours and are increasing, they render you neither useless nor unfruitful in the true knowledge of our Lord Jesus Christ" (2 Peter 1:4–8).

2. "But the day of the Lord will come like a thief, in which the heavens will pass away with a roar and the elements will be destroyed with intense heat, and the earth and its works will be burned up" (2 Peter 3:10).

Second Timothy

Second Timothy was written about AD 67.

This was the last of Paul's letters from Rome, and it was written toward the end of Nero's reign (AD 54–68). Paul was evidently arrested, possibly from Nicopolis, Greece, if he made it that far, where he had intended to spend the winter after his letter to Titus. He was then returned to Rome under sentence of death (2 Timothy 4:6). This imprisonment did not resemble the first. Instead he was under close confinement. He was difficult for his friends to find (2 Timothy 1:16–17). He had been deserted by those in Asia Minor (2 Timothy 1:15) and by others as he attempted to make his legal defense (2 Timothy 4:16). Some of his companions were sent away on specific errands, and only Luke remained with him (2 Timothy 4:11). This far more personal letter asks Timothy to bring him his cloak, which he left in Troas, his books, and parchment and together with Mark to come quickly (2 Timothy 1:3–5). Despite the feeling of urgency one gets from this reading, it isn't known if Timothy and Mark made it to Rome in time to see Paul before he was martyred by beheading.

Paul's final letter addressed to Timothy sounds to me like a father confiding in and encouraging his beloved son. It's like he is saying to Timothy, Be strong. Things do not always go as they should or as you would like them to. Don't be ashamed of the gospel. I suffer here in prison as a criminal, but the Word isn't imprisoned. Don't become engaged in foolish conversations as they produce quarrels. Preach the word, follow what you have been taught, and be ready. I so wish I could see you again. Only Luke remains with me. All have deserted me. I feel Paul's sadness, but I don't believe it was for himself. It is more likely that he grieved that some had fallen away.

Paul's theme for this last letter of his life is equally depressing for us because we know that he knows his life is finished and he "so wants to see Timothy one more time." Somehow I can't see Paul down because he is alone or almost alone, having been deserted by some. I think he is down because of the souls that have left their first loves and are in danger. He also talks about the coming apostasy and gives final instructions and encouragement. Yes, he would be down about the safety of his 'children.'

His purpose in writing was to ask Timothy "to come quickly" and to urge him one last time "to be steadfast."

1. "Be diligent to present yourself approved to God as workman who does not need to be ashamed, accurately handling the word of truth" (2 Timothy 2:15).

2. "All scripture is inspired by God and profitable for teaching, for reproof, for correction, for training in righteousness; so that the man of God may be adequate, equipped for every good work" (2 Timothy 3:16).

Jude

Jude was written about AD 67.

He also was a brother of our Lord and wrote this letter to a general audience about AD 67–68. There is little that is known about Jude except that he became a follower after the resurrection (Acts 1:14).

False teachers had become such a problem in the church that Jude writes this severe letter of warning on how to avoid them, using Old Testament writings to remind his readers of God's judgment against the ungodly. Jude is similar to 2 Peter in its warnings against false teachers. His is the only gospel devoted exclusively to confronting apostasy.

Jude's chosen theme is the godlessness of false teachers. His purpose is to warn that apostasy leads to sinful living, and his emphasis is to hold fast to faith.

1. "But you, beloved, ought to remember the words that were spoken beforehand by the apostles of our Lord Jesus Christ, that they were saying to you, "in the last time there will be mockers, following after their own ungodly lusts." These are the ones who cause divisions, worldly-minded, devoid of the Spirit" (Jude 1:17–19).

2. "But you, beloved, building yourselves up on your most holy faith, praying in the Holy Spirit, keep yourselves in the love of God, waiting anxiously for the mercy of our Lord Jesus Christ to eternal life" (Jude 1:20–1).

Hebrews

Because Hebrews was written about AD 68, it is possible that some of the readers of the book were second-generation Christians. The destruction of Jerusalem would take place in about two years (AD 70) during the reign of Vespasian (AD 69–79).

From a Jewish perspective Hebrews is a defense of the Christian faith to those who would waver, in which the blessings of the new covenant are compared to the inadequacies of the old covenant. It is a logical, systematic message of the superiority of Christ over angels, Moses, Aaron, the old covenant, the sacrifices of bulls and goats, and the legalism of the law. It is an exhortation to Christian duty. The author is unknown.

The theme of this magnificent book is the superiority of Christ and the new covenant, and its purpose is to confirm those who are in the faith, warn and exhort those who waver, with emphasis on steadfastness by holding fast and pressing on.

1. "Therefore, He had to be made like His brethren in all things, so that He might become a merciful and faithful high priest in things pertaining to God, to make propitiation for the sins of the people, For since He Himself was tempted in that which He has suffered, He is able to come to the aid of those who are tempted" (Hebrews 2:17–18).

2. "Therefore, let us draw near with confidence to the throne of grace, so that we may receive mercy and find grace to help in time of need" (Hebrews 4:16).

First John

First John was probably written from Ephesus by the apostle John toward the end of the first century. Whether he wrote it before or after his prison sentence on the Isle of Patmos is unknown. I would guess the letter came before this event from the sheer amount of writing he did on Patmos (the Revelation letter), and many are fairly certain he wrote the gospel of John after he was released in AD 96. It seems to be a general exhortation to live in a godly manner. It is the most intimate of the letters and treats sin as a family matter that has been taken care of at the cross by Jesus, who is now our advocate with the Father. Whereas Paul deals with our relationship to the Father as rightful sons, John deals with it as an intimate nearness with beloved children. He exhorts us to live lives befitting true believers, lives made evident by mutual love, godly lives, and obedience. This is a deeply spiritual letter.

John's theme is to reassure Christians in their love. His purpose was to warn against false teachers, specifically the Antichrist. His emphasis is on faith and love, which will overcome the principles of an evil world.

1. "If we confess our sins, He is faithful and just to forgive us our sins and to cleanse us from all unrighteousness" (1 John 1:9).

2. "And this commandment we have from Him: that he who loves God must love his brother also" (1 John 4:21).

Second John

This letter from John was written near the same time as the first and appears to be a summary of his general letter with a personal note at the end. It is somewhat more personal in nature and has occasioned discussion because it is addressed to the chosen lady and her children. It isn't known if this was an individual or if the term is symbolic for the first century churches. In this short letter he identifies the Antichrist again, and in verse 7 he warns against those who don't accept the incarnation of Jesus.

John chooses as his theme the truth in relationship to Christian living. He warns against false teachers and emphasizes love.

1. "This is love that we walk according to His commandments. This is the commandment, that as you have heard from the beginning, you should walk in it" (2 John 6).

2. "For many deceivers have gone out into the world who do not confess Jesus Christ as coming in the flesh. This is a deceiver and an Antichrist" (2 John 7).

Third John

This book of John seems to have been written at the same time as 2 John, and it is addressed to an individual named Gaius, who was apparently a leader in the church, possibly the church to which the second letter was addressed.

He is commended for his hospitality and the fact that he walks in the truth. It demonstrates concern for the individual and Christian relationships. These three letters show that John was actively writing in his advanced age at Ephesus.

John uses the same theme as in 2 John, the truth in relationship to Christian living. It's purpose is an exhortation to a church leader with emphasis on good works.

1. "Beloved, do not imitate what is evil, but what is good. He who does good is of God, but he who does evil has not seen God" (3 John 11).

2. "Beloved, I pray that you may prosper in all things and be in health, just as your soul prospers" (3 John 2).

Summary

Jewish Christians were scattered by Roman persecution, burdened by the weight of misunderstandings regarding the law, unsure of their responsibilities as fledgling Christians, and harassed on every side by false teachers, and yet they were in possession of that most precious gift, the good news that the Messiah had indeed come. These twenty-one letters witness to that event in a powerful way. Not only was the young church able to continue its expansion, but these letters also provided definitive guidance for daily living both then and now.

As these letters end John is the only apostle still alive.

Study Guide—Chapter 18

Q. Name at least two reasons James is known as a practical book of knowledge.
A. The book of James is known for its moral and ethical teaching. James style reflects the Lord's teaching, similar especially to the Sermon on the Mount, but it also reminds me of Proverbs with its terse terminology.

Q. What two books are considered to be companion volumes because of their salvation by grace and justification by faith?
A. Of course, both books are written by Paul, and their subject matter almost of necessity weave in and out creating a whole. Paul writes masterfully regarding salvation by grace alone but doesn't neglect to point out then the *how* by which it works is through faith. In Galatians Paul defends the doctrine of justification by faith both theologically and in practicality.

Q. What three letters deal with the second coming?
A. The books of 1 and 2 Thessalonians and 2 Peter deal with the second coming of the Lord.

Q. What is the main subject of 1 Corinthians?
A. The Corinthian church was a mess, but I want you to note that Paul still called them *brethren* and ends by saying, "My love be with you all." He talks with them about division between them and moral conduct.

Q. What four letters by Paul were written from Rome during his imprisonment?
A. During his imprisonment in Rome Paul wrote Colossians, Philemon, Ephesians, and Philippians. You would think he would be the recipient of letters of encouragement. Paul was quite a warrior for Christ.

Q. Which letter deals principally with the church as the body of Christ?
A. This is the book of Ephesians. Paul encourages them to use their spiritual blessings.

Q. Which two books deal with church organization and conduct?
A. When Paul dropped Titus and Timothy off at the Island of Crete and at Ephesus respectively, he charged them with "setting in order what remains," which sounds as if they were having some rough times.

Q. Who wrote about suffering and victory to the dispersion, and in which book?
A. Peter wrote to those who were "scattered throughout Asia" to remind them of the blessings they had in Christ, their responsibilities as Christians, of growing in faith, and of godly living.

Q. Both Peter and Paul wrote letters predicting their deaths. Name them.

A. These two books are great examples of devotion and perseverance. Both letters are the second ones of the same name, 2 Peter and 2 Paul. Tradition says they died on the same day in Rome, but I've found no concrete evidence. It must have been devastating to the still-fledgling church scattered all over.

Q. Which book compares the blessings of the new covenant to the old?

A. This is the incredible book of Hebrews. It is said that the author of Hebrews is unknown, but I have recently learned that this is not necessarily true. Early Christians believed it to be Paul, but the reigning bishop at the time wouldn't allow it to be said for what reason I'm not sure. It wasn't until the time of Origen (early church writer) that the *truth* was revealed (Eusebius: Maier 2007).[51] Origen's statement is as follows: "If any church, then, regards this epistle as Paul's it should be commended , since men of old had good reason to hand it down as his." However, "traditions reaching us claim it was either Clement, Bishop of Rome, or Luke, who wrote the gospel and Acts."

Q. Which apostle lived to the close of the first century?

A. The apostle John wrote his gospel in Ephesus after he was released from the Isle of Patmos in AD 96 by Nerva, the emperor who followed Domitian, who had been assassinated. Tradition says he lived to be one hundred.

Q. How does Paul see our relationship with the Father? How does John's differ?

A. Paul speaks of our relationship to the Father as rightful heirs; whereas John sees us as beloved sons.

---

51   Eusebius: Maier, copyright 2007 by Paul Maier, *Origen's Commentaries at Alexandria*, (on Holy Scripture), Book 6, Homilies on the Epistle to the Hebrews.

Chapter 19: The Final Prophecy. The Outward Struggle

⟨ornament⟩

The final prophecy deals with the book of Revelation. We will examine the book somewhat differently than the previous books of the Bible because it is written in apocalyptic language, a word not too familiar to us today but not unusual in the first century from about 200 BC to AD 200. It is a Greek word meaning *revelation* or *to unveil* (Nelson 1995).[52] Either definition refers to something that is hidden from view or understanding, something that will be revealed.

Revelation is rich in symbols and at times is difficult to understand, but its value to us is great if for no other reason than it is the last prophetic word received from our God. Think back on how many times His method of communication had to change as the world's population increased. The communication He has with us in this age is much more complete than any that has gone before because His rules under this covenant teach the inner man and involve the heart in preparation for spiritual growth. This is just one of the results made possible by the foundation He has provided for His church. When He says, "Come unto me all you who labor and are heavy laden, for my yoke is easy and my burden is light" (Matthew 11:30), He speaks to each of us not only with the tender love of a Creator for his created image but with a compassionate longing for a quality of fellowship only He is able to envision. In the process He shows us the way of eternal life and the ways to avoid the pitfalls that wait for us along the way to salvation.

There is also the understandable fact that because of its apocalyptic content, one must take a lot into consideration in order to obtain its continuity and the significance for what come before. Therefore I have provided two chapters that are divided by what I call the outward and the inward struggles. The outward struggle will deal with Satan's attempts to

---

52   Eusebius: Maier, Paul L., *The Church History*, Copyright 1999, 2007, Published by Kregel Publications. a division of Kregel Inc., Grand Rapids, MI, Book 3:18-20.

gain supremacy over God as he reached for control and dominance. Of course man was used in whatever evil manner he could devise, but the conflict was between God and Satan. The inward struggle refers to the personal battle each of us has in making the choices that enable or defeat him. That struggle takes place in the inner recesses of the mind and the heart, but it is manifest in the lives we lead.

Everyone seems to have a different method of interpretation for Revelation. My method begins with the idea that God had a reason for warning first-century Christians of danger. Therefore He counted on the fact that they would understand the message. Secondly in the same way that the Bible is a continuous revelation of truths that are interconnected, the apocalyptic message is also continuous and connected. Thirdly, you should look for God's identification of signs and symbols (Revelation 1:20). Fourth you must keep your mind in the realm of common-sense answers that apply without visitations from Mars or any kind of speculation. This brings us to the most important point. Understand that this message just like all the prophecies of old had a near interpretation and a far interpretation. A part of it would unfold soon, but the other enactment would not come until the end of time.

The book of Revelation was given to the apostle John about AD 95. He was in exile on the Island of Patmos and was *in the Spirit* on the Lord's day. I would say that this phrase means he was worshipping by focusing his mind and his heart on the Lord.

According to (Eusebius: Maier 2007)[53] John was taken to Patmos in the fourteenth year of Domitian's rule, which would have been AD 95, and he was later released by Emperor Nerva, who followed in succession after the assassination of Domitian (AD 81–96). John went back to Ephesus from where he continued His participation in serving the Lord until his death. It is thought that he died peacefully in Ephesus around AD 98–100. Before his death in Ephesus he wrote the gospel of John. The apostolic age came to a close with his death.

Revelation is in stark contrast to Genesis, where we saw both the beauty of creation and the triumph of Satan as sin was introduced into the world. In a very real way Revelation completes Genesis by showing the restored relationship between God and man, by revealing the tragedy of sin, and by promising that man will once again eat of the tree of life

---

53   Eusebius: Maier, Paul L., *The Church History, Copyright 2007*, Kregel Publiications, a division of Kregel, Inc., Grand Rapids, MI, Book 3:18-20.

and thereby have eternal life. In prophetic scenes from the final judgment Revelation shows us the conclusion of the dilemma of sin, at which time Satan and his helpers will be cast into the pit to be tormented forever (Revelation 20:10).

But what does Revelation have for us now? It is so much more than just a look at the final judgment. It was given to show God's people through John how to overcome the struggle against sin and the power of persecution. To overcome is almost a unique phrase to Revelation. It is used in all three time frames of the story, and in a way it is the theme. I call it a story because it has all the criteria of a mystery, the diverse characters, good and evil, a stage that begins small and escalates to include the world, as well as a few isolated scenes that originate in heaven. It has suspense, drama, and pathos, but don't ever lose sight of the fact that this is God's Word. His Word is never spoken lightly. The Israelite nation learned over and over that when God says it will happen, it happens.

The revelation as given to John is God's final prophetic word to man. He communicates with us now through His Son's teaching as recorded in written Scripture. Revelation is given in symbols, probably to protect those of the first century who might be found with it in their possession. Nevertheless, it had an urgent meaning (Revelation 1:1). Persecution, already a presence in the lives of Christians, was about to increase. Let me change that verb from *had* to *has*. It still has urgent meaning because we don't know when our day of reckoning will come or when the end of time will occur. The only solution is to be prepared. That the message was shown should add to its urgency in this generation, but as the years have passed, the immediacy of its import seems to have ebbed away, if not become totally lost.

As we look at the connection between the past fulfillment of this prophecy and the future fulfillment we will begin with a few words about Rome and her emperors.

Rome

Rome ruled most of the known world in the first century, and because of Rome's influence, it was a world of degradation and immorality. To degrade and be degraded was the motto within the ruling classes, which included all of the emperors in the Caesar Dynasty with the exception of the first Caesar, Augustus. Debauchery, murder, incest, and sadism were favorites of these rulers, which perhaps helps to explain some of their passion for persecution. As one emperor after another fell to the assassin's blade or to poisoning or strangling, commonly at the hand of a wife, brother, daughter, son, or mother, you are able to get the picture of the disease that surrounded the Christians of the first century.

With each new ruler, debauchery increased, and eventually, the citizens became involved, if not as participants, then as helpers who provided the many needs of a people who demanded any luxury life could provide. Read Revelation 18:9–24 to get an idea of the workers who did participate out of choice or out of economic necessity and who would be left adrift when the empire was no more. One gets the idea that even joyous occasions were hampered as ordinary production was affected by the oppressive days that followed.

In addition to the immorality of this nation there were other considerations that spread over the entire realm. Rome oppressed the world she should have served and deceived people, and perhaps the most immediate consideration was that she killed the saints.

The Book

Revelation begins with a prologue from God (Revelation 1:1–3). The prologue is important in the way that a seal on a letter is important. In it John identifies himself and brings greetings sent from the Father, the seven Spirits who are before His throne, and from the resurrected Jesus Christ (Revelation 1:1–8).The Father is the architect of this mission (as He was present in creation, and He was in the creation of the plan for reconciliation and salvation), and the task of implementation was given to Jesus, who is identified as the faithful witness, the firstborn of the dead, the one who gave His blood as sacrifice for our sins, the one who made us a kingdom of priests, the one who will come for us in the clouds.

These descriptions connect Jesus to both His past and future by the functions for which He is known; this is His identification to those who will welcome John and His message.

The first of seven beatitudes is announced. (Beatitude is a word that means *blessed*.) Those who *hear and heed* the warning will be blessed. The seven spirits around the throne are probably the same spirits mentioned in Isaiah 11:1–5, which describes the way in which Jesus will judge the world.

Vision One (Revelation 1)

This vision was received on Patmos. When John sees Jesus, he falls down before Him. Jesus identified Himself and gave him these instructions (Revelation 1:19):

1.   Write the things which you have seen.

2.   Write the things which are.

3.   Write the things which will take place after these things.

Jesus also said to John, "I have the keys of death and of Hades" (Revelation 1:18). This is so important for John to know because death had belonged to Satan. Jesus is telling him that the resurrection broke Satan's authority over death, and the power of death is again in God's hands.

Vision Two (Revelation 2–3)

Revelation 2 and 3 deal with the letters to the congregations, which set the stage for the rest of the book. Each letter follows an identical format. Each has a salutation, identification of the person who wrote the letter, a commendation (if possible), a condemnation (if necessary), a warning, an exhortation, and a promise.

Vision Three (Revelation 4)

John looked up and saw a door standing open in heaven. A voice spoke with instructions to come up, and he would be shown the things that "must take place," (Revelation 4:1). John indicates that he did not go bodily to heaven, but "in the Spirit" (Revelation 4:2).

The Magnificent Throne (vision three continued)

What John saw as he stood in heaven was a magnificent throne with an occupant who was surrounded by a rainbow (Revelation 1:3). I wonder if the rainbow might have been for John's benefit because he would have received the teaching and been familiar with the rainbow as a seal of the covenant with Noah. God set "His bow in the cloud" as a sign the earth would never again be destroyed by water (Genesis 9:13).

There are many other descriptions in this section of the glorious and triumphant Father and Son. Some of the things you read about will be in symbols that will be difficult to understand. I suggest that you look to the song and beatitudes of that section for a basic interpretation of the subject under discussion. For example you can draw from Revelation 4:3–11 that those before the throne are there to worship Him and then look at the two songs (verses 8 and 11) and realize the content speaks of His eternal nature and of His will for the creation, both reasons for that particular moment of worship.

1.   Worship and praise for the eternal one.

2.   The sea of glass like crystal is another symbol of the separation between man and God and will have additional significance in chapter fifteen. Even though separation still existed at the time of this vision, just remember that the veil of the temple was torn in two at the time of the crucifixion (Matthew 27:50), so that particular separation (the law) is in the process of elimination.

3.   The four living creatures (Revelation 4:6–8) probably represent protection. They are cherubim (Ezekiel 10:20) who make up God's army.

Vision Four
A Worthy One (chapter 5)

John saw a book in the right hand of the one on the throne, and because no one was found worthy to break its seals, he wept; however, one of those around the throne told him that Jesus had overcome and was worthy. As John watched and Jesus held the book, they listened as those around the throne worshipped by singing the song of redemption. "You were slain, and purchased for God with your blood men from every tribe and tongue and people and nation. You have made them to be a kingdom and priests who will reign upon the earth for our God" (Revelation 5:9–10), and many angels began to sing another song, this time one of exaltation for Jesus, our Lord. (Notice who it is that was purchased and who reigns on the earth with Jesus.)

Then John saw a Lamb (Jesus) as if slain (Revelation 5:6–7) and many angels began to sing a song of exaltation concerning His power, riches, wisdom, blessing, honor, and glory. This scene of the glorified Christ was not only a thrill for John but a necessity in order for him to understand what he is about to see on earth, where he will view the persecution of those in Christ. He had to recognize and realize that Rome wasn't in charge after all. God was still in charge. And what an award awaited the faithful! Seeing the redeemed in the presence of God would have instantly changed his perception of Rome's authority.

Vision Five (chapter 6)
The Opening of the Book of Seven Seals

The book of seals is a pantomime of horses and riders, what they show, and the results. There are no words spoken. Identification must be made from the color of the horse and the description of the rider. For a fuller description, you will want to read the Scripture. John sees the scene as if he were on earth.

Seal	Horse	Rider	Action	Results
First	white	the Savior	spread of gospel	salvation
Second	red	those who slay	war/persecution	death
Third	black	famine	withholding of food	starvation
Fourth	ashen	starvation	death	death
Fifth	martyrs	vindication	How long?"	rest
Sixth	terror	fear for life	seek a hiding place	can't hide

The Seven Seals (continued)

These seals represent judgments against six different classes of people who are grouped according to their activities. The seventh seal will introduce the seals that come next (in the same order), which are warnings of what is to come and how it will occur. I call the third round of seals *the enactments*, although as they are shown, each represents a *future* enactment, even for the near fulfillment of the prophecy. It is always well to note that God never leaves man without hope. Salvation as represented by the white horse is available to all, and it rests on each individual's decision. As for the martyrs, they are already dead physically but very much alive spiritually, and they do not cry out for their own loss of life but for the cause for which they died, the cause of Christ. Retribution for the cause of Christ would also avenge their deaths.

The seventh seal will be held in readiness by the angels until the trumpets are ready to sound. There is silence for a half hour followed by prayer and incense before the sounding. Fulfillment of the warnings, whether *near* or *far*, represents final judgment (Matthew 24:31, 1 Corinthians 15:52, and 1 Thessalonians 4:16). He is saying, I think, "I am the same Jesus whom you crucified".

Vision Six, Seven Seals, (continued)
Identification Aids

The rider on a white horse carried a bow but no arrows; the conclusion is that the arrow has already been spent. This fits our Savior who "used His arrow" at the time of the crucifixion and resurrection. From Isaiah 49:2 another interpretation could be that Jesus Himself *was* the arrow: "He also made me a select arrow, He has hidden me in His quiver." White generally represents purity or victory in battle, so putting it all together, I conclude this is the Savior.

- The word usually used for Jesus' crown is *diadema* or *diadem*, a crown of royalty or exaltation; the alternate word is *stephanos*,[54] which was most commonly used to designate the victor in the games (Strong's Greek). Revelation 6:2 surprisingly uses the word *stephanos* here, but it was unclear why this was done. And then I learned that the crown He wore at the time of the crucifixion was like a stephanos plaited together like a wreath except that it was plaited of thorns and cruelly placed on His head. It was explained to me as a form of mocking, and I began to see the connection. The rulers of the synagogue would hardly have mocked and mistreated him had he worn the diadem. The only other instance where he wore the plaited crown was here in this parade of horses. Think of what He represented here. He was to represent the judgment that would fall on a certain class of people, and that judgment would be the judgment of God. I think He is saying "I am the same Jesus whom you crucified."

---

54 Strong's Concordance, (Grand Rapids, MI), Hebrew, Greek 4735, Copyright by Thomas Nelson Pub., 2001.

- In regard to the second rider the color red often represents danger, and this rider's purpose was to take peace from the world. Perhaps the most telling identification for the red rider is the great sword, which in this case was a battle sword for war. Its name in the Greek is *rhomphaian*[55] (Strong's Greek) and is identified as a long broadsword, a battle sword with which to slay and be slain. It would seem that Satan feels he must take action to counteract the conquering of men by the gospel.

- The rider of the third seal rides a black horse and presumably carries a balance scale, which is used (usually) for something of value such as gold or jewels. It may only refer to the fact that amount is limited, but it could also indicate that even a weighing of wheat or barley on this type of scale would be inaccurate. Verse 6 indicates the weighing refers to food. Oil and wine were considered luxuries and were often used to barter, but in this situation, they were not available to those who were restricted. A denarius was considered a day's wage (Matthew 20:1–16). The implication here is that you could choose a quart of wheat, which would be enough to feed yourself for one day, or buy three quarts of barley, which was not as nutritious, and hopefully feed a family. The voice that gave this information came from the midst of the living creatures, so we are to assume the message that starvation leads to death came from God.

- The fourth seal involves several methods of death, which are often mentioned throughout the Old Testament—death by sword, hunger, disease, and wild beasts. In those situations death was not usually deliberately forced on the victims, but starvation in a time of plenty is quite different. This rider is on an ashen horse and is called Death, and where death is, Hades follows (the place of the dead).

- The fact that the martyrs of the fifth seal cry out for vindication says that their cause is just, as the guilty seldom, if ever ask for vindication. The implication here is that martyrs who gave their

---

55 Strong's Concordance, (Grand Rapids, MI), Greek 4501, Thomas Nelson Pub., 2001.

lives for the cause of Christ go directly to heaven to await the day of the Lord. They are given white robes as one of the promises in the letters to the churches for those who die.

- Please don't view the sixth seal as the end of time because the people in this scene scurried for shelter, hunting for a place to hide. That will not be a possibility in the final judgment as it will happen in the "twinkling of an eye" (1 Thessalonians 5:3). This preview no doubt refers to the judgment against Rome, the near enactment of the prophecy. As the inhabitants all tried to hide from the "face of Him who sits on the throne and from the wrath of the Lamb" it is pronounced that "the great day of His wrath has come, and it had for those who were targeted as having no more time, and the question was asked, "who is able to stand?" 'The great day' refers to the near enactment, and is corroborated by the next phrase 'who is able to stand?' At the final enactment when time will be no more no one will stand, time will be up for everyone. Chapter 11 will reveal to us who will remain standing after this 'near' enactment.

Vision Seven, (chapter 7)
An Interlude

God gives us a short break in the activity to give us an overall view of various things that are happening and that will continue to affect us after the tragedy of this eventual happening. We must keep in mind the many attempts to bring the rulers of the city to repentance and the result of those attempts. Whatever happened when the enactment came, it was by God's intent as punishment for failure to repent of the wickedness that permeated Rome and the realm.

We are privileged to see how God utilized angels to allow or prevent things from happening in this world we live in. The situation is that God wanted to seal those of His children who were on land or sea even before anything was damaged and trees were probably symbolic of the damage that would occur, so He sent another angel as a messenger to tell the angels waiting for the message to begin that they were to wait to release the winds because He was not yet ready. It is my opinion that the sealing was for those mentioned in verses four through eight, those who were labeled as the saved.

Secondly, He indicates that those who will be saved are not all Israelites as one might at first think because of the tribes listed. However, from that list it is easy to grasp that they were from all nations.

1. The children of Levi are never included in a census or a numbering because the inheritance for the Levites comes from a portion of each of the other eleven tribes (verse sevenb).

2. God knows those who are His and there is an implication (from verse nine) that this 144,000 accounts for *all* the redeemed (from the beginning of creation until the end of time) which means that this is not a literal number.

3. Jacob adopted Joseph's sons Manasseh and Ephraim, who took his place in the census, so Joseph as the head of a tribe would not be in this census.

4. Verse 9 indicates that the groups that stand before God "are a great multitude that no one could count." They are from every nation and all tribes and peoples and tongues. "Standing before the throne and before the Lamb, clothed in white robes" (Revelation 7:9).

5. If we have not already surmised that this group is comprised of all of the saved, take a look at the fifth song: the rewards they sing of speak of the perfect care of God which is promised for the home with God in eternity (verses 15-17.) "The song they sing is a song of praise, as they take a look into the future, our future. They sing of no hunger or thirst, no discomfort, plus the presence of our Lord and it occurs to me that perhaps this song of encouragement is for our benefit as much as for those who were suffering then. Just as He did for those who were persecuted He is doing for us, "this is what you can expect" He is saying, "don't forget your goal.

6. At the end of chapter seven there are promises of perpetual care, "they shall neither hunger nor thirst anymore...the Lamb who is in the midst of the throne will shepherd them and lead them to living fountains of waters, and God will wipe away every tear from their eyes" (Revelation 7:16-7).

So we have seen the different types of judgments that God can use against His people. We don't like the way they sound, but remember that God has tried many methods and nothing has yet worked that has been important enough to Rome to convince her to change.

It is perhaps a bad metaphor but nevertheless true at least with many people who believe that they are above the rules that apply to other people. This is a matter of humility. It would be well to remember that God loves the humble but resists the proud.

Vision Eight, (chapter 8:1—5)
The Golden Altar

In the previous section John was shown a multitude that couldn't be counted standing before the throne, so we know that his point of reference was once again what he was seeing in heaven (Revelation 7:9-17). This section introduces the trumpets but postpones the sounding for a half hour of silence in which he saw a golden altar before the throne and an angel with a golden censer (a vessel to hold incense) standing before the altar on which were our prayers. Another angel came and gave him much incense for his censer, which he poured on the prayers on the altar, and the smoke of the incense mixed with the prayers of the saints (that's us) went up before God out of the angel's hand. Then the angel took his censer of incense and filled it with fire from the altar and threw it to the earth, and there followed lightning, thunder, and earthquakes. This is an example of ritual cleansing, and it is also demonstrated in Isaiah 6:6, where a seraphim (angel) takes a coal from the altar with tongs and places it on Isaiah's mouth and says "Your iniquity is taken away and your sin is forgiven." In Revelation 8:3–5 this cleansing was followed by peals of thunder and flashes of lightning and an earthquake.

We are left to wonder at the significance of this moment of silence and the reason for the cleansing at this particular moment. I have heard several ideas presented such as honoring the moment of 'calm before the storm', 'honoring God whose omniscience allows Him to make such decisions,' and 'honoring the serious nature of what is to be seen as the trumpets sound.' Each is a valid idea and there are probably many others from which we could once again observe the nature of God.

Vision Nine, (Revelation 8:6—13)
The Trumpets and the Seventh Seal

The seventh seal introduces the trumpets. Remember that the seals were judgments that dealt with the choices people made in life. We could call them promises, but they are not the same as contracts (covenants). These seals of Revelation are what we might call cause and effect. If you do this, then this is what will happen. The trumpets will reveal the nature of the punishment.The seven angels holding seven trumpets prepare to sound them (Revelation 8:6).

- The seventh seal is ready to be broken. The trumpets will reveal six of the seven warnings. Trumpets one through four will illustrate natural disasters. The fifth will bring judgment from the throne of God on the authority of the beast (the emperor), and the sixth will announce war (invasion by a foreign power). All are warnings that in the absence of repentance judgment will be enacted. Let me remind you again that the happenings that occur as a result of a trumpet sounding are not yet the final enactment. God's faithfulness in assessing judgment plus a warning should have been sufficient to bring about repentance. Let me also point out that His faithfulness assures not only promised blessings but also justice. As a consequence of this trumpet and the outpouring on the earth of hail, fire, and blood, there will be one third loss of all earth. (This as with all numbers in Revelation is not a literal number, but it means the damage is limited.)

- On the sea a great mountain (perhaps a volcano) burning with fire is thrown into the sea. One third of the creatures will die, and one third of ships will be lost (Revelation 8:8).

- On freshwater and springs a great star fell like a burning torch and polluted freshwater sources. The star's name was Wormwood. The result is a loss of one third of freshwater.

As a conclusion to this half of the warnings, a threefold warning has been issued to those who dwell on the earth. They are called *woes*.

Vision Nine, (continued)
The Trumpets (continued, Revelation 9:1–12)

- Wormwood and Apollyon and Abaddon of trumpet five are names for Satan.

- Wormwood is a bitter pollutant that tastes of gall and can cause death when it is mixed with water. It comes from the Artemisia plant.

- In the heavens one third of the sun, moon, and stars are struck and darkened. A third of the day and a third of the night are darkened (Revelation 8:12). This speaks of all manner of heavenly disasters. Some could be man-made, or they could all be natural.

- With judgment on the authority of the throne the fallen star (Satan) has the key to the abyss, which he opened, and smoke billowed out like the smoke of a great furnace, which darkened the sun and the air. Out of the smoke came swarms of locusts with the power to inflict pain and disease with damage only to those who do not have God's seal upon their foreheads. They claim as their king Abaddon (Hebrew) or Apollyon (Greek) (Revelation 9). Think for just a moment how any darkening element can cloud our thinking. I've been in both sandstorms and snowstorms that took away all intelligent thinking. It literally clouds the mind. Now think about a swarm of locusts, that you can't keep out of your eyes, nose or mouth. They are formidable opponents.

- Scripture doesn't make the distinction, but it is likely that this is the Wormwood of trumpet three. John does say, "A star from heaven which had fallen to the earth" (Revelation 9:1).

- It has been suggested that the winds being held back were beneficial to the invasion by the Parthians who then came across the dry riverbed to invade an unprepared Rome. I have not been able to confirm or refute this assumption but felt it was worth including since one of the methods that God promised would be a part of the Roman downfall was invasion by external enemies. The

Euphrates River would have been a normal deterrent to invasion from the east. Dry it would have been a different matter. The invasion force spoken of by God was to include two hundred million (not a literal number). This number as with all of the predictions of loss indicates two things. It would be a limited loss. (One third is a partial amount and not a complete loss, but it would be enough to get the job done as two hundred million *could* be considered a *complete* number.) There was no repentance. The text will usually tell you what a number refers to.

With all six of the trumpets sounded, we have two of the predicted woes revealed.

- Woe one: Those who participated in enacting this woe were told not to hurt any grass, any green thing or any trees, or any who had the seal of God on their foreheads; also, in tormenting those who did not have the seal, they could not kill anyone (Revelation 9:5).

- Woe two: This consisted of internal war and disease, but there was no repentance.

Vision Ten, (Revelation 10)
The Strong Angel and the Little Book

This chapter is actually a second interlude and it would appear that what John is seeing is on earth, so in my mind I see him approaching the mountain on which the angel stands. Actually this is a very large angel as he set one foot on the sea and the other on the land. There is no action except for the angel's voice by which to move the battle along, only the frustration of the strong angel. And when John saw him, he realized that he was strong because he had been in God's presence. (Do you remember that John had seen Moses take on the glory of God when they were on the mountain?) And this angel probably looked to him in much the same way. He glowed from having been in the presence of God. John would never forget that. This angel was clothed in a cloud with a rainbow upon his head (covenant relationship), and he carried a little book and cried out with the voice of a lion. And when he had finished, suddenly the seven peals of thunder uttered their voices, and as John started to write, a loud voice from heaven instructed him to "seal up the things which the seven peals of thunder have spoken and do not write them" (Revelation 10:4–5), and then the strong angel raised his right hand to heaven and swore by Him, who lives forever, that there would be no more delays. "In the days of the voice of the seventh trumpet when it is about to sound, the mystery of God will be finished." This use of the term *the mystery of God* is thought not to refer to the unveiling of God's church (which has already happened) but to victory in the battle between good and evil, the war in which we are engaged. That war is what the book of Revelation is about, and the delay, so emphatically pointed out by the strong angel, refers to a time limit. There will be no more judgments assessed and no more warnings granted. When the seventh trumpet begins to sound, the mystery of the end will be revealed. That is when the final enactment will begin.

In the meanwhile a voice from heaven instructed John to take the book from the hand of the angel, and as John obeyed, the strong angel told him to eat it and said, "It will be sweet as honey in your mouth, but bitter in your stomach," and when he had eaten it, the strong angel told him he must keep on prophesying (teaching) to all people (Revelation 10:8–11). In Ezekiel 3:1 there is a similar message to Ezekiel, and we are able to conclude from it that the message of the scroll (salvation) is sweet but that rejection of the message is bitter to handle.

As God brings us to repentance, His methods are the same. Natural disasters bring us to the reality that we need repentance. The immediacy of disaster can open the mind to truth. For a descriptive use of natural disasters against Israel I would recommend the reading of the Old Testament books Joel and Nahum. You can also experience God's use of evil against evil in Revelation 9:4, where we probably would be inclined to comment, "Served them right."

(John is still in a vantage point on earth in Vision Ten. Watch for the shifts back and forth in this next section).

Two Witnesses (Revelation 11:1–14)

John was told to measure the temple, the altar, and those who worship within but not to measure the outer court because it had been given to the nations who will trample it down for forty-two months. What is God saying here? The key, I think, is in the second statement. The people who belong to the nations are not His, but the ones inside are. This counting is both an indication that He knows His own and protects them. Of course the physical temple was destroyed in AD 70. So what temple was John to measure? If you said the heart, you guessed correctly. The Greek word used is *naos*[56] which refers to *the inner habitation of God. Hieron,*[57] the other word for *temple*, refers to the whole structure, outer court, porches and all (Strong's, 2001).

Those who are outside in the courtyard belong to Satan and will receive no protection. Nevertheless, Satan's forces are about to win a battle, and God's people are about to be trampled. Though God's side will not be victorious this time, Satan's victory will be limited to forty-two months. It is his number for victory and does not specify a length of time. Nor does the opposite number, 1,260 days, which is the same length of time, but it indicates victory for God's followers.

Let me suggest that chapter 11 is the specific time of which John wrote. The church is in disarray, frightened, and unsure of the future. Domitian's persecution was taking a heavy toll.

The history of Domitian's reign is rather sketchy, and at times historians have been hesitant to blame him for the deaths brought about by his hand in part because the record was extant. This came about following his assassination. By order of the Senate a call was made for an edict called "the damnation of the memory," which meant his entire reign was wiped out. His record was so damming it seemed advisable that it be destroyed, so the edict expunged his name from all official records. Thinking he still had not done enough to rid Rome of Domitian's memory, Nerva restored property that had been unjustly confiscated, melted down coins that had his image, had Domitian's statues smashed and the inscriptions erased, as he continued to make amends[58] (Kerrigan, *Dark History* 139–140). The horror of this period of history was sufficient for God to include the aid of the Spirit in the form of His two witnesses.

The identity of the two witnesses is rather vague, but Scripture does reveal that their prophecy would last long enough to be effective in the ways that were needed (1,260 days). Their identity hangs on Zechariah 4, where

---

56 Strong's Concordance, Greek, Copyright 2001 by Thomas Nelson Pub., Hebrew, 3485.

57 Strong's Concordance, Greek, Copyright 2001 by Thomas Nelson Pub., Hebrew, 2411.

58 Kerrigan, Michael, *The Roman Emperors, from Julius Caesar to the Fall of Rome, A Dark History, copyright 2011 by Metro Books 2011, 2008,*

an angel brings a message from God to Zerubbabel about a lampstand and two olive trees. Zerubbabel's responsibility was to finish rebuilding the temple. God's message is that neither power nor might can accomplish the task, but it can be done by the Spirit (Zechariah 4:6). The interpretation for our situation is that neither can the gospel survive by power or might, but with the Spirit, who dwells within man and helps Christians proclaim the Word, it will survive because the lampstand is also identified as the church (Revelation 1:20) and the Word is the message of the church.

From the rest of Revelation 11 we read of persecution, death, and of rejoicing by some; however, after three and a half days the dead come back to life, and great fear came upon those who watched. When a voice from heaven said, "Come up here," the martyrs rose up into heaven in a cloud as their enemies watched, and in the same hour, there was a great earthquake. In the Old Testament the earthquake would have signified the demise of a nation. Whether this demonstration is figurative, prophetic, or metaphorical for the decline of Rome, I can't tell you. However, the book of Revelation refers to the martyrs as being in heaven and reigning with Christ for one thousand years (Revelation 20:4, 5:9, and 17:6). (Remember numbers are symbolic of completion.)

There is an interpretation that fits the purpose of the book and satisfies history, so we'll leave the decision about what happened to the martyrs up to God and examine the alternative interpretation. After the period of intense persecution when the church was in disarray and it seemed that the gospel had been crushed, the Spirit enabled it to be resurrected and preached again. It is probable that this is the intent of Revelation 11:11–13; however, with God, all things are possible, and I don't rule it out. I do believe that at some point martyrs were taken directly to heaven. Perhaps at this point as well.

The Seventh Trumpet (Revelation 11:15–19)

The seventh trumpet *foresees* the reign of Christ, and from Revelation 11:15 we know that the heavenly kingdom is the one that is being celebrated. The kingdom on earth is already in effect, and while the two are not yet joined, they are joined in this vision that looks forward.

The twenty-four elders sing the song of victory, which says in part, "We give you thanks, O Lord God, the Almighty, who are and who were, because you have taken your great power and have begun to reign" (Revelation 11:17). This indicates that the redeemed have experienced resurrection, which is termed victory, and the kingdom of the world becomes the kingdom of Christ. Suddenly, the temple of God opens. Do you recall what the temple is? There is no physical temple. This temple is made up of the hearts of the redeemed in heaven. How do we know? This section is looking forward, and the King (Jesus Christ) is reigning in the heavenly kingdom.

This event is also accompanied by "flashes of lightning, peals of thunder, and an earthquake and hailstorm" (Revelation 11:19).

Summary

We looked briefly at the book as an apocalyptic writing and at John as the transcriber. We looked at his life outside of Patmos, broke the message into visions as nearly as possible (a purely subjective matter), and spent a little time looking at Rome's reputation in the first century.

We examined connections to past history as seen through the lens of the resurrected, exalted Christ, the worthy Savior, recognized God's behind-the-scenes involvement in advancing and securing His plan, and acknowledged the glory and peace of the heavenly home as His.

It was necessary to dig into the history of the two witnesses, the lampstands, and the olive tree to learn that in this Christian walk it is not might and power that succeed but the indwelling Spirit. Although the seals and the trumpets took a great deal of time to explore fully, I feel it was beneficial in helping understand God's communication with us regarding the need for repentance. Revelation connects God's continuity to both past and future events, and this book takes us a step further into the knowledge of the existence of darkness, from which He rescues mankind.

Study Guide—Chapter 19

Q. What type of book is Revelation?
A. Revelation is a book of prophecy in apocalyptic language. This means that something will be revealed that has been hidden.

Q. What is the main difference between Genesis and Revelation?
A. Well, the main difference is that Genesis tells of our beginnings and Revelation tells us what our endings will be like, but what I was thinking of is that the beginnings showed us the beauty of the creation and the end will be either beautiful for some and horrible for others.

Q. Can you think of a reason why John was taken to the throne room immediately before he was shown anything else?
A. You need to remember that John is still in prison at the time when God sends an angel to him with this commission to write. Persecution is still intense; Domitian is even persecuting members of his own family that are following Christ. Before John saw how things were on earth, he needed to know how it was with God. The resurrected Jesus sat on the throne, reigning after His exaltation, with worshipers and a rainbow surrounding Him. It was magnificent. It was impressive. It was awesome, and the message was this: "This is how it is. Don't forget when you come before the people because this is why they endure. Tell them what awaits them when their persecution ends. Tell them what you saw."

Q. Why is it thought that Revelation was written in symbolic terms?
A. It was probably written in symbols to protect the reader if caught with it by Roman authorities.

Q. To what does the term *outward struggle* refer?
A. The outward and inward struggles are my perception of the division of Revelation. The outward battle is the one Satan waged against God, thinking he could bring the Lord down or compromise Him in some

way. The inward battle is against you and me and takes place within our souls.

Q. What do the seals and the trumpets represent?
A. The seals are six types of judgments against six groups of people of consequences of the choices they made in life. The trumpets represent warnings to those same groups with a graphic illustration of what will happen when those consequences come due.

Chapter 20: The Final Prophecy: The Inward Struggle

～✦～

The first part ended as the angels rejoiced that our Lord had "taken His great power and begun to reign" (Revelation 11:17); however, I reminded you that this scene is under the category of "things that will take place after these things" (Revelation 1:19). In other words the angels are foreseeing this event. My understanding of the kingdom is that the heavenly kingdom will begin when all the redeemed are together in heaven. In the meantime in His kingdom here on earth we serve as priests, and He is our High Priest with direct access to the Father.

Let me remind you that words in apocalyptic writings may have more than one meaning. Watch for that and practice choosing the one meaning that fits the scene best. There may seem to be more than one, in which case there may be a double meaning or a near and a far interpretation as we have seen in the previous struggle.

God's focus up to now has been the revelation of His Son's exaltation and why He is worthy to receive it. That focus has shown a connection to the old covenant through examples and knowledge of happenings, but it has also warned of the persecution that is coming to the young church that will be so intense that maintaining principles will become a matter of life or death, eternal life or death. The struggle for obedience can't be made externally. It must come from the heart, an internal battle of the soul.

This is the point at which the focus of the book of Revelation changes. We are going to witness so much in such a short period of time that you may struggle to keep up. I'm sure you'll have no difficulty because the remainder of Revelation is directly about you and me.

You may have noticed these *sign posts* to keep us up to some degree with where John is. It is at best a subjective matter, but there is no doubt that he has gone back and forth in his focus to earth and back to heaven. And as I tried to visualize the different scenes, I felt it did make a difference from which direction he looked, so I gave numbers to the visions and located where he stood in my mind. I hope it helps you, but if it doesn't, ignore it, the divisions are not revealed in scripture.

Vision Eleven (vantage point heaven)
The Eternal Struggle (Revelation 12:1–6)

As described in Genesis 3:15 woman has been on a direct path to this clash with Satan since the curse. I would imagine Satan is delighted by the opportunity to get even for all time, but this is a point at which we need to stop and evaluate. This 'happening' is in symbols, so the woman is a symbol as is her description.

This text is compressed, which means our entire knowledge of this information requires only six very short verses, while Jesus' life from birth to ascension is taken care of in one sentence.

Now let's put it together. That the woman is clothed in the sun would indicate she is from God. She wears a crown of twelve stars, and she is pregnant (Revelation 1-2). The twelve stars represent the prophets who prepared the way and the twelve apostles who were the original messengers for the church, so the woman isn't a female but God's covenant people, which would indicate both sets of covenant people, the Israelites and the Gentiles, representing both the law and the church.

That she fled to the wilderness (the church), prepared by God (the presence of the Spirit), and was nourished for 1,260 days (victory for God) says that she (the church) was taken care of as long as it was necessary to survive. Drop down to Revelation 12:14, and the "wings of the great eagle" echoes Exodus 19:4, where the same term is used to describe crossing the Red Sea in the flight from Egypt. Another usage is in Isaiah 40:31, where the term again indicates power and strength.

The dragon has seven heads, ten horns, and seven crowns, and he is a great red dragon whose tail swept away a third of the stars of heaven and threw them to the earth. And his purpose is the destruction of the child when born. I would think that one third of the stars refers to the angels Satan corrupted and took with him when he fell, but I suspect that it is also tied to the third trumpet, where the star fell in freshwater sources and was contaminated by wormwood. I suspect as such it is an allegory with the angels from heaven as the freshwater that was contaminated and with Satan the cause for both situations. This guy isn't difficult to identify, although I had always thought the red part was a fictitious rendering for his cartoon representation. Because seven in Scripture is a perfect number, my guess is that he (Satan) is claiming both perfection and victory (the crowns).

He has already tried to destroy Jesus as an infant (through Herod, who issued the proclamation that all infants under two be killed) (Matthew 2:16–18). He commands a following from among the angels who are fallen (Revelation 12:7), and he aspires to be God (Revelation 14:13–14).

The woman gave birth to a male child (Revelation 12:5), who was Jesus, and it is stated that He would rule with a rod of iron. This phrase may have been intended to identify the child as the promised Messiah because the Old Testament refers to Him frequently using the phrase. It could also refer to the manner in which He will render His judgments against evil. And finally He is caught up to God and His throne (the ascension), which probably refers to His own throne as other passages say He is "seated at the right hand of God." If you are confused that the child is no longer a child, remember that He is the head of the church and therefore necessary to the function of the church.

Vision Twelve (vantage point heaven)
War in Heaven, Revelation 12:7--12

Did you notice Jesus was born, ruled, and ascended all in one sentence! That's really condensed history, isn't it? By the next sentence Satan is in heaven, declaring war on Michael and his angels. My belief is that this battle took place following the resurrection and ascension, but this verse is the nearest thing to proof that I have. I just know that until that happened Satan still entertained the thought of winning, and after that we are told that he came down to the earth "having great wrath, knowing that he has only a short time" (Revelation 12:12). And I might add, knowing that he was defeated and tied to a war that was lost with no prospects of it getting any better didn't help his frame of mind. His only recourse was to contaminate whatever he could touch, and by so doing he would take as many souls with him to his punishment as possible.

There is no way of knowing the length of the war between Satan and Michael. I readily concede it could have been a very long time; however, my heart doesn't believe that it was. God gave him opportunity to prove his point that man would choose him over God, and yes, some did; however, it wasn't the big rush to his side that he thought it would be. He was egotistical enough to think he could bring God down or at least replace the

Son, and that didn't work either, so now he has used his final asset, battle with the heavenly host, and is defeated once again.

The text doesn't give us a lot to think about other than the fact that they waged war Michael and his angels with Satan and his angels, "and they were not strong enough, and there was no longer a place found for them in heaven. And the great dragon was thrown down, the serpent of old who is called the devil and Satan, who deceives the whole world; he was thrown down to the earth and his angels were thrown down with him." (Revelation 12:7–10).

There are three points of interest here regarding the battle.

- Satan and his angels were not strong enough to defeat Michael and his angels. We tend to think Satan can do anything he wants to do. Actually he can only do what he is allowed to do, and too often, we are his enablers.

- They lost their home in heaven. We don't know how long Satan had lived outside of heaven, but we do know that he could go back as often as he wished (Job 1:6). That is no longer possible because there is no longer a place for him there. They were cast down to earth. I don't believe Satan was as angry about being cast out as he was over recognizing his defeat.

- Satan deceives the whole world (Revelation 12:7–10). This is possibly the worst punishment of all, as he was bound already by the limitations God had placed on him, and he lost his power over death because of the resurrection, so now he is bound in such a way that he can no longer deceive. No wonder he is full of wrath, for which we'll examine causes and circumstances as we move forward to chapter 20.

What does it mean to be bound as Satan was bound? I think of lying as his big tool of deception with knowledge as our big defense. Here are two pieces of information that relate to each other in regard to Satan's activities. On the one hand he is depicted as "prowling about to see who he can devour" (2 Peter 5:8). In the other picture he is bound and thrown into the abyss, and the door is sealed (Revelation 20:1–3). In doing any kind of analysis we have to remember that this book is written in symbols.

One of the rules of understanding such a study is to be consistent, so if things are symbolic, they must remain symbolic. We have pointed out all through this study the symbols that had reference to the Old Testament or to God's nature. We've also pointed out where symbols have been identified by God in the New Testament. Therefore we must consider that Revelation 20 speaks symbolically in regard to this subject.

- First, why did God place limitations on Satan to begin with? I think the answer was to level the playing field for man. Satan has powers beyond those we have, so man needed ways to protect himself. The powers given to Satan are effective only with those who choose to follow him. I hope you had noticed that. The limitations placed on him revolve around the individual's faith and spiritual growth.

- Second, how is he bound? Is it a physical binding with a rope or a chain? Is he incarcerated behind bars? If we use his previous limitations as an example, it is not too difficult to realize that he has no choice in this matter. God placed the limitations and they have to be obeyed. Perhaps this is a consequence that goes with his use of the choice that was originally granted him. Perhaps it was a stipulation he had to concede when he challenged God for the right to test Job. We'll never know, but I believe we must agree that Satan has to abide by the limitations placed on him. That being the case we can draw a conclusion that location is immaterial to obedience. It is fairly obvious that handcuffs and bars were not necessary to be sure of his obedience.

- Third, why did God choose the prevention of deception as an additional limitation? Of course we can't know for sure, but we can make a fairly good guess based on the fact that the resurrection and thirty to thirty-five years into this new age had changed things, such as the facts listed below.

  o There is a new age, and with it, forgiveness is now possible.

  o The Word was being circulated by letters from the apostles and scattered among Christians wherever they went. Plus some of the law and some of the prophets were available in scroll which gave added opportunity to know God.

- Fourth, what kind of seal was used at the abyss? We've studied seals that were on the outside and seals that were on the inside, seals that show physically and seals that can only be seen by a changed life. What kind of seal did God use to close the abyss? Regardless of the method, a seal gave proof of authenticity and ownership, and it was a down payment for something that was to come. It would seem that the seal God gave to Satan was not one to keep him inside the abyss, but one to show authenticity and ownership of the created one, Satan. The seal was a promise and proof that God was superior to Satan and could make decisions without Satan's approval. It is not a promise in the sense of eternal life for Christians but a promise to Satan of where he is going. Why would God choose to fight the battle over again? The battle was won when Christ came out of the tomb, proving that He was the Son of God. The resurrection fulfilled the law, and the new era began. These by God's own words are the *latter days*, especially in light of the fact that Satan has already been judged and condemned (Hebrews 2:14).

Will man suffer the same outcome as Satan? Only if he did not participate in the first resurrection, and let me remind you that in the first resurrection man traded his decaying body for life in Christ and was resurrected from death to life. Revelation 20:6 is the reminder of that. Although the body itself would eventually die physically, the spirit would live on to receive a spiritual body. From life to life or from death to death, it is our choice.

I've come to understand Satan's restrictions as if he is an animal bound or tethered to whoever controls him. That would be God. I don't see the sealing of the abyss as a preventive action by which we might ask, "Does the abyss have a door?" but rather as a restriction that will be obeyed just as other restrictions from God had to be obeyed. So in my mind he is tethered without choice by the power of God. So what is the explanation? It is simply to understand that the primary thought of this twentieth chapter is that Satan is bound with another restriction. Does he *have to obey God?* If the answer is *yes*, obedience does not depend on where he is.

Vision Twelve (continued)
Satan Overcome, Revelation 12:13-7

John sees the rejoicing in heaven over Satan's defeat at the hands of Michael and his angels. There were three reasons given for this defeat.

1. He was defeated because of the blood of the Lamb.

2. He was defeated because of the word of the testimony of the martyrs.

3. He was defeated because the martyrs loved God more than they loved their lives.

The result of this defeat was that Satan was thrown down to the earth where he went with great wrath "knowing that he has only a short time" (Revelation 12:12).

Vision Thirteen (perspective: earth)
Persecution, (Revelation 12:13-17)

Satan's first thought was to go after the woman; after all, she gave birth to the child. She is the one who is responsible. Do you see how we have utilized this tactic? Failure to accept responsibility comes straight from Satan. Let's see what happened.

Scripture says that "the two wings of the great eagle were given to the woman so that she could fly into the wilderness to her place, where she was nourished for a time and times and half a time, from the presence of the serpent" (Revelation 12:14). If we go back to God's deliverance of the Israelites from Egypt we see that these same words were used regarding their deliverance (Exodus 19:4), "how I bore you on eagle's wings and brought you to myself." The eagle is symbolic of God, the time element does not mean forever but as long as His protection was necessary. The woman in this instance is the church that was under protection of the Holy Spirit but may represent instead or 'as well' the priests, etc. of the law who taught about His coming. There is no reason it could not represent both.

Unsuccessful in this attempt to do away with the woman, Satan was enraged and refocused on "the rest of her children, who keep the commandments of God, and hold to the testimony of Jesus" (Revelation 12:17). And that is how Christians became the focus of Satan's persecution.

Defeated first by God and then by Michael and his angels, Christians are his final target. He knows he is defeated, but he wants to take as many with him to his punishment as he possible can.

Vision Fourteen, (vantage point, earth)
Satan and the Beasts, Revelation 13

I wonder how long Satan continued to harass Christians before he devised the plan below.

In time Satan joined forces with a particular partner who had the same inclinations for evil that he had. The implication of Revelation 13:1 is that he may have stood on the seashore for some time, waiting for just the right person to use in his schemes. As John watched he saw the dragon, and he saw a beast with ten horns and seven heads. The horns were adorned with ten diadems, which was normally what a person of royal birth would have on the head. In the Jewish community horns represented strength and power in part because of their placement on the altar. To have several crowns would be making a statement of power. Normally the diadems were for those of royal birth, though many claimed them and wore them who won their position and power in battle. Those would be rulers by reason of power and not because of birth. It was also symbolic of some national rulers even without the royal heritage or warfare. The horns of the altar in the Old Testament were a symbol of strength if one was strong enough to claim what he wanted. This, I believe, is what Satan was looking for—strength but without preexisting values.

The dragon (Satan) was pleased with his choice because he immediately offered to give the beast his own power and in addition his throne and his authority (Revelation 13:2), and I expect that sounded pretty good to the beast. As the beast mulled it over, he probably thought, *This guy is pretty crafty, but I will have the upper hand because with his power and his authority I can do whatever I want with my throne.* There was a problem though. Satan didn't really give him anything except the necessity to do exactly as he told him to do. However, Satan managed the scheme. He is still in charge. That must surely have been a surprise to the two beasts.

"And (John) saw one of the heads (on this ten-headed beast) as if it had been slain, and his fatal wound was healed, and the whole world worshipped him" (Revelation 13:3), "and they worshipped the dragon because he gave his power to the beast" (Revelation 13:5–8). And then we found that there was a second beast (with the appearance of a lamb), and though he didn't come up out of the sea, he came out of the earth. And there was a strange thing about him, too. He had two horns, which gave him a *holy* look; however, when he spoke, it was like a dragon, and the voice revealed that he belonged to the dragon and not the lamb.

This second beast is not without power himself. He was something of a magician and could make all sorts of things happen. He was the one we might call the enforcer. He saw to it that everything the beast/emperor said was obeyed. He could make fire come down out of heaven and make the beast whose fatal wound was healed speak, and he even gave breath to the beast/emperor's image so that he was made to speak and people were anxious to worship him. And he decided to bring on a famine against those who would not worship the emperor. He did this by causing everyone to receive a mark either on their forehead or their right hand before they could buy or sell, and the problem was that many people only earned one day's wage, so how did they feed a family?

Soon people would be starving. Scripture says the beast was "arrogant and blasphemous, and was given authority to act for forty-two months, and he blasphemed against God, His name, and those who dwell in heaven" (Revelation 13:5–7). What does all that mean? It meant that lives were going to be lost and none of it was going to be nice. God warned His people to prepare their minds and to remain faithful to death, and He said that they would then earn a crown of righteousness. Why do you suppose He didn't just throw up a seal of protection or destroy those who were destroying? It is simple. God created the world and the people in it to have the choice of how they would live. Each individual would still have the choice over his or her own life.

Things were going to get bad. You need to keep in mind that God is speaking in apocalyptic language here. What was really happening could have been much worse. What has to be recognized is that the situation was life-threatening and it seemed with no way out. Forty-two months is a time of victory for Satan. In the letters to the Asian churches it seemed that different cities had different problems and punishments. God was encouraging them, telling them to look forward in preparation for the eventuality of losing their lives. There will be losses; therefore focus must remain on the end result of remaining faithful. After all, Satan's forty-two months could be only a week, or a day. Focus would be the key.

Satan, the emperor (the first beast), and the conciliar (the enforcer otherwise known as the sea beast or the false prophet) worked together through their common goal of persecution, robbing the citizenry and general mistreatment of anyone when it was advantageous or amusing. In the meantime, they lived lives of self-destruction, which was amusing to Satan as he watched and waited. He would take what he could get from this new relationship and not worry about anyone else. *Let them look after themselves* was one of his favorite mottos.

You've not yet met the one remaining personality in this group. She is called the woman, the scarlet woman, or the harlot (Revelation 17:18), but she is actually the city of Rome.

Vision Fourteen (vantage point heaven)
Jesus and the 144,000, (Revelation 14:1–5)

Jesus is with the 144,000 standing on Mount Zion (a reference to Jerusalem specifically and to the entire area in general), and he hears them singing the song of the redeemed. We might say today that this song belonged to the redeemed as no one except the redeemed could learn it. These are the faithful ones. We saw them before in chapter 7. They represent all of the saved, so this is a projection into the future. I can't help but wonder what is going on in John's mind. Perhaps there is nothing beyond what is happening. There may not have been room for anything else. One of the things that is so compelling about this scene is the fact that it is our future. I am not surprised to learn that no one can learn the song of the redeemed. How would it be possible to relate either the trauma or the joy of that experience? And to be with our Lord would be the crowning moment of happiness.

Next we witness John as he sees three angels flying in *mid-heaven* with the news of the gospel. I'm not exactly sure where mid-heaven begins and ends, but I'm willing to take John's word for it. This scene strikes me as most unusual. The last warning has already been given in chapter 10, so this is not a warning. I thought perhaps it might be a summary of what's happened before, but Babylon has not yet fallen. So what we have is the first angel's admonition to follow God and worship Him as the Creator because the "hour of His judgment has come." The other two angels show the fall of Babylon and worship of the beast as examples of what can happen (Revelation 14:6–8). I believe this is a demonstration that some have not as yet repented, but those who have persevered are applauded.

Again John is told to write. The text says, "Blessed are the dead who die in the Lord from now on!" And the Spirit adds, "Yes, so that they may rest from their labors, for their deeds follow with them." This is the second blessing (Revelation 14:6–12), and it refers specifically to the harvest that is about to be taken of the redeemed, specifically those who die in the Lord.

Vision Sixteen (vantage point heaven)
The Harvest, (Revelation 14:13—20)

One like the son of man wearing a golden crown came out carrying a sharp sickle and sat on a cloud. Another angel came out of the temple and shouted that the harvest was ready, and the one on the cloud put in his sickle and harvested the earth. Two more angels came out of the temple. One carried a sharp sickle and the other came from the altar and had the power of fire. He shouted to the one with the sharp sickle to harvest the clusters from the vine because the harvest was ready. The grapes harvested were thrown into the great wine press, symbolic of God's wrath.

Although it is a gruesome description, it helps us understand the feeling God has regarding those who reject His Son. "The blood (that) came from the winepress (came) up to the horses' bridles, for a distance of two hundred miles" (Revelation 14:20). This simply means that the destruction of the wicked was complete. Hebrews 13:11–14 gives the comparison to the crucifixion of Jesus.

In the continuation of this vision John sees another scene in heaven in which seven angels stand ready to pour out the plagues on the world below to finish the wrath of God. Then John saw the redeemed standing on the sea of glass, which was mixed with fire, and they were singing the song of Moses. In part it says, "Great and marvelous are your works, O Lord God, the Almighty … you alone are holy; All the nations will come and worship before you, for your righteous acts have been revealed" (Revelation 15:3–4). As John continued to look the temple of the tabernacle in heaven was opened, and the four living creatures brought out the bowls of wrath. The angels took charge of these bowls, and the temple was filled with smoke from the glory of God and from His power. And no one was able to enter the temple until the seven plagues were finished.

We've looked at the judgments that will fall on these people if they fail to repent of their wickedness, but there is no repentance. Drunkenness and dissipation and all manner of immorality fill their lives as they make life as miserable as possible for others.

The judgments were followed by warnings in which God graphically demonstrated the judgment to John as it will happen, which was a terrifying experience.

The first six enactments will again be a *dress rehearsal* for this demonstration, but God will use the six as He sees the need to use. Now we can understand why the *real* enactment of the seventh trumpet is held until the end of time because when the voice of the seventh trumpet sounds everything will be revealed and time will be no more.

Vision Seventeen (vantage point heaven)
Six Bowls of Wrath, (Revelation 16)

Please notice that each pouring corresponds by number with the seals and the trumpets, first on the land, next on the sea, etc. I can't tell you if there is a reason for this pattern.

A loud voice from the temple instructed that the wrath of God be poured out on the earth (Revelation 16:1).

The first angel poured. "And God's wrath became a loathsome and malignant sore on those who wore the mark of the beast and who worshipped his image" (Revelation 16:2).

The second angel poured into the sea, and "it became blood like that of a dead man; and every living thing died" (Revelation 16:3).

The third angel poured into the rivers and the streams of fresh water, "and they became blood" (Revelation 16:4–7).

The fourth angel poured upon the sun, "and it was given to it to scorch men with fire. Men were scorched with fierce heat; and they blasphemed and didn't repent" (Revelation 16:8–9).

The fifth angel poured on the throne of the beast, and "his kingdom became darkened and they blasphemed the name of God who has the power over these plagues, and they did not repent so as to give him glory." (Revelation 16:10–11).

The sixth angel poured out on the great River Euphrates, and its water was dried up, so that the way would be prepared for the kings from the east (Revelation 16:12).

Notice that the bowls of wrath are not mentioned as having caused harm to Christians.

Vision Eighteen (vantage point heaven, continued)
Deception and the Gathering of the Armies (Revelation 16:13–16)

This interlude is extremely interesting because it deals with deception. I wonder if Satan assigned these responsibilities as a way to get around God's announcement that he would no longer be able to deceive the nations. This is the place at which the three participants in the evil plot conspire against the great day of the Almighty, of which we refer to as the day of judgment.

- There are three participants: the dragon (Satan), the beast (emperor), and the false prophet (the land beast).

- An unclean spirit comes out of the mouth of each of these participants in the form of a frog and are identified as the spirits of demons who are capable of performing signs. Since the frog in ancient times was considered unclean, the imagery suggested is that of deceptive propaganda that will convince the acceptance of the cause of evil (Leviticus 11:10).

- Their assignment is to gather together the kings of the world for the war of the great day of God (judgment), and they gathered them together to the place called in Hebrew *Har-Magedon*.

I think I would be frightened out of my wits if in the middle of a conference God suddenly began to speak. The three plotters did not even acknowledge God's voice. I think this says that it is possible to refuse to hear Him for so long that suddenly you no longer can. He just isn't there for you. That's scary for me. I hope it is for you as well.

The voice of God intervenes to remind the world that He is coming "like a thief in the night" (Revelation 16:15). Can this event be planned? I don't think Satan's demons are going to know when they need to be at Har-Magedon. Consequently this is an exercise in futility. Be sure to watch what happens when these two armies meet. The blessing of this verse is for those who prepare and are therefore ready for God's coming. As indicated those of the sixteenth verse are preparing, but their preparation is for war, so this verse has a dual meaning

Same Vision (Eighteen) (same vantage, heaven)
The Seventh Bowl of Wrath, (Revelation 16:17-20)

Some of these references happen prior to the event of which they speak—the second fulfillment or enactment of the bowls, the gathering of the armies at Har-Magedon, the identification and viewing of the Harlot. Watch for these time discrepancies to better understand.

"Then the kings were gathered together at the place that in Hebrew is called Har-Magedon" (Revelation 16:16). And the seventh angel poured out his bowl on the air, and a loud voice came out of the temple from the throne and said, "It is done." And there were flashes of lightning, sounds and peals of thunder, and an earthquake greater than any that had been on the earth since man had inhabited it. It was so great that the city split in three parts and the cities of the nations fell. Every island fled away, and the mountains were not found. There were huge hailstones of one hundred pounds each, and men blasphemed but did not repent. It is possible that *Har-Magedon* here refers to the plains of Har-Magedon, which is an actual place where many battles had been fought, or it could also be a symbolic term that applies to the total destruction of evil by God (Revelation 17:16).

This illustration is so graphic I feel it is definitely a 'showing' rather than a 'telling'. This is what would eventually happen to Rome, but before relaxing too much, it is also what will happen to the world we live in at the end of time. The message is, "Be prepared."

Vision Nineteen (vantage point in a wilderness)
Identification by an Angel, Revelation 17

This chapter includes almost all of the personas who are involved in this part of Revelation. It will help your understanding of the message if you study this chapter until it is almost second nature to you. Enjoy!

An angel takes John to a wilderness to show him the harlot (remember, the harlot is the city of Rome). She sits on a beast with seven heads and ten horns. This is the first beast to come up out of the water. He had a fatal head wound but it had healed. The angel says he is about to go to destruction, which means that he will die soon. He was assassinated soon after this prediction to John. Let's take these points one at a time.

1. The sea beast is known by seven heads and ten horns. She wears rich clothing at the expense of the people of the city and brags about her immorality.This is not a literal description as she is

245

described as a wanton woman. In reality she is a city unmindful of her responsibilities to her people. She lived at the expense of her people who were in need. She not only persecuted the saints, she killed them by wicked and cruel methods for entertainment.

2. The harlot is the current emperor. (She is not a woman.). She/he is vile, immoral, and she/he is not only corrupt, he corrupts others. He is soon to be assassinated and will go to destruction.

3. His name is Domitian He/she wears many crowns because he has conquered many kingdoms.

4. The head that had a fatal wound was the first emperor (Nero) who persecuted the Christians. He was feared and hated. He was more than a little crazy and tried to burn down the city of Rome. A short time later he committed suicide and died. Because the people were superstitious they feared that he might come back, and because Domitian's heart was even blacker than Nero's he took advantage of the situation. With the help of his conciliar (sea beast who was the false prophet) he capitalized on the story to make the people think he *was* Nero come back with his fatal wound healed.

5. In addition to being Domitian (the emperor), he claimed to be the reincarnation of Nero, who had died and come back to life. He didn't know that he was about to go to destruction by assassination (Revelation 17:8).

6. The harlot has no power of her own, but she gets her power from the emperor. She causes others to be drunk on the wine of her immorality while she is drunk on the blood of the saints. She wears names on her body to flaunt her immorality. She is dressed richly in purples and scarlets to designate her importance, and she wears costly jewels and drinks from a gold cup that is full of the abominations of her wickedness. The one who was and is not was an emperor but is now dead (Nero) and is the one whose number was 666 and who is still remembered and feared and whose memory is therefore used by the current emperor (Domitian) (Revelation 13:18) to promote his own evil reputation.

The angel identifies for John the seven heads as seven mountains (the mountains of Rome) (Revelation 17:9). The number seven is also identified as seven kings of Rome. Five of them are dead (fallen). One (is) the one who is reigning Vespasian (AD 69–79). One is coming (Titus) (AD 79–81). One will arise after the seven and will remain a while and is also the beast who was and is not (Nero), and he is himself an eighth (refers to the five fallen plus Vespasian and Titus plus himself). (Revelation 17:8–11). The ten horns are identified as ten kings without a kingdom because they gave theirs to Rome (which probably means they were defeated). They have no authority, and they hate the beast and the harlot. They will also be a part of Rome's destruction (Revelation 17:16–17). The waters the harlot sits on are her people (Revelation 17:15). (She is rich on the poverty of her people). And she is the great city of Rome (Revelation 17:18).

You may wonder why I identify this passage with Rome. I believe she was the only city that ruled over a large number of kings at the time and had a dynasty of rulers, a dynasty that fits both the number of the kings and the years of their reigns (e.g., the Caesar Dynasty from 27 BC to AD 96). There is also the historical fact that Rome began as a network of seven hill settlements on the eastern bank of the Tiber River. Her designation as the city on seven hills is commonplace among Roman writers (e.g., Virgil, Martial, Cicero) (Archaeological, 2066).

There were actually three more emperors who reigned very short periods of time all within less than a year before they were each assassinated by their successor. They are not included in John's vision, but were included in Daniel's vision. You might be interested in studying that vision in Daniel 7:7—27). Daniel says that the three who are not counted in John's vision were "pulled up by the roots" before Domitian's time (though he does not use John's name or Domitian's name.)

Vision Twenty (vantage point, earth)
Babylon, (Revelation 18)

Do you remember what the strong angel of chapter 10 said? "In the days of the voice of the seventh angel, when he is about to sound, then the mystery of God is finished" (Revelation 10:7). I believe that time has come in this vision of the future. Let's see what will happen in the enactment.

The first thing I noticed about this chapter is that John was taken to see Babylon (Rome) before her destruction. That can only mean that he saw her (Rome) in her glory not as she will appear by the end of this chapter after her punishment. It also means that the demons called up by Satan to gather kings and armies for a showdown with God had some time, and back a little further whatever the message of the three angels of chapter 14 was, it allowed time for repentance. After the vision of the harlot John saw an angel coming down from heaven, and the earth was illumined with his glory. This angel announced the fall of Babylon which was a pseudonym for Rome and what she had become, and another voice was heard from heaven, one imploring God's people to come out, indicating they didn't have to participate in her judgment. Her plagues would include disease, mourning, famine, and fire (Revelation 18:1–8).

Sadly there were those who were sorry to see her go—kings who had participated in her immorality, merchants over their loss of income, shipmasters who lost cargoes of great value, passengers on ships who went to and fro, sailors whose income was dependent on ships, as well as all who made their living by the sea. God's people, however, rejoiced because God had pronounced judgment for them against her (Revelation 18:9–20).

After these things John heard a great multitude singing a song of vindication. "His judgments are true and righteous; for He has judged the great harlot who was corrupting the world with her immorality and He has avenged the blood of His bond-servants on her" (Revelation 19:1–4). This song was immediately followed by another, a song of praise. "Hallelujah! For the Lord our God, the Almighty reigns. Let us rejoice and be glad and give the glory to Him, for the marriage of the Lamb has come and His bride has made herself ready." She was clothed in fine white linen for that is the righteous acts of the saints (Revelation 19:6–8).

And John was told to write, "Blessed are those who are invited to the marriage supper of the Lamb" (Revelation 19:9). Notice that *invited* seems to be a key word, so let's watch to see what happens next.

Vision Twenty-One (vantage point heaven)
The Coming of Christ Revelation 19

Heaven opened, and John saw a white horse. And the one who sat on it was called "Faithful and True," and it was said of Him that "in righteousness He judges and wages war." His name is called the Word of God. The armies, which are in heaven and clothed in white linen, follow Him on white horses, and from His mouth comes a *sharp sword* (the Word of God), which is for discerning truth. And with it He will strike down the nations and will rule them with a rod of iron (Revelation 19:13). This phrase doesn't mean harshly or unfairly. It simply means there will be swift, righteous judgment[59] (MacArthur 2005).

John saw an angel standing in the sun who called out, "Come, assemble for the great supper of God." Remember that the last blessing was for those who were invited to the supper (Revelation 19:19). Now we will see if anything of importance happened as John waited. Suddenly he sees "the beast and the kings of the earth and their armies assembled to make war against Him who sat on His horse and against His army" (19:19). "But as he watches, the beast and the false prophet are seized, and were both thrown alive into the lake of fire which burns with brimstone. The rest were killed with the sword which came from His mouth, (the Word of God), and the birds were filled with their flesh" (19:20–1).

This is the great war we hear so much about. These guests were obviously not invited, and their plan to make war with the Lamb at this critical moment didn't work. We saw instead the doom of the beast, the false prophet, and their armies. Satan is evidently still alive. Watch for the enactment of his punishment.

Vision Twenty-Two (location the abyss and heaven)
The Thousand Years, Revelation 20

John witnessed an angel coming down from heaven, one who held the key to the abyss and a great chain in his hand. He "laid hold of the dragon," bound him for a thousand years, threw him into the abyss, shut it, and sealed it over him so that he would not deceive the nations any longer until the thousand years were completed. After this completion of time he would be released for a short time.

(The scene switches to heaven.)

In heaven John saw the following:

- The souls of the martyrs who had given testimony for Jesus and had obeyed the Word of God.

- Those who had not worshipped the beast or his image.

- Those who had not received the mark of the beast on head or hand.

---

59 MacArthur, John, MacArthur Bible Commentary, copyright 2005 by Thomas Nelson, p. 2032.

These came to life (the martyrs and the persecuted) and were sitting on thrones where they reigned with God for a thousand years. Thrones, crowns, authority, and white garments were some of the rewards promised to the overcomers of the Asian churches who received the letters God had sent through John. Let's take a look at those instances:

- Smyrna and Philadelphia were promised a crown of life (Revelation 2:10 and 3:11).

- Thyatira was promised authority over the nations (Revelation 2:26–7).

- Sardis was promised white clothing (Revelation 3:5).

- Laodicea was promised to sit down with Him on His throne (Revelation 3:21).

These overcomers of Revelation 20:4 are alive. They are in heaven, ruling with Christ during this thousand year period because they were willing to give up their physical lives rather than give up Jesus. When did they come to life? As far as we know a believer comes to life through obedience. These martyrs were never dead because they went from physical life to spiritual life. Those who never come to life on earth are the living dead or those in their graves who had no faith. The fact that the martyrs didn't die is a dramatic illustration of going from death to life. We may not all go straight to heaven as these martyrs did, but we do go to Paradise, which is not death.

The other ingredient of this somewhat difficult equation is Revelation 20:7–10, which says, "When the thousand years are completed, Satan will be released from his prison and will come out to deceive the nations again." Again I have two points for two separate time periods.

> In my wildest imagination I cannot imagine God saying to Satan, "Okay, Satan, you've served your thousand years, now go on about deceiving the nations again. After all, that's your job." God says in 20:7 that that is exactly what Satan will do when his limitations are removed. So, He tells us what will happen. When they all meet up for the war, "fire came down from heaven and devoured them,

and the devil who deceived them was thrown into the lake of fire and brimstone, where the beast and the false prophet are also; and they will be tormented day and night forever and ever" (Revelation 20:7-10)Revelation 20:6, "Blessed and holy is the one who has a part in the first resurrection; over these the second death has no power, but they will be priests of God and of Christ and will reign with Him for a thousand years."

- In this text God gives us the blessing, and it speaks to us of the part we play as Christians during the thousand years in which Satan no longer has the power of deception. We are priests of God and Christ here on earth. Just as the martyrs reign with Him in heaven, our reign with Him is on earth. The first resurrection is by the obedience engendered by faith. We trade a decaying body for spiritual life. And when death comes, it is of the physical body. It may surprise you to know that punishment will not be primarily because of sin, because sin can be forgiven in the presence of repentance. What cannot be forgiven is the failure to accept the Son of God, who died on behalf of sinners—you, me, and all humanity. He cannot forgive that because without belief, there is no sacrifice for sin and we are dead even while we live.

Compare this with Eve's situation. She had no idea about anything, didn't even know that she should be on guard. Why? It was because she had yet to be taught. We, on the other hand have had teaching, we have sources from which to study and learn, we have direct access to God through our high priest Jesus Christ, so what is out excuse? We don't have one. God does not take ignorance for an excuse not to believe and obey. Again, I ask why? It is because He has provided avenues for belief. He has taught us and shown us His love. It is time for us to show our gratitude and praise Him as we do for Him whatever we can do.

My understanding is that we are in the one thousand-year period to which chapter 20 refers. It began on the day of Pentecost, and it will end when God decides that it is complete, meaning there is no reason to continue because it will no longer benefit His purpose, which has always been the salvation of souls. When the thousand years are complete, Satan will be released from his limitations for a short while. In the meantime we continue to preach the gospel in all the ways that we can.

These are the ways by which Satan is limited (bound). He has known of these limitations probably since Jesus' resurrection but certainly from the day of Pentecost.

- He has been bound by God's grace to all men (Ephesians 2:8–9 and John 1:12), from which comes justification (Titus 3:7) and mercy (Hebrews 4:1).

- He is bound by Jesus' prayers of intercession on our behalf (Hebrews 7:25).

- He is bound by God's promise to Abraham (Genesis 12:3).

- He is bound by the crucifixion, the resurrection, and the ascension from which he lost the power over death (Hebrews 2:14).

- He is bound by the Christian's spiritual birth, which makes man a priest of God and gives him the privilege of reigning with Him in His earthly kingdom for one thousand years (Revelation 20:6).

- He is bound by time, which is limited (Revelation 12:12).

- He is bound by the Christian's access to God as priests and to the written word of God.

- He is bound by the Christian's humility (James 4:6).

- He is bound by the Christian's faith (James 4:7).

- He is bound by the Christian's resistance (James 4:7).

- He is bound by the Christian's love (Revelation 12:12).

- He is bound by the armor provided us by God (Ephesians 6:13–17).

- He is bound by the Holy Spirit, who instructs us in how to walk (Galatians 5:16).

- He was bound by the defeat of Rome's power, Hitler's power, Stalin's power, and the power of every persecutor who has ever ruled a nation instead of serving it.

If this seems too long a list, thank God for it. I'm sure there are things I've missed in listing these. The length of the list should be an indicator of God's love for us. It is also a demonstration of the reason for Satan's great anger. The most successful way not to become entangled with him is to spend regular time in study and prayer and stay away from him.

Though Satan is tethered, he still has access to us if we get too close to him, if we are not strong enough in faith and prayer, or if we forget that we are Christians. However, it is my belief that because of our access to God and the Word, he cannot actually deceive us. This is one of the promises of the thousand-year reign, so let's examine it. What does the seal mean? It is not a contract because there is nothing in it for Satan. However, it is a mark of authenticity together with a promise that we can no longer be deceived. But why? Deception requires ignorance, and we have the source of knowledge, God's Word. Besides we have access to Him not only through His Word but through prayer. The promise is that after the thousand years, he will be released, so let's see what the final prophecy says he will do.

Vision Twenty-Three (vantage, a great high mountain)
The New Heaven and New Earth (chapter 21:1–9)

In the next visions John was shown the new heaven and a new earth after the first heaven and earth and the sea passed away. John saw the holy city, Jerusalem, coming down out of heaven, and she was adorned as a bride (the church). And a voice from heaven identified her as His people among whom He would live and care for their every need. An angel took him to a great, high mountain an showed him the city with its beautiful walls and gates, and he was privileged to see paradise restored with the water of life coming from the throne of God and the tree of life with its twelve kinds of fruit.

Another angel took him to view the bride, the wife of the Lamb, and he saw the holy city of Jerusalem coming down out of heaven from God, having the glory of God (Revelation 21:19). And John said that there was no temple in it, for the Lord God the Almighty and the Lamb are its temple, and there was no need for the sun or of the moon to shine on it, for the glory of God has illumined it, and its lamp is the Lamb" (Revelation 21:22). And he heard the final blessings and the final admonitions:

- The Spirit and the bride say "come" (the Holy Spirit and the church).

- The one who hears the message says "come" (all who hear the gospel).

- To the one who is thirsty, "come" (all who hunger and thirst for righteousness).

- Any who wish to drink may come and drink of the water of life at no cost (the cost was paid by Jesus blood).

"Blessed is he who heeds the words of the prophecy and of this book" (Revelation 22:7).

"Blessed are those who wash their robes so that they may have the right to the tree of life and may enter into the gates of the city" (Revelation 22:14).

Summary

For the purpose of analyzing what we've learned here's another question: Why did Rome fall from a nation that had conquered and ruled? I think we can agree that she was like a wanton, luxurious, immoral woman who oppressed the world, deceived the nations, and killed the saints. Think how things could have been different had she assumed her role as a leader to serve rather than to be served. God tolerates and puts up with things hoping to bring man to repentance, but His patience is not limitless. Eventually he had to weigh the good against the bad to determine that her role had passed the point of no return. In doing so He placed His purpose of reconciliation and salvation before her right to survive as a world power.

I must point out that many of the things that happened to Rome had double meaning, what we have called a near and a far fulfillment. Our showing from Scripture serves as a duplicate for what John saw at the hand of God. This is why I wanted us to be able to see the visions in pictures if possible and why the concluding visions were word pictures for the most part. The warnings to her are our warnings, even to the extent that we must accept the fact that our time is near. We have no knowledge when God will take us home, assuming that our time comes before the last day He has so vividly described for us. There will be no announcement. We are promised that He will come to us as a thief in the night, unexpected and suddenly. The only solution is to be ready.

The one thousand years spoken of in Revelation is not a literal time in the same way that the other numbers we looked at are not literal. If we do not choose to follow Him now, we will not be ready when He comes to claim those who are His. If we understand the concept of complete, we take by faith the assumption that when He comes for us, the war will be over because He will not come until everything is done that must be done. The fact is, though, more than the war will be over, this age in which we live will be transformed into the new heaven and the new earth, where there will be no pain, no more death or dying, no tears, no crying or mourning. In addition there will be the beauty of that home He has prepared and fellowship with our God. Our relationship with Him will be restored as it was in the garden with Adam and Eve, the way He intended it to be for all man. As with all things there must be an end, and I am confident that "the best for us is yet to be." God bless.

"He who testifies to these things says, 'Yes, I am coming quickly'" (Revelation 22:20), and John replies, "Amen. Come, Lord Jesus."

It is time for me to leave you now. There was no way for showing (or telling) all that is in this book. To begin with I don't know it all. Nor does anyone, I'm quite sure. All that any of us can do—and this is in reference to the entire book—is read it regularly, and as we are ready, the Spirit will reveal new things to us. I hope you will begin your own study to fill in the gaps. In the meantime my thanks for sharing the journey with me, and I pray that you have found new meaning and renewed purpose for your goal in this life.

Study Guide—Chapter 20

Q. Do you have any idea why so many things are presented in groups of sevens?

A. Seven is a number that represents perfection in the Bible. Groups of the seals and the trumpets are examples, but it really comes down from what I would call numerology of the day. The Romans were very much into numbers and had meanings for combining numbers. Seven was for perfection, which came from combining Father, Son, and Holy Spirit, plus the cosmic number for the universe which is four which represents north, south, east and west. As far as I know it is a symbolic number that God uses, or perhaps numerologists took the number from God. However, in Revelation numbers are symbolic. A complete number can be divided evenly by units of ten. If you check it out, it is consistent. In our study the *perfection* idea fits with all that God does. He doesn't overdo. He does just what is needed. In a way it is like the word *complete*. We have seven seals, seven trumpets, seven bowls of wrath, and perfection where punishment is required. Not too much and not too little. Just what is needed.

Q. What historical event marked Satan's defeat, and what did he do about it?

A. Jesus resurrection marked the point at which Satan knew he was defeated. He immediately went to heaven and challenged Michael and his angels to battle.

Q. Why does the war continue?

A. Please remember that God's purpose is to save souls; therefore, the war will continue until all things are *complete*, which means no more can be done toward that end.